HD8036.F45 1981   245?

FELDSTEIN
HOME, INC.

HOME, INC.

HOW TO START AND OPERATE A SUCCESSFUL BUSINESS FROM YOUR HOME

STUART FELDSTEIN

GROSSET & DUNLAP
A Filmways Company
Publishers • New York

To my sons, Jason and Aron—my most important home business.

Contents

Introduction

The winds of economic change are blowing across the United States. Unfortunately, they have caused an unhealthy draft for most people, because the U.S. standard of living is declining under a redistribution of world wealth.

It is no surprise that in such an environment, the sellers of get-rich-quick ideas are coming out of the woodwork. Instant riches, so they say, are awaiting us all through investment in real estate, or gold, or commodity futures. If that's true, of course, we are living in really paradoxical times. Most people can still afford the cost of a magazine or book to learn all about these new techniques, yet the statistics tell us that the average wage earner continues to be clobbered by inflation.

This book is about a more traditional way to make money: working. But it is also about a very special way of working. This is the story of people who have discovered ways to utilize a portion of their paid-for living space to house a new, income-producing business. Home-based businesses are sprouting up across the land, to supplement or replace money earned outside the home. What follows on these pages is actually a combination of tales—an attempt to describe how existing home entrepreneurs run their operations, and how you can start one, too.

A team of nine researchers, plus the author, went to the doorsteps of home-based businesspeople in cities all over the nation to ask the most personal questions imaginable. At the outset, we fully expected that many would not answer the nitty-gritty questions, those not-so-subtle inquiries like, "How much money do you make at this business?" and "How in the world does your husband (or wife) put up with this?" To our surprise and pleasure, the majority of the interview subjects, friendly and open people, knew exactly why we were asking and were happy to answer.

Many of those interviewed happened to live in the same cities where the research team members live: Akron, Chicago, Denver, Fort Lauderdale, Houston, Los Angeles, New York, Seattle, and Washington, D.C. There were others, ranging from Connecticut to Arizona, but finding home businesspeople nearby was an easy chore. Early in the research, it became clear that almost everyone, everywhere, knows somebody who is doing something to make spare cash at home.

By combining the experiences of home workers with the expertise of accountants, marketing executives, lawyers, and others, the project became a mixture of descriptive journalism and "how-to" nonfiction. Part 1 of the book concentrates mainly on the ways to start any home-based enterprise: how to change family relationships successfully when more time is spent at home; how to avoid common small business problems; how to handle taxes, company structure, and government regulation; how to perform home-based marketing; and the like. Part 2 is primarily the story of how others run their home operations right now, in ten different categories of activity. The focus is on profit potential, identifying risk, and making the business enjoyable.

It is possible, and even likely, that by press time, some of the real-life home businesses described in this book will have changed. Many small businesses are volatile creatures. One of the advantages to running one from home is that it can be started or stopped with comparative ease. Our best wishes go with the hard-driving pioneers mentioned here. They have given us a recent look at their operations, and we hope that their prosperity has increased by the time they have a chance to read their own stories.

Those who worked on the book are all part-time or full-time home businesspeople. We are home-based writers, at least some of the time, and this volume is certainly a homemade product. We think the topic is a very important one today. As the manuscript was being completed, home working was very much in the news. A new national organization had just come to life for women who run businesses at home. In Washington, the Reagan administration was lobbying to throw out old labor laws that prohibited some kinds of home work, especially in the garment industry. Aside from all this, our own research made one thing clear: There is a burgeoning movement in this country toward self-employment at home, for women and men, in spare hours or full time. You can be part of it. You may not get rich quick, though that has been done, but you are certain to live a little better.

Part 1

Making Money with Your Own Best Asset

CHAPTER ONE

The Hidden Opportunity inside Your Front Door

In 1977, a rich recipe for a new business was discovered in the kitchen of a Tucson, Arizona, housewife. "Sugar" Cane Birdsall, a one-time Manhattan real estate agent with a yen to return to profitable work, was hostessing a New Year's Eve dinner party. She made something special—a mustard sauce that brought raves from her guests. They suggested she bottle and sell it. She did.

That launched Sugar's Kitchen, and its line of Arizona Champagne Sauces. Prime among them was Arizona Champagne Mustard, but the list also grew to include another mustard preparation, a vegetable dip, and a relish. Within four years, Birdsall had lined up 200 accounts, including some of the most prestigious New York City department stores. Annual sales topped $100,000. Birdsall's laundry room became a separate business kitchen (washer and dryer were banished to quarters outside the house) and another room was converted to cold storage. The study was turned into an office and the garage became a sanitary warehouse for jars.

Sugar's Kitchen stayed at Birdsall's home, and that meant a number of things: She paid no rent for an outside shop; she did no commuting; and she had the opportunity to take tax deductions for home-related costs that were legitimate expenses of the business. Also, it was the handiest of locations for Birdsall's husband to pitch in and help, drawing the couple together to work meaningfully on a mutual enterprise. By 1981, he was putting in three hours a day, ordering ingredients, handling invoices, taking charge of other day-to-day duties.

Mr. and Mrs. Birdsall may not have known it at the time, but they also were pioneers—trailblazers in a movement that has picked up incredible momentum. Their home business became one of hundreds of thousands—more probably millions—that have grown up all across the United States. The variety of these businesses spans the imagination. And, at a time of economic chaos, when inflation, high interest rates, and periodic

5

recession afflict everyone, and when American workers are villified in some quarters as unproductive, the home business movement proves that something can be done to change things. Without going the risky route of investment, the average person can help himself financially by combining ingenuity and industriousness with a simple economic principle: There is no good reason to underutilize paid-for living space if even a tiny part of it can be converted into a profit center.

By doing that, home business people are showing that American entrepreneurial instincts are alive and well inside the front doors of houses in every community. In fact, these instincts are thriving in spare rooms, back yards, garages, cellars, attics, dens, and even living rooms. Home businesses are producing goods and services—in every kind of excess space, working full time or part time, and ranging from the commonplace to the obscure. Some of the enterprises are easy to categorize: food processing, garments, animal breeding, plant production, and professional services, to name just a few.

Others range to the esoteric. These show an almost boundless inventiveness. There is, for example, Charles Zanichelli, a Harris Park, Colorado, musician and salesman, who, in his spare time, raises wolf cubs to sell as pets. Jack Smith, an Akron, Ohio self-made man, grows bean sprouts in his basement for Chinese restaurants, builds furniture, and operates his own wood-splitting business to supply neighborhood fireplaces. James Martin, a Washington, D.C. policeman, spends his spare time maintaining a home inventory of metal detectors, which he sells at shopping malls and other marketplaces. Grover Criswell, in Fort McCoy, Florida, has parlayed a childhood hobby into an eminently successful mail order business, buying and selling Confederate currency. Criswell says he grosses more than a half-million dollars a year, and he employs five people in three rooms of his house.

Like Criswell, there are home businesspeople who earn top dollar as full-timers. Others merely supplement their regular income by starting a business doing what they enjoy—on their own schedule and in the comfort of their homes. As self-employed business people, they can set prices to make up for inflation as well as being victims of it. "If my rent and food go up, so will my prices," declares Louise Brogdon of Takoma Park, Maryland, a professional at-home seamstress.

Raising the prices of one's own products is one way to fight inflation. Another way is to put an end to commuting and exhorbitant gasoline bills. Advantages such as these have caused a surge of interest in home-based businesses unheard of since the era of the agricultural society, when most people worked and lived harmoniously on their own property. Surprisingly, the U.S. government, usually a paragon of number-crunching and people-watching, has no clear fix on the number of home businesses in operation. But there are enough statistics and some recently-discovered trends to hint strongly that the scope of the home-working movement is expanding dramatically.

The Census Bureau, for example, has chosen to track businesses owned by women, and one recent tabulation showed that well over 300,000 women's businesses were operated out of the owners' homes. This number represented nearly half of the total number of businesses owned by women in the United States. Strikingly, some 357 of the home-based businesses in the group had annual receipts of $1 million or more.

In a study in 1980, researchers at the U.S. Department of Labor's Bureau of Labor Statistics were surprised to find a major increase in the number of Americans self-employed in or out of their homes, on a full-time basis. They found that between 1972 and 1979, more than 1.3 million nonagricultural workers moved over to the self-employed column, making a total of 6.65 million self-employed, not including farm owners. "The numbers have experienced sustained growth for the first time since World War II," they noted, and the most rapid part of the growth came in the last few years of the decade of the 1970s—the same years when inflation became endemic to the economy. Similarly, Internal Revenue Service figures show that the number of people filing tax returns that include business and professional income (separate from wage and salary income) jumped suddenly in the 1970s. According to this measure, the number of full-time or part-time, nonagricultural self-employed hit 8.2 million by 1978, and was on a fast upward track.

None of these statistics, however, tell the whole story. A vast number of home businesses are performed in secret, a part of the murky world of the underground economy. The motives for this are diverse.

Some are underground for all the wrong reasons. Much of the illegal trade in drugs is performed, of course, inside homes and apartments, and in recent years there has been an upsurge in unscrupulous garment companies that have "subcontracted" to home workers—often illegal aliens—simply to obtain products at piecework rates that are less than the minimum wage. Some home businesses, too, have been created to lose money as tax shelters. These businesses are really hobbies or recreations, such as horse breeding or art collecting, which the taxpayer would engage in anyway, but whose expenses he wants to write off as losses against his other income. Legal crackdowns are going on in all these areas, including a new effort by the IRS to separate businesses from tax-shelter recreations.

Unfortunately, however, the majority of underground home businesses are kept secret because of government regulations and laws whose only effects are to stifle productivity. Unreasonable zoning regulations in some cities, and a federal tax structure that did not change enough in the 1970s to compensate for the damage done by inflation, have helped to drive tens of thousands of legitimate home entrepreneurs into what amounts to a clandestine life. Eventually, these workers may rejoin the economic mainstream as the nature of work locations changes drastically in America.

In the future, the clear separation most people now set between living places and working places will vanish in the death throes of the Industrial Revolution. Electronic devices will allow more and more people to be stationed at home instead of the office, whether they are employed by others or themselves. A growing demand, too, for custom-made goods will lend itself to home-based work. Not all jobs will be worked at home, but, undoubtedly, by the early part of the twenty-first century, many will. This trend has already begun, and it begs an answer to one prime question: If you are going to work at home, will you choose to do it for your own profit?

Home businesspeople already in operation have made that choice. Many of them, like countless thousands of others, had long desired self-employment as a means to control their own destinies. But right now, the fear of failure, the up-front costs, and the risks of becoming self-employed deter most of the hopefuls. Costs and risks can be cut by striking on a business idea that can come to fruition at home. A part-time home business can be even safer, adding to income while outside employment, with fringe benefits bought at group rates, continues.

The current wave of home businesspeople is motivated by economics and the desire for particular kinds of life-styles. In 1976, for example, Bruce M. Wilkinson sought to meet a mainly economic goal by searching for a way to supplement his income as a writer for the Denver *Post*. He set up a home office to run a map-selling business. Wilkinson bought some map vending machines and a supply of maps, and placed them in book stores, gift shops, and drugstores. Two years later, he says, this side business grossed $58,000 in sales. Meanwhile, in New Freedom, Pennsylvania, George Theofiles, a former teacher and illustrator, says he simply "didn't want to get up early in the mornings" any longer. "And," he adds, "I didn't like putting out other people's fires." Theofiles began a mail order business, selling valuable posters and graphic advertisements, often antiques. Set up to accommodate Theofiles' life-style goals, the business, nonetheless, became extraordinarily lucrative.

Like all businesses, those run at home span the possibilities of success, from smashingly good to utter failure. Most of the turf lies in between. Home businesses are hard work, and, if anything, require qualities tougher to find within one's self than those needed to work for others. "Sometimes you enjoy it, and sometimes you don't. You try to make a living," says Constance Pitchell, who runs ABC Papers, an editing and typing service for doctoral dissertations, from her living room and bedroom in Chevy Chase, Maryland. Pitchell may even be understating the point. Operating a home business requires not only steady toil, but a spate of other fuels: a marketable idea to begin with, the readiness to act without prodding of other people, the courage to take on ultimate responsibility for yourself, a desire to manage instead of being managed, and plain grit for the long pull.

The same can be said for many kinds of self-employment, and home businesses can function as a starting place for enterprises to be grown and later planted on the outside. By the time a business is ready for this kind of transplant, it is usually on solid footing.

Among home businesses that have outgrown their original quarters, some of the biggest surprises have emerged from the smallest of towns. In May 1975, in the tiny hamlet of Big Sandy, Texas, Annie Gentry sat down at her kitchen table and looked proudly at two 18-inch pillow dolls she had made with needlecraft. She and her husband, Jerry, a former advertising consultant, then made a momentous decision to put together a mailing list and distribute ads to sell patterns for making these dolls, which they named Sunbonnet Sue and Overall Sam. The response to the initial mailing was strong. Before long, the Gentrys were selling not only the patterns, priced at about $2.75, but also complete kits for making the dolls, priced at about $6.95.

"Annie's Attic" was born, and, according to Mrs. Gentry, growth came so quickly that the business literally "ran us out of our house within two or three years." By then, Annie's Attic was a mail order house selling patterns and kits for dolls, pillows, wall hangings, puppets, knickknacks, aprons, potholders, and dozens of other items. In 1980, Gentry says, the operation took in an astonishing 380,000 orders for merchandise. The Gentrys moved to a new home, and Annie used the entire third story as her design studio. The old house became company headquarters. Four additional homes in Big Sandy were converted into warehouses, sorting rooms, offices, and other work areas. By the end of 1980, Annie's Attic employed 90 full-time workers.

The Gentrys' success was greater than most, of course. Typically home businesses stay at home. But properly conceived and carried through, ordinary home businesses can bring in a desired level of income, and answer other needs as well.

They can be an answer for women or men torn between staying home to raise children and the need to help earn extra family income. They can remove people, too, from the syndrome of wasted time involved in most out-of-home jobs, which separate spouses from each other and parents from children. Commuting alone can waste years of time spread over an entire career.

Thus, the lure of starting a home business often catches the fancy of experienced workers rather than novices. There are those who know the rat race all too well, and have decided to step away from it. Irving M. Seidner, a former Chicagoan who moved to Denver to set up a home-based public relations agency, makes an eloquent spokesman for this group.

Seidner now operates Irv Seidner Public Relations out of his strikingly modern condominium overlooking Cheesman Park, a large, graceful park in the center of Denver. He recalls: "I had spent twenty years in Chicago in a conventional corporate-business setting, where I went to the office every day, had a secretary, had a half-dozen people working for me. I had a job.

"One of the reasons I left Chicago was that I wanted a

totally different business structure. I did not feel that having a fancy address or a nice office was important. What was important was the end result of my work. I wanted to leave behind a lot of the frustration of having a group of people working for me and having to deal with administrative problems, management problems. I wanted to do what I liked to do."

Seidner was able to achieve that goal. His one-man office handles half a dozen clients, whose payments range from $1,200 to $2,500 per client per month. When the work gets hectic, Seidner farms out some of it to free-lance writers (often home businesspersons themselves), photographers, and a secretarial service. In the meantime, he enjoys a number of home business fringe benefits:

"I avoid rush hour traffic, and wading through two feet of snow to get to the office. I've avoided unnecessary overhead. I don't need the overhead to say to the world that I am a legitimate businessman. My energies go into my work, and not into keeping up an office or getting to the office every day. And, I don't have to set an example for other employees."

Working late, he says, is easier when it has to be done, because work is a few steps away. Peace and quiet in the office are at his own command. "When I have to concentrate on a piece of work, the office becomes a kind of ivory tower," he notes. If he wants, Seidner can break up his day with a business lunch with clients; otherwise, he can be his own chef at home. "I eat less, and I don't have a drink," he says. "It's healthier than having lunch downtown." Work at home is still work, but for Seidner, it is under his own control and in the surroundings he has chosen. Conventional formalities of outside employment can often be discarded. "I get calls from New York or Washington as early as six A.M., which is eight A.M. Eastern time," he observes. "The person I'm talking to probably visualizes me in a coat and tie, but I'm standing here in my bathrobe."

The experiences of Irv Seidner, "Sugar" Cane Birdsall, and Jerry and Annie Gentry are merely a sampling. Their stories are being reenacted daily by others, though the names, occupations, and locations differ. The experiences of thriving home businesses are no guarantee of success for others, but they do establish the hard fact that a path is available—a low-overhead route—to become your own boss, to step out of the office or factory grind, to stay closer to the family, or simply to make some extra cash in your spare time. The opportunity for self-employment is closer at hand than most people realize, hidden for the moment inside an inventive mind and the four walls of every home.

CHAPTER TWO

Shelters and Dollars

It is often said that buying a home is the biggest investment most people will ever make, and is probably the wisest as well. But since the onslaught of serious inflation in the early 1970s, home ownership has taken on an added, mystic aura, and that aura is colored green.

Inflation—more specifically the superinflation of home prices—has clouded the notion of what a house represents. We are led to believe that the single-family home is no longer just a dwelling place, but a fast-growth financial market instrument, like shares of IBM during that company's infancy. Everyone has heard the tale of someone, living on some nearby street, who paid $25,000 for his house in the 1950s and who just sold it for $90,000. These are not boring stories. In the faces of the storytellers, and usually the listeners, all eyes have turned up dollar signs.

The old homestead, once valued for its comfort, its gift of rootedness, and for the nostalgia of shared family experiences, has changed. The whopping new prices are simply too great a temptation away from the old ideas, and we pick between two courses of action. We sell the place when the market is hot, or we hold on, feeling secure in the thought that whatever else might happen—the loss of a job, sickness, injury—we can always fall back on selling the house as a financial cushion.

The trouble is that the green aura is largely a dense fog comprised only of hope, and when it lifts, we find very little has really changed about pricing and costs for housing. The selling price, however high, is likely to be less than the purchase price for the next house, presuming the seller wants a slightly better location and more modern place, as most do. For every dollar of profit retained from the sale of the old house, instead of being placed down on the new house, the new monthly mortgage payment increases. And, with interest rates perhaps double what they were on the former mortgage, the new monthly payment is already a shock. The alternative to all of this is to sell the house and then rent. This mortgages the future instead of the present, as escalating rents over which the apartment dweller has no control gradually draw down the profits of the home sale. In the meantime, the renter discovers there is a real impact on his taxes when he can no longer deduct mortagage interest payments.

There is money to be made in real estate—by buying, developing, and selling properties other than the one you live in. The plain fact is that the main attribute of home ownership is still as it always was: It affords dwelling space whose use is at your own discretion. Thus, at a time when inflation and periodic recessions are making life miserable for most, the home as an asset to sell provides no easy way out.

But there is another way to look at what a home represents financially, and at what rented space can represent, too. Both can be used as assets that can generate income now.

In business, the generation of income is the only purpose of fixed assets. It is ludicrous to imagine General Motors building an assembly plant for the purpose of allowing it to sit idle until it can be sold at a higher price. Some would say, of course, that it is equally silly to compare housing to factory space when the purposes behind the two are so totally different. Yet the definition of "home" already has leapt from dwelling place to temporary quarters maintained until liquidation at a higher price can be arranged, despite the fallacies in this view. The real question is: Has the time come to combine shelters and dollars through a new double-utilization of the home as living space and working asset, instead of as living space and market investment? For an increasing number of people who have set aside portions of their homes to house operational businesses, the answer is yes.

This is not so much an idyllic view as it is a realistic one. The old values hold the home as a place of retreat from income-producing work. This is an attractive scenario, except for the person at home who does the housework, home repairs, and maintenance, and for those who find themselves spending their time at home not retreating from the vagaries of the outside world, but worrying about how to cope with a shrinking paycheck.

Economics have put leisure time and the usage of leisure time at cross purposes. The average work week continues to shrink, as it has for decades, but to what end? Because of inflation, there is frequently less disposable income to use to enjoy the leisure hours. More people are spending more time off-the-job than before, but it is hard to discover any automatic financial benefit, or even much social or personal benefit. For whatever reasons, the divorce rate has skyrocketed. Husbands and wives may be spending longer evenings together, but the lack of meaningful communication and nonfulfillment of expectations have been enough to spawn an entire industry: marriage counseling.

For employees of manufacturing companies, the average work week has remained relatively stable in length since World War II. But the U.S. economy has become increasingly service-oriented, and work weeks for nonmanufacturing jobs (retail and wholesale trade, finance, government, and other service sectors) have undergone a precipitous decline. The net result is an overall reduction in work hours (see Table 1). There may even be a second factor at work increasing the amount of time available for leisure activity. As U.S. population, industry, and jobs have migrated from the congested cities of the Northeast to the smaller urban centers of the Sunbelt, fewer Americans have to cope with commuting times lengthened by heavy traffic and failing public transportation systems. In New York City, for example, commuting can easily use up two hours or more per workday.

The elimination of a long commute can cause a fundamental increase in discretionary time, a shock to the life-styles of those brought up in a transit culture. "I was born and raised in New York. I just didn't know life could be like this," remarked an attorney whose firm transferred him from New York to Columbus, Ohio in 1976. His commuting time had been cut from two hours per day to about 40 minutes.

Table 1

Average Weekly Hours of Production or Nonsupervisory
Workers on Private, Nonagricultural Payrolls

Year	Work Week in Hours
1947	40.3
1948	40.0
1949	39.4
1950	39.8
1951	39.9

Year	Work Week in Hours
1952	39.9
1953	39.6
1954	39.1
1955	39.6
1956	39.3
1957	38.8
1958	38.5
1959	39.0
1960	38.6
1961	38.6
1962	38.7
1963	38.8
1964	38.7
1965	38.8
1966	38.6
1967	38.0
1968	37.8
1969	37.7
1970	37.1
1971	37.0
1972	37.1
1973	37.1
1974	36.6
1975	36.1
1976	36.2
1977	36.1
1978	35.8
1979	35.6
1980 (October)	35.2

Source: U.S. Department of Labor, Bureau of Labor Statistics

As Table 1 shows, the average work week has declined from 40.3 hours in 1947 to 35.2 hours in 1980—an extremely meaningful change. Those who have experienced this reduction find that, during the work week, they can spend one extra hour each day at home instead of on the job. Yet, as discretionary time has increased, discretionary income has declined. Pay increases were exceeded by the general rate of inflation from 1973 through 1980, putting the nation's standard of living on a backsliding course.

THE DEATH OF THE ABMLA

A decline in hours at work—more freedom from drudgery—is a goal man has striven to achieve for generations. But attainment of the goal seems hardly worthwhile if the new leisure time can only be spent wringing hands, worrying about how to pay the bills. As important as the figures in Table 1 are, those in Table 2 are more significant. They show the erosion of earnings on an hourly basis because of inflation.

Picking 1967 at random as a year against which to measure others, average U.S. hourly earnings rose handsomely in the mid-1960s, even when adjusted for inflation. In just three years—from 1964 to 1967—wages increased by more than 6 percent over and above the rate of inflation, boosting the purchasing power of the average individual worker significantly. This increase followed right along with the post-World War II expansionary trend in the economy. Ordinary working men and women took full part in this expansion, and the regularity of the increases in purchasing power formed expectations among many for an Always-Better-Material-Life-Ahead (ABMLA).

Table 2
Hourly Earnings Index
Total Private Nonfarm, Constant Dollars,[1] Quarterly
Averages, 1964 to Present (1967 = 100)

Year and Quarter	Seasonally Adjusted HEI	Percent Change from Previous Quarter
1964:		
1	94.213	
2	94.566	.4
3	95.250	.7
4	95.563	.3
1965:		
1	96.090	.6
2	96.320	.2
3	96.816	.5
4	97.283	.5

Year and Quarter	Seasonally Adjusted HEI	Percent Change from Previous Quarter
1966:		
1	97.566	.3
2	97.853	.3
3	97.926	.1
4	98.410	.5
1967:		
1	99.196	.8
2	99.866	.7
3	100.106	.2
4	100.450	.3
1968:		
1	101.190	.7
2	101.716	.5
3	101.990	.3
4	102.370	.4
1969:		
1	102.746	.4
2	102.843	.1
3	103.073	.2
4	103.380	.3
1970:		
1	103.163	−.2
2	103.320	.2
3	104.196	.8
4	104.263	.1
1971:		
1	105.576	1.3
2	106.270	.7
3	106.853	.5
4	107.460	.6
1972:		
1	108.926	1.4
2	109.546	.6
3	109.980	.4
4	110.793	.7
1973:		
1	110.600	−.2
2	110.056	−.5
3	109.603	−.4
4	108.816	−.7

Year and Quarter	Seasonally Adjusted HEI	Percent Change from Previous Quarter
1974:		
1	107.396	−1.3
2	107.126	−.3
3	106.683	−.4
4	105.826	−.8
1975:		
1	105.610	−.2
2	106.210	.6
3	106.030	−.2
4	105.926	−.1
1976:		
1	106.400	.4
2	107.310	.9
3	107.840	.5
4	108.306	.4
1977:		
1	108.236	−.1
2	108.250	*
3	108.570	.3
4	109.143	.5
1978:		
1	109.463	.3
2	109.316	−.1
3	108.996	−.3
4	108.650	−.3
1979:		
1	107.883	−.8
2	106.370	−1.4
3	105.180	−1.1
4	104.016	−1.1
1980:		
1	102.283	−1.7
2	101.430	−.8
3	101.846	.4

Data: U.S. Department of Labor, Bureau of Labor Statistics
[1]Adjusted for movements in the Consumer Price Index.
*Less than 0.05 percent

The trend did not stop in 1967. But it did peak at the end of 1972, when wages hit 110.8 percent of the 1967 milepost year. Remember 1972; it was a vintage year for money, the last before inflation became virulent and started a long chipping away at consumer buying power. Cultural historians may well conclude that 1972 was the year of the death of the ABMLA, even though many frustrated workers have yet to adjust their thinking to the stark reality of what happened. A redistribution of world wealth began in 1973 as the Organization of Petroleum Exporting Countries (OPEC) quadrupled oil prices, feeding the rate of inflation in the industrialized West. Deep recessions failed to have lasting impact as a tool to fight inflation, which, in the United States, grabbed workers' paychecks by the throat in a longlasting stranglehold. By the fall of 1980, wages adjusted for the impact of inflation had sunk to the level of 1968, and the end was not in sight.

The waves from this economic shock have washed over a number of fixed expectations that came from deep belief in the ABMLA. What is happening is an economic trip backwards in time, all too visible and tangible to the average person. For many people, we have already passed backwards through the years when the biggest decision about a vacation was where to go rather than whether a trip could be afforded. Buying a car for the high school graduate is on the same hit list; in fact, the two-car family, a creation of the 1960s for most, may slide by in the economic rear-march as well. Vacation homes were a dream that came close for many, but have since receded from their grasp like a taunting apparition.

The death of the ABMLA means a new ballgame for family finance. For many adults, the combination of more time at home and less money to spend has been a surprise in desperate need of resolution. For those hit hardest by economic reversal, the solution, moonlighting, has been mandated by rising bills. The number of moonlighters holding two or more jobs in the U.S. hit a record high of 4.7 million in 1979, or nearly one of every twenty workers. About three of every ten moonlighters were women—nearly double the proportion of ten years earlier. And, not included in these figures, which were gathered by the Labor Department, were the multiple jobs held in the underground economy, that misty world of financial activity not measured by the government because its participants don't want the government to know. Undoubtedly in the millions, the underground economy jobs range from criminal occupations to others that are perfectly legal, but whose practitioners simply do not report income to the IRS—a taxpayers' revolution that puts California's Proposition 13 in the minor leagues by comparison.

A major reason for this nonreported income is that the federal tax structure simply has not changed to fairly account for the effects of inflation on taxpayers. Too often, extra income earned by moonlighting simply puts the taxpayer into a higher bracket (if that extra income is reported), transferring the funds to the government. "In 1965," observes Alexander & Alexander Inc., an insurance firm in New York, "only 7 percent of the taxpayers faced marginal tax rates of 25 percent or higher. By 1976, one third of all taxpayers did. This proportion has expanded rapidly since then, destroying the capacity to save and invest."

In the utterly new environment of lower income and more time at home, the metamorphosis of the purpose of living space is moving more rapidly than ever. The economic trends point to utilizing some paid-for living space for income-production, if a way can be found to do it. In the face of this trend, the old concept of home as retreat is worth a reexamination in general. The fact is that the separation of living space and working space is not truly traditional, but a result of the Industrial Revolution, an economic movement whose strength is waning in many respects.

The Industrial Revolution used mass-production techniques to centralize work places in factories and office buildings. But historically, work, leisure activity, eating, and sleeping typically occurred in about the same vicinity. Home is where early *Homo sapiens* built his weapons and tools, and the transition from hunting and gathering to agriculture changed this very little. The farmhouse was, and still is, the prime office complex for work done on surrounding property.

In the early colonial United States, home-based businesses were the rule rather than the exception, and the products of these businesses went beyond agriculture. In *American Economic History*, author Harold Underwood Faulkner notes that the colonial farmer produced not only his own food, clothing, soap, and furniture, but generated other goods for sale. Especially in the slow winter months, the colonial farmer, together with his family, made extra income by manufacturing nails, shingles, farm tools, casks, and other goods. These were used in the West Indian trade, or in the fishing industry. Now almost forgotten, there was early trade, as well, in ginseng roots, gathered in the eastern mountains and warehoused in the homes of pioneers and trappers, who shipped them to the Far East, where the plants have long been used as an herbal remedy. Indeed, trappers tended to make their homes warehouses for a variety of products, and sometimes hide-processing plants as well. Fortunately, the new home businesses are a little more clean and less pungent.

Home businesses drew families together to do meaningful work. Some families that launch home businesses today find the same thing happens, although views of marriage and relationships with marriage partners have changed too much for others. One New York woman who considered starting a home business of her own decided against it mainly because it would have kept her too close to her husband, already self-employed at home. "If I had to work next to my husband all day, and be with him at night and on the weekends, too, I'd go nuts," she remarked. Still, the bygone era that so many people seem to yearn for—when families were secure and life was "simple"— happens to be the period when home working was common.

To be sure, there is no going back to a simple agricultural civilization. Fortunately for those interested in home-based businesses, turning back the clock isn't necessary. The latest trends in household living patterns are almost tailor-made for the new home businesses. The average amount of living space per person is increasing dramatically in the United States, because the number of people per household is declining faster than the nation's housing stock is turning over. This means more extra space is available in housing units than ever before to be used for an office, production area, or storage space.

Probably the most amazing findings of recent census-takings have been the changes in the nature of U.S. households. Family living groups are shrinking with seemingly geometric speed. Just a decade or so after the American Revolution, the first U.S. census found that in a total 558,000 households, no less than 35.8 percent contained seven persons or more. One is tempted to assume that the term "forefathers" is a legacy of those days, when the average child looking at all the adult relations scurrying around the house must have thought he had four fathers somewhere among the uncles and cousins. It was literally a packed house almost everywhere; the one-bedroom apartment was not quite in vogue. A tiny 3.7 percent of the population lived alone.

A full century passed, and some change was discernible, but it didn't amount to much. More than one fifth of all households still fit the seven-plus configuration. Households of one or two persons were up to 16.8 percent of the 12.7 million family units that existed in 1890. But the Industrial Revolution, which helped foster the so-called nuclear family of mother, father, and two children, was underway, and began to speed the decline in household members.

By 1930, the really big families were still present but were a distinct minority. Medium-sized families proliferated. Since many existing U.S. homes were built in the 1930s and earlier, the changes that have occurred since are even more meaningful, because so many living spaces have stayed the same while the families inside them have dropped in size. Over a span of nearly 50 years since 1930, the Census Bureau has found that the seven-plus arrangement has practically disappeared, from more than 10 percent of the 1930 families to 3 percent or less. Families almost as large, with five or six members, declined from about one fifth of the population to about 12 percent. The most dramatic changes have happened with singles and couples. One- and two-member households have skyrocketed since 1930, from 21.3 percent to a staggering 51.6 percent by 1977.

Despite the complaints that come from some singles, who find they cannot buy much apartment space in high-rent areas of big cities, the overall statistical trends are undeniable: Fewer people are living in the same spaces that housed many more in prior times. This conclusion completes three sides of a square of facts that help explain why home-based businesses are in a renaissance. People have more leisure time to spend at home. They have more space. And, since 1972, they have less money. The fourth side of the square is opportunity.

Rather suddenly, it is possible to perform tasks at home which were once impossible for a single human being to accomplish, or even a couple working together. Technology has multiplied working power in much the same way as the internal combustion engine multiplied horsepower. New gadgetry, in fact, has had a double effect: It has reduced the labor required to maintain a home, adding to leisure time, and it has offered up new tools to begin small businesses. Just within the last 20 years, new labor-saving appliances and other household products have taken more toil than ever out of homemaking. Microwave and convection ovens, permanent-press clothing, and even fireplace logs that keep themselves burning are among the products that have cut hours of labor from housework every week. But the real power of technology shows itself in tools that can be used to make money.

Prime among these tools are electronic devices that enable a single person to do calculations and word processing that once kept whole staffs of clerical workers busy for weeks. Personal computers have, by themselves, made possible a wide range of data-processing businesses that can be operated in homes by individuals. Sophisticated stenographic services can now be operated from home with the new tools. Technology is opening up other vistas as well: better machinery for food processing and catering businesses, and vastly improved home entertainment systems ideal for child-care ventures (though not to replace old-fashioned playing).

Modern tools are not the only source of opportunity, either. Solid growth markets of the 1980s are well-designed to support home businesses. The market is strong for original and hand-crafted creative products. The U.S. population of pets is high, displaying demand for breeders and pet groomers and handlers. Houseplants, which can provide a lucrative business at home, have seldom been more popular.

In the child-care industry, the increasing numbers of working women have strained the capacity of commercial facilities. Many mothers would prefer to see their children cared for in the daytime in a home setting anyway, rather than en masse at a day-care center where employees come and go. Among the stimulants that will keep this industry hot is the child-care credit available for income taxes; as of 1980, a maximum of $800 could be deducted directly from tax liability for child care, and higher credits were being considered by Congress in 1981.

In addition, certain home-based businesses are being aided by the same economic difficulties that have caused so many families to search for sources of extra income. Inflation and the uncertainties of world politics have turned investors away from financial markets and toward collectibles, for example. The buying and selling of stamps, coins, jewelry, antiques, and art works—frequently home businesses—have become more volatile as a result, but the general trend in prices has been strongly upward for all these products. Mail order businesses are thriving for similar reasons. Spiraling energy prices have made the ordering of goods by mail more attractive simply because it is a way of saving gasoline. As the national standard of living careens backward, mail order will be helped all the more by an increasing portion of the population that has no access to a personal auto to do shopping.

Ready markets and sophisticated work tools provide the opportunities to succeed in the new wave of home businesses. The necessity to find more income through full-time or part-time work provides a motive. If the result turns out to be a redefinition of the home, as an asset to produce income as well as to enjoy life, it will be ironic. Time will have leapfrogged. The home of the near future, bustling simultaneously with work and the business of living, will be surprisingly like the home of the agricultural society of the past. Shelter and the production of dollars will coexist again.

CHAPTER THREE

The Quality of Life

"I had a taste of office politics when I worked for a museum. Now I can do what I like and nobody bothers me," declares Morris Pearson, a furniture refinisher who works out of his home in Wheaton, Maryland. Pearson, at 58, was working as much as 80 hours a week, rebuilding and restoring pieces for customers who heard about his service by word of mouth. "My work is never dull," says Pearson, and the point he makes with that statement is a critical one for all home businesses. Aside from the financial payoff, the merger of self-employment and work at home must be a happy one for other reasons if it is to last for very long. A home business must create a satisfactory level of enjoyment.

Personnel and labor specialists have come to call this issue the "quality of life" that spins off of any job. In times of economic depression, when the sheer survival of working people and their families was at stake, salaries and wages were the preeminent concerns. Working conditions, job location, safety and health, social relations within work groups—all factors that affect the quality of working life—were subordinated, to say the very least. Hopefully, such times are behind us permanently. Despite the economic uncertainties that prevail today, it is well recognized that jobs must be measured by more than dollars alone. Working is a psychic adventure, capable (like any adventure) of meting out rewards and punishments in unequal shares.

It is in the quality of life arena that home businesses stand most separately from other kinds of work. Many of the potential pleasures are unique: the elimination of commuting, complete freedom of work scheduling, being one's own boss in comfortable surroundings. But there are potential drawbacks as well that simply don't appear in jobs outside the home. Some of the questions that must be answered are:

1. Will I feel isolated?
2. Can I motivate myself to work, with neither a boss nor an office full of colleagues or employees watching?

3. Will I feel out of place, a home-based worker in a world of office and factory workers?
4. Will my spouse and children be both understanding and supportive?
5. Will the comforts of home become distractions to concentration and motivation?
6. Will customers or clients invade my personal privacy because I am located at home?
7. Will outsiders question my professionalism because I am not in a conventional business setting?

These questions, and the potential advantages of home working, are most important if you plan a full-time business. At stake will be the enjoyability of half the waking hours of every weekday. Even for part-time home businesses, the quality of life considerations are important enough that they ought to be weighed at the same time you consider the moneymaking potential—before the business begins. For moonlighters, in particular, the second job can be physically taxing enough; it had better have some redeeming qualities to balance out.

The first warning flags on quality of life can be found within the reasons for starting a home business. If your main motivation for self-employment is to get away from an unpleasant job on the outside, look out. Any venture begun merely to replace something else suggests too little planning. Consider this scenario, which is all too common: A middle-management corporate employee, whose career has spanned the bullish 1950s and 1960s, abruptly finds that inflation is eating away at his paycheck. For the first time, his family's standard of living is declining. Moreover, he is beginning to feel threatened by a nagging realization: Not everyone is destined to climb the corporate ladder, and the fact that he works long hours and seems as bright as his co-workers may not be enough to do the trick. Feeling ill-treated and even a bit panicky (after all, his over-expectations have been ripped away), he decides to strike out on his own as a self-employed businessman. He later discovers that self-employment usually requires even longer working hours, and that nothing in this world aside from his own sweat, talent, and luck can guarantee success. He may scramble to get back on the corporate ladder, even in the middle again, only to find that employers now regard him with suspicion.

Since self-employment is not for everyone, home businesses

certainly are not. On the other hand, it is impossible to evaluate the potential quality of life in a home business without first looking at how the nature of all kinds of work is likely to change in the future. Home businesses, though on the rise, are still a distinct minority, but they are certain to become more common in the future. As they do, some of the questions about isolation, feeling out of place, and professionalism, will largely evaporate.

In his book *The Third Wave,* author and futurist Alvin Toffler describes a near-term future society wherein a huge portion of the population works at home. On top of the incumbent home work force—home businesspeople, self-employed tradesmen such as plumbers who have no office other than home, company-employed field sales people, and the like—Toffler sees whole new layers of workers being added. His vision conjures up all manner of company, government, and institutional employees stationed at home, doing paperwork and computation ranging from clerical to professional tasks on electronic devices, staying in touch with headquarters and colleagues by sophisticated communications hookups across electronicized telephones and video screens. In a chapter entitled "The Electronic Cottage," Toffler predicts a shift of "millions of jobs out of factories and offices, right back [to] where they came from originally: the home."

Working at home will certainly not be universal, for a few reasons. There are types of heavy industry—steel, mining, auto-assembly, glass, and many others—in which it strains credibility to fathom any method of efficient production outside of a centralized and automated workplace. And, there are jobs that could be done at home, but perhaps shouldn't. White-collar work sectors that require team thinking and brainstorming are among them, including daily newspaper editing, product marketing, and research and development laboratory work. In addition to this, there are some counter-trends going on right now within the labor force. Many women, for example, see work as a chance to escape the drudgery of staying home, and their movement into the out-of-home work force represents an abandonment of living space during daytime hours.

Yet, despite all of this, Toffler and other believers in the electronicization of the home are probably more right than wrong. For one thing, powerful economics work in favor of home-based careers as an instrument of national policy. Energy is the key. In early 1981, the United States was consuming an estimated 17 million barrels of oil per day, a critical economic problem because the imported portion plunged the U.S. balance of trade into deficit. Of that oil, some 6.6 million barrels per day was being converted into gasoline. And, of that gasoline, about 80 percent was considered "nondiscretionary" in usage. That is, people were buying and using it because they had no choice. The nondiscretionary gasoline was being used to ferry people back and forth to work outside the home. Clearly, any significant increase in the amount of work shifted to homes would have a tremendous positive impact on the nation's financial health if only by cutting gasoline usage.

The futurists are correct, too, about the potential for electronics to make many paperwork jobs possible at home. For economic and technological reasons, the abandonment of living space in the daytime is certain to be reversed. What does this mean for the quality of life working at home, either as a self-employed or company-employed person?

For one thing, as more and more people work at home, the social amenities that make work less tedious at the office, plant, or construction site will begin to show up in neighborhoods. Isolation will diminish. Coffee breaks and restaurant lunches at out-of-home workplaces will be replaced with neighborhood visits with other home workers. Already, there are enough people operating home businesses that there is no need to feel odd, in any sense, for beginning one. Eventually, home workers will seem almost as commonplace as shopkeepers today. As that happens, any remaining doubts about the professionalism of people working at home will vanish.

Company-employed home workers, of course, will not be totally cut off from their co-workers; the whole idea is to set up communications systems that will allow fairly frequent contact, albeit electronically, in many cases. In some urban neighborhoods, where large companies employ many at home, there may even be opportunities for some co-workers to do their jobs together in one's house, perhaps trading off to work in a partner's home on odd weeks. And, for the self-employed at home, there will still be contacts with customers, suppliers, or other business associates in the daytime.

A general renaissance of the American neighborhood is one likely result of all these events. Restaurants and other service businesses will probably revive in residential areas as workers stay home. Neighbors living on the same street who have never met will meet. They will no longer be separated during the day by distance and at most other times by the reclusiveness of scurrying about, one or two at a time, in cars.

Those with a phobia about new technology worry that machinery may somehow robotize the human race, but eventually electronics are more likely to bring back some of the romanticism of the past. Naturally, there are caveats to this: First, tomorrow hasn't happened yet; second, it is a mistake to spend too much time evaluating a home business in terms of its socializing qualities. Like any job, home businesses are work, and plain labor will have to be the major ingredient of the workday in order to succeed. Motivation to do that work can be a real problem with no one else around to supervise, or to be supervised. Home businesses are ideal for "self-starters"; others must learn self-motivation, and perseverance.

"It takes discipline, true discipline, to work at home," says Marjorie Maxfield, who runs a public relations firm called the Max Agency out of her home in Houston. "More than that," she advises, "you have to like yourself as a person. You can feel isolated, and then you are tempted by all the distractions—a pool, the television, the stereo. But the key is convincing yourself that when you get up, you are going to the office, and you should prepare yourself as if you were going to any office building anywhere. When I go into my home office, I'm there until the evening, and I don't care what happens in the rest of the house. When I close that door, it's closed."

This kind of need for fine-tuned self-control can be a blessing or a curse for the quality of life in home work. Those who have great trouble getting started in the morning by themselves, and sticking to work all day without yielding to distractions, are certain to face penalties in profitability. Those who can master the discipline, however, will find themselves free in home businesses to control their own schedules to a degree seldom possible with any other kind of work. As long as working hours are spent working, they can be scheduled at any time: morning and evening shifts, nights instead of days, if desired, or on weekends to free up time during the week for shopping when the stores aren't crowded. Even the self-employed shopkeeper has no such luxury: He must remain at his counters at least during posted open hours. Those workers who decide to toil at home reiterate that their control of their own schedules is one of the greatest attractions in the work they do.

"I create my own schedule, and that's why I don't feel trapped or isolated," says Peggy W. Gowan, who runs a translating and interpreting service from her Manhattan apartment. "There are times I work from six A.M. to midnight," says Gowan, but she adds that there are other times—times of her choice— when she can arrange to have daytime guests, go out for long lunches, or visit with friends. One accountant who works out of his home in Tyson's Corner, Virginia, puts it succinctly: "I can allocate my time the way I want to. Isn't that what it's all about?"

For the people who can get over the self-motivational hurdle, schedule control is one of a long list of working-condition benefits at home. Some of the other items on the list might more aptly be described as "avoidances" of unpleasant conditions that surround most work outside the home. Home businesses mean the end of:

—the shower-dress-bolt breakfast-and-hit-the-road routine.
—punching time clocks.
—feeling like punching that one guy or gal at the shop who seems dedicated to bothering you.
—foremen or managers breathing down the back of the neck.
—back-stabbing to advance in rank
—the finish up-clean up-and-hit-the-road-home routine (too often made frantic by the knowledge that being late for dinner or some social engagement will complicate life with spouse or family).

Of all these unpleasantries, commuting to work and back is the one that is destined to grow worse with time. The cost, obviously, will rise with oil prices, and even mass transit is becoming expensive in many big cities. In 1981, New York City workers who lived as close as 12 miles away in New Jersey were paying $100 per month for bus fare. In addition, the aggravation of commuting through congested traffic is spreading to more and more regions. The older cities of the Northeast have long been famous for their traffic jams, but the movement of population to the Sunbelt is taking some commuting problems along. Boom towns like Houston are seeing their highways snarled as never before. Home workers who have grown accustomed to avoiding the commuting hassle look with horror at the prospect of ever having to go back to it. "I hate getting on freeways, and if I had to commute, I would be a mushroom by the time I got to the office," declares Jeff Sulkin, an architect who works in his loft in Venice, California.

Cost and aggravation are eliminated by the end of the commute, but far more important is what is gained: time. "The two most common commodities that people spend are money and time," a wise person once observed. "Only one of them has much potential to be adjusted upward." The very fact that so many people are willing to give up huge chunks of irreplaceable time to mindless transit is one of the inscrutable characteristics of modern civilization.

People who can commute to work in 15 minutes are the lucky ones in medium-sized and large cities, yet that 15 minutes one way piles up to 2.5 hours in a five-day week. In one year, that comes to 130 hours, or more than three full work weeks. Over the span of a 45-year working career, the 15-minute commute uses up no less than 146 40-hour weeks, or nearly three years' worth. For the much less fortunate commuters who spend an hour getting to work, the numbers, of course, go through the ceiling. In the same 45-year career, these travelers are on the road for 23,400 hours, or 11 years and 3 months' worth of 40-hour work weeks! Finding ways to utilize that time for business and industry would probably be a bigger step toward solving the problem of flagging productivity than anything else conceivable.

Home-based workers do have this extra time to use as they wish. However, like the opportunity to motivate one's self, the gift of new time can cut two ways. Full-time home businesspeople quickly discover that the end of the commute means a quantum leap in time spent inside the house, a change that can be so fundamental that some underestimate its effects.

Used unproductively, this time can add to monotony. It can contribute to the "trapped" feeling some home workers do complain about. Interestingly, while some say long days at home give them a hermit-like excess of privacy, others turn the equation around. They feel that because they are located at home, a place that ought to be private sometimes, customers are encouraged to think they are open for business day and night. "People think that because the business is in your home, they can call or come over any time. It's an invasion of privacy," says Joel Schachtel, a Highland Park, Illinois, home-based photographer. Schachtel says he has difficulty convincing customers to stick to normal working hours, so that, for example, "Some people call at ten-thirty on a Sunday night to see if their prints are ready."

There are ways for most home workers to take good advantage of extra time. Commuting time saved in the early morning can be used to work, enabling one to end the day at, say, 4:30 P.M. Late sleepers can reverse the formula. Or, to alleviate the trapped feeling, the new spare time can be turned into an institutionalized midday excursion for lunch, exercise, or socializing outside. Time saved from commuting becomes part of your discretionary schedule. Once you have decided how to use it, it is best to be firm in advising customers exactly which hours you are—and are not—open for business.

Just as the longer day at home will change a work schedule, it will profoundly change family relationships, too. Whether a home business is run as a full- or part-time occupation, it is certain to mean both closer contact with family members (simply by proximity) and a different kind of contact than is typical. Husbands, wives, and children of home workers can react in any number of ways. They may love the idea, and turn the home business into a family project of sorts. But they may also feel resentment, especially at first. Children whose mothers or fathers have always worked outside the home usually expect that when the parents are present, their time is to be shared. When one of the parents decides to wall himself off in a home office for hours at a time, children naturally can be upset that the rules have been changed, unfairly and without their consent.

For married couples whose relations already are strained, home businesses can easily push things over the brink. The woman who thinks she just might be able to cope with her mate, as long as he's only around for a few hours a day and on weekends, will not be overjoyed when he announces he is staying home for good. Even when family relationships are basically harmonious, the fundamental changes wrought by working at home can cause irritations. Home work, says one free-lance writer in Miami Beach, "is good because I can spend more time with my family, and bad because they can get in my way a lot. When my wife gets home from her job, she likes to play music, but I'm trying to write." In Houston, artist Gloria Becker plies her trade at home alongside four children, twelve cats, two dogs, and a rabbit. It can be, she says, "absolute bedlam. It's hard for me for get across to them that I must have the space where

I do my work all to myself. They just don't see it as a separate part of the house, and I constantly find my material missing, or a pair of scissors or something. It tends to get very frustrating."

If you are certain that the family would be seriously pulled apart by working at home, it would clearly be foolish even to try. Yet, it could also be a mistake to dismiss a budding business only because you think the family *might* fail to adjust. Most can, and some do even better: They thrive on the new degree of contact between marriage partners, and from the chance for children to see close up, on a regular basis, what work is all about. In the agrarian society which preceded the Industrial Revolution, this was certainly the case. Now, a surprising number of home businesspeople see a parallel. "It's like farming in the olden days, when husband and wife worked together," declares John W. Plessinger, Jr. Plessinger and his wife, Pat, work together to produce stained glass in their Denver home. "There is a better chance of having a relationship last," says Plessinger. "One doesn't go galavanting off in one direction and the other in another. Each can physically see what the other is doing. And it's good for the kids to see what their parents do."

Even when husband and wife are not operating the home business jointly, there tends to be a certain amount of mutual aid and assistance that draws couples together. Peggy Gowan, the New York City home-based translator and interpreter, says she has seen this happen between herself and her husband, William. He is a public relations executive at a large U.S. manufacturing company in the daytime, and a helping hand to her in the evenings, or on weekends, when she is often laboring over documents in any of six languages. "I feel the job has brought me much closer to Bill. He is a Harvard Law School graduate, and I do a lot of legal work. He is always there to ask if I need an answer to a question. Bill feels he is part of my work. He gives me a second opinion. After the kids grew up, we had to get used to each other as individuals." That was made easier by working, as well as living, together, Ms. Gowan says.

Others find home businesses can help solve conflicts between financial necessities and family responsibilities. Mothers and some fathers who have been homemakers and child-raisers may want to—or have to—enter the work force, but two problems usually surface. First, their working wages must immediately be discounted by costs for outsiders' child care in the home or at day-care centers. These costs can easily come to half of the take-home pay from the job. Second, outside child care produces anxiety, and sometimes feelings of guilt. Too often, outsiders are not as careful in watching the children, or in nurturing them, as parents would be. In crowded day-care centers, a lack of individual attention is understandable, but an unhappy situation nevertheless. A number of parents, especially women, feel guilt about leaving the children to anyone. This feeling shouldn't have to exist if the hired help is good, yet the guilt is hard to push aside for those who believe they are shirking a great responsibility. Some parents have set up home businesses mainly to solve these problems. It is not a perfect solution, because most home businesses do require concentration and hard work that cannot be done with children inside the work space or knocking on the door. But thanks to scheduling freedom, some home work can be structured in during children's sleeping hours, and always during school hours.

Gay G. Luke, a Littleton, Colorado accountant, chose to locate her business at home precisely because she wanted to stay with her children, and she says it has worked out fairly well. "I was able to be at home when they needed me. I didn't have to lose work being home with a sick child. I could work and still play the mother role," she says. At times, Luke concedes, the children "resented my working. But it was less of a problem than if I had punched a clock. I had to be in the office (in the basement of her townhouse, where she has employed six others as well), but I could be interrupted, and I was interrupted." And even Houston artist Gloria Becker, with her big family and hoard of pets, says the experience on the whole has been good. "When you get down to it," she declares, "I really do love being home with my kids. We manage to get by. The meals get cooked, largely because I can go to the kitchen, start them, and have one of the kids finish it, or come back later and finish it myself. All the animals get fed, too, so things work out."

Stories like these of family harmony are proof that work at home can improve the quality of life. Clearly, however, they guarantee nothing. Like anything else, and certain cooked green vegetables in particular, home business is a matter of personal taste. It will meld well with the personalities and circumstances of some individuals. Before starting a home business, it is best to ask some hard questions about yourself, and to answer them honestly. Some questions that might help are listed below as a general quiz that you can score.

Take out a sheet of clean paper, and number it from 1 to 30. Next to each number, mark your answer "A" if you agree strongly; "B" if you agree; "C" if you feel neutral; "D" if you disagree; and "E" if you disagree strongly. If the statement does not apply to you, such as one about children if you have none, mark it "F."

THE HOME-BUSINESS QUIZ

1. I have ideas right now about what my home business could be.
2. The reasons I would like to start a home business are very important.
3. My motivations include a belief that I would enjoy working at home.
4. I have at least one hobby I enjoy.
5. I enjoy being my own boss.
6. I have proved in the past that I can complete projects, even when no one else is asking me to do them, or expecting me to do them.
7. I find my present work unfulfilling.
8. I believe I could find enough extra space at my home to set aside for business use only.
9. My spouse would support my decision to launch a home business.
10. My children would support my decision to launch a home business.
11. I prefer tasks that I decide to do myself.
12. I am happy working by myself.
13. My family could learn to allow me privacy in an office at home.
14. I have already told somebody else that I want to start a job at home.
15. In group working situations, I prefer being the person mainly responsible for success or failure.
16. I find I can take care of housework and home maintenance chores and still have time left over.
17. I feel I might have too much time on my hands.
18. My children are well disciplined.

19. I want to learn new skills that are financially profitable.
20. I believe I have some skills that could be used to make money.
21. I enjoy being at home.
22. I like individual sports as much or more than team sports.
23. Trying to make extra money by investing makes me more uneasy than making extra money by working.
24. I prefer my surroundings at home to those at an office building or plant.
25. I have friends in my neighborhood.
26. I dislike commuting to a job.
27. I do not need an outside job for romantic connections.
28. Socializing with co-workers is not too important to me.
29. I think I could make a substantial income in a home business.
30. I would like to get to know more people in my neighborhood.

SCORING:

Count the number of answers marked "F". Subtract this number from 30. The remainder is your *base* number.

Now, give yourself four points for each answer marked "A"; three points for each "B"; two points for each "C"; one point for each "D"; and no points for each "E." Add up the total number of points, and divide this sum by your base number.

If your score comes out between 3.5 and 4, your home business may be ready to bloom. If you scored between 3 and 3.5, you still are well-suited to try. If the score was 2 to 3, you should do a good deal of thinking before starting a home business. At the very least, discuss it with your family and friends. For a score of 1 to 2, a home business is probably not right for you. If you scored less than 1, working at home would be a grave mistake.

Whatever your score was, take a second look at your answer to question 14. If you have actually gone so far as to tell some-body—anybody—that you want to start a business at home, be especially encouraged. Verbalizing something you desire is a key step in starting out. It shows some motivation, and invites feedback from others that could help. Nothing is more impor-tant than the desire to achieve success at a new job. If that feeling is strong enough, all other hurdles shrink, and enjoyment will become a by-product of your labor.

CHAPTER FOUR

Mopping Up the Cold Sweats

In Conshohocken, Pennsylvania, the winding, narrow roads make it hard to find the Pennsylvania Turnpike even when it is nearby. The operators of a service station were taking advantage of that fact to scare up some business from among the lost motorists passing by. They erected a large sign near the curb, and on that sign was this hand-printed message: "Free Knowledge. Bring Your Own Container."

It was a perfect message to bring in traffic. And it is not a bad message, either, for prospective home business operators, who may feel lost as they face a host of great unknowns. Knowledge about how to proceed, carefully and with a feeling of security, is available to those who bring a clear and industrious mind to the task. Self-confidence, staying power, and eagerness to learn are more important than money.

It would be abnormal, of course, to feel no anxiety at the beginning. There are potentially explosive difficulties that can sink any new business: lack of financial planning, production problems, inadequate markets and poor marketing, and a lack of personal commitment. At home, there are extra considerations. Family relationships and life-styles must be adjusted, and there are special problems which include the arch-enemy of home business: the local zoning ordinance.

The fledgling home entrepreneur who delves deeply into all the sources of his fears and worries, learns what the hardships ahead will be, and then decides not even to start, is probably making a wise decision. He is acting on good information. On the other hand, it is tragic when anyone who has a good business idea and real desire to be his own boss quits on the basis of bad information, lack of information, or merely fear. Unfortunately, this is often exactly what happens. Worry and lack of drive kill more business ideas than economic conditions. There is a Fear of Failure Syndrome that can take hold early on, a condition with progressive steps that run something like this:

1. Inspiration.
2. Enthusiastic extrapolation from concept to imagined wealth and happiness.
3. A night's sleep.
4. Sobering second thoughts.
5. Worry about failure and its consequences.
6. A drop in self-confidence.
7. Immersion in other day-to-day work.
8. Emplacement of inspiration on the back burner.
9. Death of the idea, before it has had a chance to live.

Like that unforgettable character of fiction, Walter Mitty, everyone has some dreams—and schemes—that come to fruition only in the mind. Yet it is a hard fact that the dreams and schemes of individuals have built the great business enterprises of the United States; most large corporations are living testaments to that. A little girl once asked her father, Edwin Land, why finished photographs couldn't simply come right out of the camera. Land decided to try to make that happen, and Polaroid Corp. was the result. On an even larger scale, the son of a patent-medicine salesman decided during the Civil War years that there might be a real future in petroleum, especially if he could win control of the refining and marketing of the substance. His name was John D. Rockefeller, and the Standard Oil Trust he created (though long ago broken into separate companies) now has annual revenues of more than $200 billion. Giant companies have grown from home businesses, too. IKEA, a Swedish furniture retailer that is one of the world's largest, began as a mail order operation in the farmhouse of Ingvar Kamprad in the mid-1950s.

These, of course, are tales of incredible success, duplicated rarely. The men and women of real vision are outnumbered by those whose sight is blurred by trembling from within. "Most people don't have enough confidence in themselves," observes Craig McTyre, a home-based mail order seller of books in West Miami, Florida. Gary Hartzler, who runs a home data-processing service in Maryland, suggests that businesses atrophy for two reasons: "Fear of failure. And fear of success." Indeed, success means responsibility for something big, a bothersome notion, and even a scary one for some people.

Still, a general, hazy fear of business is most common, and is partly understandable. Like other specialized human endeavors, business has come to be surrounded by linguistic mystery. Like the government, business represents power and authority seemingly out of grasp for most people, and it is further clouded by strange language. Everyone can understand what is happening when the local supermarket advertises a big discount on a brand of dishwashing detergent. But let's say the detergent was a trial product that didn't work out. Its manufacturer has decided to scrub the project, and is selling its remaining supplies to supermarkets at less than the cost to produce it. The manufacturer might describe what has happened as a failure in test marketing that will result in a $5 million pre-tax write-down of inventory, causing an extraordinary one-time charge against net earnings in the current quarter. Suddenly, the local grocery store seems connected to a chain of events hip-deep in odd jargon to those unaccustomed to the tongue of corporate finance.

Business jargon probably will not change, unless it is to grow more complex. It is best for a home business beginner to familiarize himself with enough to get by. There are plenty of tools to accomplish this in the public library, and some brokerage houses carry explanatory pamphlets, too. Merrill Lynch, Pierce, Fenner & Smith Inc., for one, publishes a brochure entitled *How to Read a Financial Report*. It is a worthy document that takes the reader step-by-step through the toughest pages of corporate financial statements.

Aside from the language of big business, there are learning tools to explain terms and practices in small business. Your local office of the Small Business Administration is a fine first stop. You can buy, order, or obtain for free a wide range of books and pamphlets published by the SBA which are chockfull of explanation and advice. The *Handbook of Small Business Finance* and *Managing for Profits* are two of the books sold at a fraction of the price of commercial books. The public library, again, most likely carries a number of titles about small business, and most large universities offer small business courses.

If lack of business knowledge is a problem for you, it will become clear, after some digging around and learning, that financial language is only a code—though admittedly almost conspiratorial in its capability to befuddle the untrained. The real business skills—marketing, accounting and taxes, planning, production management, general management, and the like—are touched on in this book and in many others. Having some experience in business helps, but is not necessary for an ordinary-sized home business.

Even so, it is a mistake to underestimate any of the potential problems ahead. A pole apart from the timid who do not even try to launch their businesses are those who do underestimate the problems, and they are in for much more trouble. Naïveté combined with overexpectations can lead to the loss of a significant investment, not to mention time and self-esteem. Examples of this are not as common as failure by fear, but they are common enough.

Almost everyone who has led an exciting or unusual life, for example, thinks at one time or another about writing an autobiography. Publishers find that an astonishing number do exactly that. These rarely sell, of course, and they illustrate the fatal lure of overestimating markets and underestimating skills. In recent years, the success of mail order distribution has been a typical draw to the overconfident. George Theofiles, the successful home mail order entrepeneur mentioned in Chapter 1, issues this warning: "People believe mail order is placing a nondescript ad and then watching the mailman with a bowed back bringing crates and crates of orders to your door. But you have to find your niche."

Overexuberance and timidity mark the extremes of the spectrum; in between are most new home businesspeople. They know what they have an urge to do, and they know what they are able to do. A bit later, they may wonder about the market for their product or service, and how to reach it. It is a natural progression to decide on the product first and the market later, and it will work as long as you make certain that both decisions are based on solid knowledge *before spending or borrowing that first dollar.*

If your business is still in the inspirational stage, there are three clear analytic steps you should take before making another move. These steps alone can take you a long way toward mopping up the cold sweats that come with a lack of thoughtful preparation. The first two steps are projections of your goals and of your market acceptance. The third is financial: a listing of your personal condition right now and projections for the cash flow of your business.

You can begin Step 1 immediately. Take out a single sheet of paper and entitle it, "Description and Goals." Force yourself to stick to this one page of writing—summaries force clear and concise thinking. You will write four short paragraphs.

In the first paragraph, *define* what your business will be. In the second, tell why you think you have the *capability* to operate the business. In the third, write *why* you have decided to start the business. Watch out in the third paragraph if mostly negative reasons come to mind ("So I can quit the job I have now." "Because I haven't found anything else I enjoy." "Because other people think I could never get ahead."). Your motives must be primarily positive to succeed in the long run.

In the fourth paragraph, *set forth your goals* as specifically as you can. Come up with a minimum financial goal in dollars per week or month. Set forth a career achievement goal that tells what you would find ultimate satisfaction in creating, producing, selling, or doing for money, all regardless of whether you won't quite be there as the home business begins. If it is very important to you to limit the amount of time you spend on the home business, you should also write down a maximum time allotment goal. As you do further preparation, you will get a better feel for how much time the business will actually take, and you can then glance back at your written goal to compare.

Step 2 is equally important, but you should postpone taking it until you have read Chapter 6, Home-based Marketing. It's a mistake to start any business without first gauging market acceptance as best you can. If you employ some of the inexpensive market-research techniques suggested in Chapter 6 (or any others you can think of), you will begin to find out in advance whether applause or utter silence will greet your venture's early performance. After you have done your research, get out a second sheet of clean paper and title it, "The Market." On this page, you should write why your product or service will fill a real need for the customer group at which you are aiming. Feel free to include the key facts and figures you have gleaned from your research, but don't forget to write a couple of sentences about the generic need of the market. A restorer of antiques, for example, might note that there are a lot of people who love the look and feel of original furnishings, yet many pieces have been painted-over or damaged with time. Use this page, too, to state what your target market is (antique owners, for instance), and do your best to describe that target market's demographic characteristics: numbers of potential customers, ages, income levels, location, sex. Describe the pricing typical in this market, and what you propose in pricing and distribution method.

Step 3 is the longest of the pre-business evaluations. The first part of this step is designed to highlight your personal financial condition before you plunge into the potential risk of a new venture. The second part involves making financial projections for the business. In Step 1, you set a financial goal for the business, and now is the time to make some estimates about how close you may come to reaching it. As you wend your way through Step 3, you should keep a conservative, or even moderately pessimistic, attitude. If you make your estimates conservatively and the numbers still look good, your business is much more likely to survive a rocky start. Wild optimism in financial projections is a sure road to trouble.

PERSONAL CASH FLOW

When you borrow money, one of the things a lender usually requires is a statement of your monthly income and expenses. He wants to get an idea of your ability to take on more debt for which you will have to make monthly payments. Some people don't like to provide this kind of data, viewing the request as something of an invasion of privacy, or even slightly insulting. But if you are going to coordinate your personal finances with a new business, you will have to be more demanding of yourself than any banker would be.

A lending institution usually asks that you tell what your income and expenses are in an "average" month. Similarly, when most people sit down and compute the family budget, they try to figure at least the expense side on the same kind of prorated basis. The problem is, in the real world of bills due and payable, there is no such thing as average or prorated. Christmas bonuses, tax rebates, extra jobs in the summertime, and sales of stocks and bonds can all cause sudden lurches in income

Monthly Income	Jan	Feb	Mar	Apr	May	June	July	Aug	Sept	Oct	Nov	Dec
Take-home pay												
Interest												
Dividends												
Bonuses												
Rental income												
Other												
TOTAL INCOME												

Monthly Expenses	Jan	Feb	Mar	Apr	May	June	July	Aug	Sept	Oct	Nov	Dec
Food												
Utilities and heating												
Housing/rent												
Telephone												
Education												
Taxes other than payroll taxes												
Medical (not covered by insurance)												
Insurance premiums												
Debt repayment to lenders												

	Jan	Feb	Mar	Apr	May	June	July	Aug	Sept	Oct	Nov	Dec
Debt repayments on credit card balances												
Transportation												
Car payments												
Clothing												
Entertainment												
Vacation												
Gifts (include toys)												
Furniture												
Charitable contributions												
Child care												
Home and car repairs												
Other												
TOTAL EXPENSES												
PROFIT OR LOSS (difference between income and expenses)												

in certain months and not in others. The same is true on the expense side. There are quarterly or biennial insurance premiums to pay, vacations, quarterly water bills, and winter heating or summer cooling costs, among many others that occur sporadically during a year.

You will have a much more accurate picture of personal cash flow if you make up a month-by-month real income and expense chart. Not only will the focus be more clear, but you'll quickly see which months are most lucrative and which are most costly, before you start the home business. Then, as you make plans for your business, you can seek what businessmen call "contracyclicality"—the arrangement of income sources that balance each other in swings. In other words, you'll be able to see which months your personal non-home-business income is really eaten away by expenses, and try to design the business to yield the most cash at those times to balance things out. During the months when your personal cash flow is most positive, you may wish to invest in your home business rather than draw cash from it.

You can start on the road to contracyclicality by making 12 separate monthly statements of income and expense. As you do so, think hard about the long list of irregular items that usually show up on the expense side. If you have a budget plan with your utility company and make regular monthly payments all year, this will simplify things, but don't forget about the rest: Christmas gifts, back-to-school clothing in the fall, and the others mentioned above. This chart may seem tedious, but it should fit onto a long sheet of paper turned sideways. Across the top, list the 12 months of the year and along the left margin, list the items shown in the chart.

Fill in the chart, and you will see your real monthly cash flow, which is more likely to show waves rather than a straight line. The purpose is not to suggest you should be highly solvent before starting a full- or part-time home business; indeed, the whole reason for your business may be to improve a troubled cash flow. But you can now try to tailor your business income to try to fill the valleys in the chart. You should also have a feel for the degree of risk you should take on in a home business. If the personal cash flow is not very positive, avoid a home business that may have to operate in the red for a while, or that requires up-front borrowed money that would increase expenses by adding a new monthly bank payment, sending your cash flow into deep red ink.

PERSONAL BALANCE SHEET

Lenders also typically ask customers for figures on total personal assets and liabilities. This is to check out your net worth. They want to make sure that if something should happen that cuts into your monthly income, you have enough value in owned assets to fall back on to cover a loan.

Your purpose in drawing up a personal balance sheet is similar. If something terrible should happen in your new business, do you have assets that can cover the cost? If you intend to operate your business as a sole proprietor, you will be personally liable for debts of the business, even if you keep separate personal and business bank accounts (see Chapter 5). The risk of this unlimited liability is serious enough that, once again, you should be tougher on yourself than a banker would be if you want to get at real answers.

Bank loan officers, especially mortgage loan officers, are often surprisingly generous as they assign values to your possessions. At the time this author applied for his first home-mortgage loan, a banker smilingly insisted that *everyone* had at least $7,000 worth of furnishings, and he jotted that figure down. The real marketable value of those furnishings, had their owner been forced to sell them, probably wouldn't have paid that banker's salary for three weeks.

A truer picture comes from comparing debts that are real to assets that are real. That means assets should be stated at actual market value rather than at original or replacement cost. In other words, you should state non-cash assets at the amounts you could get for them if you sold them, rather than at the amounts you paid to get them, or that you would have to pay to replace them. This can make your balance sheet look more positive or more negative, depending on your personal circumstances. Long-time homeowners will benefit by showing a high market value for their real estate compared to the balance of their mortgages. Owners of certain kinds of furnishings and personal items—oriental carpets, jewelry, antiques—will benefit from the effect of inflation on market valuation. But furniture should be discounted to real-world prices for second-hand pieces. And, owners of gas-guzzling automobiles should discount their market value to levels that others would be willing to pay for used transportation that carries a high operating cost.

With that in mind, fill in the blanks as follows:

Assets	*Liabilities*
Checking accounts _____	Current mortgage balance _
Savings accounts _____	Current unpaid bills _____
Stocks and bonds	Installment loan(s)
(current market value) __	balance _____
Real estate _____	Owed on car(s) _____
Car(s) _____	Taxes owed _____
Household furnishings _____	Other debts owed _____
Personal items _____	TOTAL LIABILITIES _____
Vehicles other than cars __	Minus total assets _____
Loans (owed to you) _____	NET WORTH _____
Other _____	
TOTAL ASSETS _____	

Keep in mind that if you borrow money to help finance your home business, both your assets and liabilities will rise; but, considered realistically, they will not rise equally. For example, Mr. Pierre borrows $10,000 to buy equipment to set up a home beauty shop. He'll owe every dollar of that money back to the bank, and, therefore, the entire principal amount adds to the liability side of his personal balance sheet. With the money, he buys equipment for $8,000, and keeps $2,000 in cash to pay bills and maintain his inventory of supplies. The cash goes directly onto the asset side of the balance sheet, but the $8,000 of equipment should probably be discounted in value; after all, it is now used equipment. Pierre puts his equipment value at $7,000, the amount he might get if forced to sell it. His net worth has dropped by $1,000 in the process.

The way the arithmetic works out, you can use your pre-business net worth figure as a benchmark for borrowing. As long as you have a positive cash flow before the business begins, you'll be relatively safe if you borrow less than your personal net worth to get the business started. Your lender will tell you how much less is apropos. If things go badly in the business, you should still have salvageable assets of some sort, and you are sure to have a positive net worth even after paying the bank.

BUSINESS FINANCIAL PROJECTIONS

Good market research will tell you a great deal about the likelihood of success or failure for your new business. Unfortunately, the best research is imperfect; it will not give you a specific and reliable set of figures for your future sales volume and profit. Indeed, there are some home businesses in which financial projections of future results are impossible. Book writing is one example. Another is collecting and trading in gold or silver coins, whose values will be affected by inflation or even worldwide political strife. The business categories where financial performance is unpredictable should also be the ones in which the proprietor seeks to reduce risk by cautious investment.

There are ways, however, to get some feel for future results in many home-based endeavors. If your business is one in which you will set the price for a product or service, you can begin by calculating maximum sales volume. Check back to the goal you have set for time spent on the business in Step 1. Total the maximum amount of time per month that you would like to spend, and determine how many units of your product or hours of your service could be produced in that period. Add in the maximum monthly production by any employees you plan to hire. Multiply the total number of units of product or service by the price you set forth in Step 2. The dollar figure you come up with will be the very highest sales volume you can achieve in a month. If it seems too low, you may have to increase your working hours or your prices, if the market will bear the raise, or your number of employees. Another option is to improve your production system so that it can turn out more product or service per man-hour.

The maximum sales volume really ought to be an impressively high figure—higher than you can realistically hope to achieve at first. No manufacturing business sells literally every piece of product turned out, and no service business is so efficient and successful that every man-hour invested is paid for by a customer. Before a business begins, it is impossible to estimate accurately how much product will be manufactured but not sold, or will be destroyed or fouled up in production. As a very generalized rule of thumb, you should deduct at least 25 percent from your maximum sales volume to obtain a more down-to-earth monthly sales estimate.

To get an indication of profits, you must deduct all expenses of business from the monthly sales figure. Home businesses have the advantage here of low overhead—office and production space are already purchased or rented. But other expenses come in all shapes and sizes. A list of direct business expense categories is shown on page 64 in Chapter 5. Deduct estimates for them all in a given month and you will be left with before-tax profits. Multiply this monthly figure by 12 for annual before-tax profits, and add this figure to your projected year's income from sources outside the home business. You can then use IRS tax tables or tax rate schedules to estimate the percentage of your total income payable to the government. Take this percentage and deduct it from your monthly home business before-tax profits to estimate your business after-tax earnings—something comparable to take-home pay if you were a company employee. Check this figure back against the financial goals you set in Step 1. If the profit seems low, you should once again reconsider some of the numbers you crunched to make these calculations. Can you raise your prices and get away with it? Can you increase production per man-hour? Work longer hours and still enjoy it? You may even want to reconsider the nature of your product or service. If projected profits are disappointing, can you make or offer a different product or service that is truly more valuable in the marketplace, and could, therefore, carry a higher price?

A prime objective of your financial planning should be keeping control of your cash flow. The better you are able to adjust and control money flowing in against money flowing out, the better you will be able to tailor your home business to be contracyclical to your personal cash flow. You will maintain control best by eliminating all possible elements that are left to chance, and the premier one is customer billing. If it is in any way possible, your business should demand payment from customers on delivery of products or services. And, you should be vigilant about accepting personal checks; try to take them only from good-risk customers. If you allow customers to pay bills at their discretion, count on having almost no money flowing in during the first month of your business. Future months will depend on many things: loyalty of your customers to you, quality of your customer group, and general economic conditions. In times of high inflation, customers can be expected to stretch out payments as long as they can. The cash-flow advantage of the cash-on-delivery business is hard to overstate.

BEATING THE REGULATORS

Home businesses actually face two separate kinds of potential difficulties. There are those related to business operations—your own skills and motivation, financial management, production, and marketing. These are the internal question marks before a business begins. But there will also be external forces with which to cope. Government has been the fastest growing and the biggest business in the United States for years, and its agents at several levels will be knocking on the door.

There is plenty of irony in this. If only by accident, home business operators happen to be the most patriotic citizens. By eliminating commuting, they save more oil per person than anyone else trying any other conservation method. Home working thus becomes the least expensive and most immediately effective solution to overconsumption of oil, which together pose one of the most serious economic dilemmas ever to face the nation. And, in a society that honors hard work, home business people who work two or more jobs ought to be the object of official praise. Unfortunately, under a system of skewed and old-fashioned government regulation, things don't work out that way.

To begin with, home businesses are subject to all the myriad regulations of other businesses: taxation by federal, state, and local agencies; environmental restrictions; health and safety rules; labor regulations; licensing and registration at state and local levels; and, of course, all the paperwork that can come along with these rules. Beyond that, there are special external forces that come to bear: zoning regulations, and even laws in some states that try to prevent certain kinds of businesses from being run out of homes, such as food processing.

Our system of law requires adherence to all these rules as though they were equally just, but, of course, some are really more just than others. Among the excesses in home business regulation, zoning laws and certain IRS practices stand out. The IRS has even sought to stretch the law to punish home working. In the late 1970s, the tax authorities began a long effort to prevent some home business practitioners from declaring legitimate expenses of an office in the home, even though the agency's drive was not clearly supported in law (see Chapter 5).

The fact that there seems to be no simple and unburden-

some way to conduct even the smallest of businesses undoubtedly drives many home entrepreneurs underground. Once
secret, home businesses have their revenge: Federal and state
governments lose millions in income taxes yearly, and cities
with local income taxes (but also with zoning laws that seek to
obliterate business use of the home) lose revenue as well. It is
an all around unhappy situation in which all parties are losers,
especially the secret home businesses ferreted out in tax audits
and zoning inspections.

One solution for home workers is to learn from bigger businesses. The leaders of U.S. corporations have complained loud
and long about the interference and cost of government regulation. Some of these companies really are materially hurt by
regulation, especially those that must spend millions to comply
with environmental and health and safety restrictions. But relatively few corporations fail because of these entanglements.
This is because the big companies have learned systems for
Beating the Regulators (BTR). They employ specialists trained
to cope with government. On a smaller scale, the home entrepreneur can do the same. BTR skills do not enable anyone to
avoid compliance with the law, but rather to live with regulation
safely, under the smallest possible financial penalty. Here are
some easy ways to develop beginning BTR know-how and avoid
becoming overmatched against the government:

1. Find out exactly what all levels of government expect from
   you. For the federal government, one way to start is by sending away for two free "advocacy publications" of the Small
   Business Administration: the *Catalogue of Federal Paperwork Requirements* and the *Guide to Record Retention Requirements for Small Business*. You can address a letter
   requesting these publications to: Director, Office of Infor-
   mation/Associations, Office of Advocacy, U.S. Small Business Administration, 1441 L Street, N.W., Washington, DC
   20416.

   Check with your city or town law department, and with
   county or township officials, to find out about zoning and
   other local business regulation. The closest office of the state
   tax department is a good place to start finding out about
   state business regulation. Personnel there may direct you to
   other agencies, such as the offices of secretaries of state,
   where corporate records often must be filed.

2. Be prepared to hire professional help. Government is nothing if not complex, and while many people have the capability to unravel the intricacies of regulation, few new business-people have the time. As you budget for the start of business, set aside money for an outside accountant's service, and also a legal aid contingency fund. Accountants who specialize in handling the books of small enterprises may want you as a client. Ask one if he will give you some free consulting time before your business begins, in return for future tax or book-keeping service compensation. Use this consultation to get a detailed description of record-keeping requirements, tax regulation, and other paperwork.
3. Don't ignore the written word. Letters and forms sent to you by government agencies should be answered by you, your accountant, or your lawyer. Documents left untended will tend to haunt you later.
4. Cheat the IRS at your own risk. The underground economy is big, but a perilous place to do business. You risk serious fines—if not worse—by failing to file tax returns or falsifying returns. It will be safer to learn how to use tax laws to your advantage.
5. If only to soothe the mind, try to understand the motives of the regulators. A seasoned labor-relations executive in the steel industry once conceded that the rights granted to unions by Congress undoubtedly stemmed from a real need to correct abuses, oppressive working conditions, and low pay. The same is probably true of most government intervention. Some amount of legitimate need is at the root, though the government's decisions and methods for resolving problems are often debatable.

ZONING: THE SPECIAL PROBLEM

Zoning is a good example of a governmental solution to a societal need. It is also the perfect example of regulation gone amok in many cities. For innocent, quiet, and unobtrusive home-based businesses, local zoning ordinances have become regulations that punish without doing good.

Zoning laws in many places represent the reactions of cit-

izens decades ago to the booming spread of U.S. industrialization. The Industrial Revolution created the factory, a marvel
of efficiency preferably admired at a distance. Industrialization
was productive but ugly, dirty, and dangerous. Automobiles,
especially dangerous where children played, crowded the commercial districts as well, replacing pedestrians. Residential property owners, anxious to protect their children, and their real
estate values, were especially hopeful in the suburbs of living
quietly and free from industrial and commercial sprawl. They
supported the creation of restrictive zoning maps, which cut
many cities and towns up into portions prohibiting heavy industry, light industry, or retail or other commercial operations,
finally creating the pristine residential neighborhoods. Even the
residential neighborhoods were sliced into those reserved for
single-family dwellings versus two-family, apartments, and con-
dominiums.

Understandable as their creation was, zoning laws were too
often drawn hard and fast, leaving them inflexible in an era of
growing home-based businesses. One recent case illustrates
this. A Los Angeles woman received a whole gallery of art work
from her husband, as part of a property settlement in a divorce.
Faced with the need to earn extra income to raise her teen-age
son, she decided to make a modest business of selling a few
pieces of art each year. The customer traffic she brought into
her residentially zoned neighborhood to see the works was no
more than a few social gatherings each year would have caused.

Still, she wanted to do business above board. She carefully
obtained licenses for retail and wholesale trade, plus an art
broker's license. Every cent of tax due on income from the sales
was paid. She suspects that a neighbor with whom she did not
get along called city officials to point out the zoning violation—
one of the ways zoning law typically becomes used to intensify
personal squabbles.

The City of Los Angeles served her with an order (without
prior warning) to put an end to the business or face a $500 fine
or six months in jail. "I just couldn't believe my eyes when I got
this slip," she says. "I called the zoning officials and told them
I do about as much business out of my home as most people
do with garage sales. They told me I would need a permit for
garage sales. Los Angeles is consumed with archaic rules and
regulations."

The harassment didn't end. Our art dealer moved her pieces

to a small shop away from home. Zoning inspectors made un-announced appearances at her home, nonetheless, to check up. They also showed up at her new shop, and took photographs in front of startled customers for evidence of the dealer's compliance. More municipal manpower and tax dollars were spent on all of this than on some police investigations of crimes of violence, in a city with enough real problems to keep its employees busy enough.

Fortunately, the same economic forces that are bolstering the work-at-home movement will probably make such horror stories obsolete in most places. Popular demand created zoning. As increasing numbers of corporations employ people at home, swelling the constituency of the at-home self-employed, popular demand will modify the ordinances. The national priority of energy conservation will push the process along. Quiet, non-polluting, and low-traffic kinds of home businesses will grow acceptable in most municipal codes.

In the meantime, there is no reason to overreact to the first revelation you hear that a business in your home would violate the zoning code. Find out at your city hall or county courthouse whether your home is really in a strictly residential spot. If it is, check into how your town defines the residential classification with a phone call or visit to the city or county law department. It may well be that the kind of business you envision will not violate the code.

If your business would be an apparent violation, you might still want to check with an attorney who specializes in zoning law to look for a way out. Most cities have zoning boards of appeals, often peopled with elected officials, who can grant variances and exceptions. Or, you may be able to alter your business plans to make the operation fit the law. For example, if the law restricts businesses in your neighborhood that employ people other than the owner at home, you may be able to subcontract your employees' work to them at their own homes. If retail traffic is the problem, you could switch to another scheme of product distribution. Or, you may be able to organize a drive to change the law. At last check, that is what was on the mind of our heroine in Los Angeles. "I will speak up before the city and try to change these rules," she declared. "I wasn't disturbing anybody."

This kind of determination is a powerful weapon on many battlefronts—against wearisome regulation, against a poor early showing by the new business, and especially against one's own fear of failure. Combined with knowledge of how to run the business and of potential problems ahead, a stiff resolve to succeed at home can be a happily self-fulfilling drive. Contrary to popular belief, motivation is not a quality that merely occurs in some people and not in others. In small business, it also flows from good information, diligently gathered and clearly perceived, about the substance of the business concept. If the idea is sound, location at home becomes an added attraction.

CHAPTER FIVE

Structure and Taxes

If you have carefully considered what lies ahead for a home business you are planning, you should be ready to proceed on the basis of solid market information, sound financial projections, and a serious evaluation of yourself and your goals. The next question is: What form should the business take?

You may know exactly how you are going to produce the goods or services you plan to sell. But no matter how well you do your job, the amount of benefit you derive—and the amount of risk you take—will depend on other factors, too. You must decide how to structure your business: as a sole proprietorship, a corporation, or a partnership. And you should know some rudiments of how to handle the IRS, which otherwise may handle you. Even if you plan to use a professional accountant or tax service, you must know what records to keep and how to keep them. And, in order to know what to expect in profit, you should have at least a rough feel for how much you will be able to deduct from income for the business use of your home, among other things.

Most home businesses that bring in moderate incomes are set up as sole proprietorships. But that does not necessarily mean that this form is always right, even for the smaller business, and it may not be right for you. How to structure your business is among the first decisions you have to make, although it is true (and very important) that you can change your business structure later.

Each business structure has built-in advantages and disadvantages. Look for the one whose advantages match best with what you are hoping to achieve, and whose disadvantages are least threatening. To begin with, there are basic theoretical differences that separate each business structure.

A sole proprietorship is a business typically owned and run by an individual. The law regards such a business as a direct extension of the owner's personal property and financial life. It is the easiest form of business to start, and the easiest for which to account. The law views regular partnerships in much the same way, except that these businesses are mutually owned, and, typically, mutually operated, by two or more individuals. Again, the partnership is literally a part of the personal financial circumstances and property of its owners.

A corporation is quite different. It may have one owner or many owners, but in no case is it part and parcel of the personal lives of its owners in terms of their liability for how well the corporation performs. Under the law, a corporation is a sort of individual of its own, an entity that rises or falls by itself, can sue or be sued, and so forth. From this philosophical and legal distinction flows a spate of consequences that remove corporations from the rest of the pack.

The single most important difference is the concept of limited personal liability. As a sole proprietor or partner, if your business fails and you owe money to creditors, they can take what's left of the business *plus* cash and property assets that you personally own. Consider, for example, a hypothetical Jane Smith who decides to start a full-scale catering business. She takes the direct route of a sole proprietor and simply plunges forward. Jane takes some money from a savings account and uses it to make a down payment on cooking ovens, food processors, utensils, and other equipment. She also borrows some money from a bank to provide some extra working capital.

But things go awry. It turns out, let's say, that Jane never was a very good cook, and the women at the Ladies Social Club quickly spread the word that a catered meal by Jane is rather like an afternoon of grazing in the north 40. Jane soon discovers she has no customers, but that she does have a bank and restaurant-equipment company unwilling to wait for their monthly payments. Jane may have set up separate bank accounts for her business, and they may be empty. That doesn't matter. Her creditors may seize funds from her personal checking and savings accounts, other liquid assets, or even personal property— Jane's jewelry or a second car. Jane cannot be certain of protection under bankruptcy if her personal assets are ample to cover the debts of the business she has begun as a sole proprietor. The same would be true if Jane's business was a partnership.

This cannot happen with a corporation. Had Jane formed one, her corporation would have bought the equipment and taken the bank loan. Corporations are more complicated to set up and run, so Jane would have had to cope with extra red tape, aggravation, and additional expense for outside tax and accounting services. But when Jane's strogonoff was discovered to require steak knives and soup spoons, she would not have been personally liable for the failure of her business. Jane's Creamed Delights Inc. could be forced to pay off its creditors only until its own capital was used up. As a separate and distinct individual, her corporation would have fallen alone, and its creditors, after having caused its liquidation, would be stuck with any remaining debts.

There are other differences between corporations and sole proprietorships, but the importance of limited liability cannot be overstated. If you plan a business with clear financial risk ahead, forming a corporation is a logical route to protect yourself. Even if you simply have developed a home business of significant size in sales and profits, it is certainly worth your while to incorporate it if you have not already done so, just to get the safety of limited liability.

On the other hand, if your home business is one that has little potential risk of financial failure in tandem with high debt (writing, garment repair, and some creative products businesses seem likely candidates, to name a few), then you certainly should go on to consider the full list of advantages and disadvantages for each type of structure. The sole proprietorship is extremely handy, and it is an inexpensive way to start a home business. Although it is never a bad idea to hire outside tax help, a sole proprietor who is deft with numbers may be able to do his own bookkeeping and taxes. It is wise to register even the sole proprietorship with local or state authorities, and you must obtain legal licenses, such as vendor's permits, if appropriate. But such registrations and licenses are usually cheap. As a sole proprietor, you can, in effect, simply start doing your business, selling your products, and taking in earnings, quickly and without much up-front cost.

This cannot be said for corporations. They usually must be registered with additional governmental agencies, typically a secretary of state. You will probably need an attorney for this, and the cost will shoot up. You will need copies of legal documents prepared—articles of incorporation, for example, and a set of by-laws of the company. You also will have to select a board of directors, and conduct regular meetings of these directors. You can be chairman, and you may want to rope in your spouse and friends to fill out the board. Professional tax and accounting services will become almost a must, and record keeping will become very complex.

Part of the reason is that you will have created a new individual, and that individual is not you. You might conduct the business day-to-day exactly as if it were a sole proprietorship, but as an incorporated home business, it will have to do some things on its own: pay you a salary, for example, and pay you rent for the space it uses in your home. Legally, the corporation is required to deal with you as someone who gets no special favors, though you may be its owner, chairman, and president. This kind of treatment is known as an "arms-length" arrangement. It means you cannot manipulate the corporation by doing such things as having it pay you thousands of dollars per month to rent some space in your den. In your various charges to the corporation, nothing can appear to have been done for purposes of your personal gratification or aggrandisement. The costs must be reasonable and necessary or they cannot be deducted from income for tax purposes.

Financially, the corporate structure can both reward and penalize in ways different from the sole proprietorship. On the penalty side, corporations are plagued with a form of double taxation. Profits of the corporation are taxed, and the dividends you receive as the company's owner are taxed, too, on your personal income-tax return. At first glance, it may even appear that the corporation is triple-taxed, though this is not true. The appearance comes from the fact that, in addition to taxes on corporate profits and dividends, your salary will be taxed on your personal return. This third tax, however, is cancelled out by the fact that your salary is part of the corporation's labor cost, and is, therefore, deducted from revenues of the company, lowering the corporate profits before they are taxed. Still, double taxation is vexing enough if you choose, as most corporations do, to pay yourself dividends from the company's after-tax profits rather than putting all the money back into the business.

Corporate financial advantages, though, are also worth considering. The law allows corporations to do many things to reward employees (you), things that sole proprietors cannot get away with. For instance, as a sole proprietor, you may set up your own pension plan, but, as of 1981, you could only do so with 15 percent of your profit, not to exceed $7,500 per year, set aside and tax-sheltered for later use when you retire. A corporation has no such limit. It can choose to pay much higher pensions, and may even do so with cash plus profit-sharing plans that can be quite lucrative.

A corporation also typically buys insurances (health and life) for its employees as a fringe benefit. It can deduct the expense of doing so as part of its labor costs. This maneuver cuts down profits, and, therefore, the amount of tax that will be levied against them. As a sole proprietor, your purchases of health and life insurance cannot be deducted as business expenses.

Your benevolent corporation can also buy you a number of other fringe benefits. These do not interfere with the arms-length principle, because corporations typically do offer a wide range of benefits. For example, your corporation can offer a death benefit covering you and members of your family (deductible from corporate revenues as labor cost when spent). The list of fringes that corporations provide grows ever longer with time. In 1980, the *Wall Street Journal* reported that General Mills was offering employees at its Minneapolis headquarters discounts of 10 to 20 percent for auto repairs and car washes performed by a company staff. Corporations also typically give their employees discounts on the company's own products or services.

The ideal home business structure would be one that provides the limited liability and fringe benefits of a corporation, but avoids double taxation and other difficulties, which also happen to include a special tax on unreasonably large accumulated corporate earnings. Fortunately, a structure that fits this description pretty closely is also available. It is called the Subchapter S Corporation.

SUBCHAPTER S CORPORATIONS

Created by law in 1958, Subchapter S is a sort of hybrid between sole proprietor and standard corporation in terms of its tax treatment. To get a basic knowledge of Subchapter S, go to your local IRS office and request Publication 589, entitled *Tax Information on Subchapter S Corporations*. This brochure explains fairly clearly what this form of business can do for you, and it even includes sample tax returns filled out for a hypothetical company. The key thing to know is that Subchapter S does protect you with the privilege of limited liability. It has these other primary advantages:

1. No regular corporate taxes.
2. If the corporation suffers a loss, its shareholders (owners) can deduct pro-rata portions of that loss directly from their personal earnings in determining their income tax liability. Losses by an ordinary corporation cannot be deducted on the personal tax returns of its owners. The regular corporation can only use losses to shield some future years' profits.
3. The tax on unreasonable accumulations of earnings usually does not apply. Also, you need not be concerned about the IRS's often troublesome "reasonable compensation" test for officers' salaries, applicable to regular corporations.
4. Corporate profits are ordinarily not taxed, but are allocated on a pro-rata basis to shareholders. This eliminates double taxation.

To qualify for Subchapter S, the corporation must meet certain conditions. But these will not be hard for most home businesses. Generally, the conditions are an attempt to make sure Subchapter S corporations are small businesses, real operating businesses instead of sham corporate shells, and are owned by U.S. citizens or resident aliens. A Subchapter S corporation must:

1. Be domestic.
2. Be a free-standing corporation. That is, it cannot be a part of a parent corporation, and it cannot own active subsidiary corporations.
3. Have only one kind of stock.
4. Have shareholders who are either individuals or estates, and not other corporations or companies.
5. Not have a nonresident alien as a shareholder.

There are other details about Subchapter S with which you should become familiar through Publication 589 or a professional accountant. This business form can be a solution to many structure problems, and home entrepreneurs who have used it tend to be strident supporters. In Stamford, Connecticut, for example, Roger Clark has run businesses since the late 1960's with Subchapter S status. Right now, Clark has a home-based computer service business.

Still, like other corporations, Subchapter S is not as easy

or inexpensive to set up and to account for as a sole proprietorship. There is still a choice to make, and you can do further free research at the local IRS office, which should be able to supply you with tax treatment details on all forms of small businesses. Though most taxpayers tend to regard the IRS as an adversary, it is true, at least, that the agency is willing to explain itself. In fact, in the United States it is often forgotten that people in many other industrial nations view the IRS and the laws behind it as amazingly liberal, if only because the system is based on voluntary reporting by taxpayers and the occasional audit. Some other governments have an unpleasant tendency to tell you what you owe and collect it forcibly.

RECORD KEEPING WITH THE IRS IN MIND

You have the right to tell the IRS what you owe. The caveat is that you have to be ready to back up what you say if challenged. Record keeping in your home business is a matter for more than light concern, as those who have been audited can attest. As a home businessperson, you will have to be aware of the full range of deductible expenses available to you—and aware of those you cannot take—in order to know what records to keep.

Using care with business records is more important in a home business than in any other enterprise. Without good books, you stand the risk of being considered a mere hobbyist by an IRS auditor, especially if your business is small in scale and is related to an activity usually considered a hobby. Coin and stamp collecting and trading are perfect examples. Both can be volatile home businesses—likely to produce big profits or big losses. But without solid business records, these occupations and others can slip into the hobby trap, and that can be costly indeed. If the IRS decides that what you doing is only a hobby, then any earnings you derive will be taxed. But you will not be allowed to deduct losses from your annual income when tax time comes around.

If you pick a corporate structure, it will be relatively easy to convince the IRS that you are truly in business. As a sole proprietor at home, there are two ways you can still prove that your business is a business. First, you can register your business with local or state regulatory authorities. Check your city hall or county courthouse to find out how. Second, keep records of all transactions that involve expenses or bring in money. This means making detailed entries in ledger books of income and spending, plus keeping and filing receipts, cancelled checks, copies of bills and invoices, and all similar papers. Pick a name for your business, and have some stationery printed under that logo: billing forms, envelopes, letterhead paper, and business cards.

The business ledger book need not be complicated, only complete. It will require almost no expertise, but it will require the time and effort to keep it current. You can pick up business ledger books in drugstores, office supply shops, or department stores. Don't forget that the purchase price of ledger books and business stationery is a deductible expense.

Your business supplies fall into one of two basic categories of expenses. Supplies are one of the *direct expenses* of business. Home workers should keep such expenses separate from those related to the *business use of the house or apartment.* The reason for the separation is this: Direct expenses of your business—labor and raw material costs, for example—cannot be challenged if they are properly documented. But the costs of maintaining a home office, production area, or storage area—costs including utility bills and other items—can be challenged for a number of causes. Rules about who can and who cannot deduct home-office expenses got tougher in the mid-1970s, although they may get more liberal again. Debate over this issue has raged for years, and we'll examine the issue more closely in a moment. First, here is a list of some direct business expenses you can always deduct from revenues, as long as you have documentation:

DIRECT EXPENSES

1. Wages or salaries for your employees, including the cost of fringe benefits you provide.
2. Costs of raw materials, components, or products used to make the products you sell.
3. Purchases of finished goods you buy and resell.
4. Automobile (or truck) expenses for a vehicle used for business purposes. Include gasoline and oil, lubrication and

washing, repairs, tires and supplies, garages and parking, insurance, interest payments, taxes, tolls, depreciation (see section on depreciation, pages 71–72), and any other auto expenditures. If your vehicle is used only partly for the business, then only a similar portion of expenses is deductible.

5. Transportation costs for your products.
6. Business-related travel expenses—lodging, meals, and transportation. Obtain receipts for all lodging, regardless of expense per night. Get receipts for transportation whenever possible.
7. Postage
8. Office supplies.
9. Business-related entertainment expenses. Obtain receipts for meals, drinks, gifts, or other items that individually exceed $25.
10. Advertising and promotion.
11. Interest payments on business debts.
12. Insurance premiums for coverages strictly related to the business, such as product liability insurance. (See Business Use of Home concerning premiums for homeowner's and renter's insurance, page 70.)
13. Protective clothing you must buy for employees.
14. Depreciation of business equipment (see section on depreciation, pages 71–72).
15. Business service costs, including legal, outside secretarial, stenographic, answering service, or related.
16. Information services required for your business. Include subscriptions to periodicals, newsletters, electronic information services, or related. You must be prepared to show why these services are really important to the business.

BUSINESS USE OF YOUR HOME

Controversy has embroiled the issue of the legitimacy of tax deductions for the business use of a home. As inflation took firm hold of the United States in the early 1970s, taxpayers searched as never before for ways to shield their ravaged wages from the final bite—that of the IRS. The wealthy, of course, could afford some neat tax shelters—large investments in oil and gas drilling projects, or setting aside big trusts for future use by children, to name just two. But the middle class and the poor were economically barred from most shelters, and more and more of them found an alternative: writing off the expenses of an "office" in the home. Rules for substantiating the active use of the home office were liberal and in some cases ill-defined. Company employees could fairly easily set aside rooms at home for a desk and chair. Then, they could declare that they were often required to bring work home, and this was hard to prove or disprove under the old rules. This made possible all manner of new, deductible expenses: keeping the home office warm in the winter, cool in the summer, supplied with electricity, fitted out with office supplies, equipment, and so on. Undoubtedly, the letter of the law was being abused by thousands, particularly employees whose work was not based at home in any way.

Congress moved to tighten the rules in the middle of the decade. In the Tax Reform Act of 1976, it set up stringent new regulations. The Act said that taxpayers could deduct home office expenses only if their work at home met specific tests. The IRS describes these tests in Publication 587, *Business Use of Your Home.* Failure of any one of them means you cannot deduct any home office expenses. The primary tests are paraphrased below:

Regular Use. You must use the home office on a regular basis, and not just incidentally or occasionally.

Exclusive Use. Your home office or work area must be a separate space used exclusively for business purposes. If the office space is also used, even now and then, as living space, you fail this test. The only exceptions involve space used for storage of inventory in some circumstances, or for home-based day-care facilities (see Caring for People, Chapter 9).

Employer Convenience. If you are a company employee, you can deduct home-office expenses only if your office exists for the convenience of your employer. If you set up and use the office only because it is helpful to you or convenient to you, you fail this test.

Principal Place of Business. This is the toughest rule. It says that if you have more than one business location (such as the lawyer who really has to bring work home, but does have an outside office), your home office must be the principal place of business to qualify for deductions. In determining whether your home office is the principal place, there are three questions to answer, and your position will be strongest if each answer is, "More at home." The questions are:

1. How much time do you regularly spend working at home, compared with your other business location(s)?
2. What is the general degree of business activity at your home, compared with any other place?
3. How much income do you derive from working at home versus outside?

In essence, all of these tests seemed tough but relatively fair when Congress set the new criteria. The trouble was, there was a loophole big enough to snare a bear in the principal place test. It did not differentiate between taxpayers who had one job, and those who had two jobs, one of which was a part-time, home-based business.

The principal place test was clear enough for a hypothetical Jane Smith who worked all day as a newspaper reporter at an office building, but who also handled a few reportorial phone calls at home each night. Before 1976, Jane might have declared home-office expenses, but now she could not, since her main location obviously was outside the home. But what if Jane, after a day at work at the paper, came home and changed hats to become the sole proprietor of a mail order business selling door knobs? Jane would then have two principal work spots: one as reporter and the other, at home, for Jane's House of Handles. Could she take deductions for the clear business use of her home? Logic, and any sense of fair play, shouted yes. The IRS said no. The agency began using its own broad interpretation of the principal place test. It decided that taxpayers could have only one main place of business, and that place was where most income was earned. If Jane made more as a news reporter, she could not declare deductions for using her home to make or sell door knobs.

This ridiculous interpretation discriminated against whole trade groups at a time. Book authors and free-lance writers were two of them. In these occupations, only the most efficient and successful practitioners can succeed as full-timers. Most authors and free-lancers who like to eat and pay the rent find they must ply their trades part time, from home, moonlighting after regular jobs outside the house. Many home businesses are run as second jobs only, and while everything about the American culture finds such diligence praiseworthy, the IRS sought, in effect, to discourage the practice.

Still, the IRS attitude was only its opinion, and U.S. Senate investigators report that some taxpayers have beaten the IRS in court on the principal place interpretation. In the meantime, the patent unfairness of the situation caused a powerful group of senators to introduce a bill on January 5, 1981, to prevent the harsh policy from continuing. In Senate Bill 31, Senators Dole, Mathias, Goldwater, Boren, Exon, and Armstrong sought to change the legal definition in the law to read: ". . . principal place of business for any trade or business of the taxpayer." Speaking for the group, Senator Armstrong declared, "This anti-small-business policy [of the IRS] is unwise." Senator Dole added: "If an individual feels he must moonlight at a business operated from his home, he should not be denied a business deduction merely because he may hold another full-time job. No one should be penalized for having the industry to hold more than one job." The senators reported that they were reacting to a deluge of mail from constituents. What is unfortunate is that so many others have been scared away from home-office deductions nonetheless. "They make it so difficult for a guy to get a deduction when he works out of the home that I figured it wasn't worth the trouble," says a self-employed carpenter who does much of his work in a shop on his property in Los Angeles.

There are two critical things to note about the IRS wrangle. First, it has nothing to do with direct business expenses; they always are deductible. Second, it does not threaten home-office deductions for full-time home workers who have no other principal place. At the time of this writing, it also appeared that the IRS principal place interpretation was headed for reversal by a Congress and White House opposed to the kind of silly government discouragement of productivity that the agency was engaging in. If you have not followed the news about the results of this fight, check with a tax accountant for a quick update on your rights as a moonlighter. Meanwhile, you should certainly be ready to identify home-office deductions, as opposed to direct expense deductions, since you might qualify to use them.

How you deduct the expenses of using your home for your business depends on whether you choose to be a sole proprietor or to incorporate. As previously noted, the incorporated business will pay rent and other office costs to you as lessor of the property. In any case, however, you will need to know which kinds of expenses can be deducted legitimately and which kinds cannot. The range can be broad, as you can imagine.

For many home-office deductions, it will be necessary for

you to calculate exactly what percentage of your total living space is being used for the home office, production area, or storage or warehousing area. Just walk off the length and width of your work area, and multiply for square footage. Divide this figure by the square footage of the entire house. This gives you a ratio you will need to use several times. You should express the ratio as a percentage for easy arithmetic, and for simplicity's sake we can call this proportion your HB/TH ratio (Home Business/Total Home).

MORTGAGE PRINCIPAL AND INTEREST

As a homeowner, you CANNOT deduct any portion of the mortgage principal payments on your home because of a home business. This is because, in theory, the HB/TH ratio of your mortgage principal payments represents your investment in ownership of your place of business: in other words, your purchase of a fixed asset. When businesses invest in fixed assets, they are not encumbering an expense of doing business so much as they are transferring cash wealth into property wealth, incurring no loss of value. Loss of value (an expense) occurs only gradually for fixed assets as their useful life dwindles, but this is depreciation. See the section on depreciation on pages 71–72 for methods of deduction.

You CAN deduct as an expense your interest payments on your mortgage. These payments are not an investment, but a payment to a lender, a clear cost of doing business. Multiply your total interest payments on your home mortgage during the year by your HB/TH ratio, and take the result as a business deduction. Don't forget that the balance of mortgage interest can be declared as an itemized deduction on Schedule A of your tax return.

LEASE OR RENTAL PAYMENTS FOR PROPERTY

If you rent an apartment, house, or other dwelling place, you are entitled to deduct a portion of your rent or lease payments for your home office. This is because you are not spending money to acquire a fixed asset; you are making payments to another owner, and these are a cost of goods sold. Multiply your total rental or lease payments by your HB/TH ratio for your deduction. However, note that you cannot depreciate your home business property, since you don't own it.

REAL ESTATE TAXES

Simply multiply your annual real estate taxes by your HB/TH ratio for your deduction. But check with an accountant if your property includes a substantial lot. Taxes are levied on your entire property, and you may be advised to deduct only the HB/TH ratio of the taxes on the house alone as a business expense. As with mortgage interest, the balance can be taken as an itemized deduction.

HOMEOWNER'S INSURANCE

Fire, theft, and related coverages of homeowner's insurance or renter's insurance also protect home business property. If you have not changed your policy because of the home business, then simply multiply your premium payments by your HB/TH ratio and deduct the result. If you have increased your coverage—and the cost of premiums—because of the business, you may be able to deduct the extra expense as well. To do so, the extra coverage should be specific to your business and not apply to the rest of your home, too. For example, a home-based beauty shop might specify in an insurance policy extra coverage for certain pieces of equipment. The additional premium costs for this equipment would become direct expenses of business.

UTILITIES

Deduct the HB/TH ratio of your home's heating, electricity, and cooling expense. Also deduct the HB/TH ratio of your telephone service expense if your business shares a phone with the rest of the house. Long distance business calls are direct expenses, fully deductible. To thoroughly validate your telephone expense, it is a good idea to install a separate business phone that can be 100 percent deductible (service and long distance cost). Similarly, an IRS auditor will be more easily convinced of your electricity expense for the business if you install a separate meter.

DECORATING, LANDSCAPING, GARDENING, AND PROPERTY MAINTENANCE

If your home business involves contact with other people (clients, customers, suppliers, salesmen, or your own employees), then you certainly have as much cause as any other business manager to provide attractive and healthful surroundings. This means that you can take an HB/TH ratio of your regular expenses for property upkeep, including lawn maintenance, gardening, and other exterior decorating. Special landscaping or decorating projects done to enhance the appearance of the home business only are 100 percent deductible. These, again, become direct expenses, and include such things as interior remodeling and repair of the home business space, painting or purchase of signs for the business, and decorating or landscaping done for business purposes only right outside a separate entrance to the work area. Also, deduct all of the cost of improvements to any parking area on your property if the space is used for business purposes only. You may want to erect signs to designate your business parking area.

DEPRECIATION

Depreciation plays a major function in accounting. It may not be as critical a factor in your home business as it is to big corporations, because depreciation is a measure of what happens to fixed assets—plant and equipment—which typically represent huge investments at manufacturing and mining companies in particular. Still, depreciation can allow you to take additional tax deductions as direct business expenses (for your major pieces of equipment) and for business use of your home.

Conceptually, depreciation is the reduction in value of an investment in a fixed asset. The value is reduced as time wears on, because the law recognizes that all assets, other than money and raw land, can be expected to last only a certain number of years. Depreciation of buildings, plants, and major equipment is regarded in corporate finance as a real expense of doing business, and is, therefore, deducted from gross revenues. Of course, the dwindling value of fixed assets requires no actual payment of cash by a company to anyone, so the dollar amount of depreciation also must be added back into other parts of annual financial statements to make them accurate. In a company's working capital statement, recently known as the Statement of Changes in Financial Position, one often finds that the decline in value of a company's fixed assets in a single year is so great that it approaches the amount of the company's profits—and sometimes exceeds profits.

For example, in 1979, the B. F. Goodrich Co. obtained most of its working capital (cash to run its business) from profits of $82.6 million, and from depreciation of $83.6 million. In actual fact, the $83.6 million worth of depreciation was cash that never left nor came back into the company. But the profit or loss statement for Goodrich was required to deduct depreciation because it is a true expense of business; the working capital statement simply showed that the $83.6 million was still in the cash box.

The purpose of the Goodrich example is to show just how large a figure depreciation can be for an operation that has heavy investments in fixed assets, as BFG does in tire and chemical plants. Depreciation works the same way for a home business on a smaller scale. Your business loses value as its major pieces of equipment depreciate, and your home office loses value as your house depreciates.

EQUIPMENT DEPRECIATION

Equipment can include machinery, vehicles, and major furnishings of your business. The rule is that you cannot depreciate investments in perishable, or short-lived, goods or equipment. In 1981, the Congress, under prodding from the White House, was working to liberalize specific depreciation rules. Below, some recent methods are described, but you should check with your accountant to get updated information. Typically, depreciation is taken for equipment whose useful life is spread over five to ten years. For example, if you were to buy a fairly inexpensive desk calculator of the sort that cannot be expected to function for too long, you may assign it a useful life of five years (the assignment should represent a close approximation of its real life). Let's say you pay $100 for this calculator. In the first year you own it, you may deduct $20 for depreciation, because one fifth of the life of the $100 investment has expired. Note that you *cannot* deduct the full $100 cost in the year of your purchase, because the calculator is an equipment investment rather than an expense. Buying it merely represents a transfer of cash wealth to goods of equal value, still owned by your business.

If you had bought a better calculator, you might have qualified for an additional tax benefit. This one is the investment tax credit—a tax allowance designed to encourage businesses to invest new money to modernize or expand facilities with long-lasting buildings and equipment. An investment tax credit of 10 percent is allowed in the year of purchase for equipment with a useful life of more than seven years. It works this way: Let's say you buy an expensive desk calculator, with a printer and all the accessories. You might expect this model to last for 10 years. You spent $400 for this model. Your depreciation in the first year would be $\dfrac{\$400}{10 \text{ years,}}$ or $40. But in that first year only, you qualify for the investment tax credit, worth another 10 percent of the $400 purchase price—another $40. The first $40, as a depreciation allowance, is a deduction that reduces your taxable income. But the $40 investment credit is even better; it is subtracted directly, dollar for dollar, from the taxes you would otherwise owe. The investment tax credit can also be applied to equipment with a useful life of less than seven years, although this must be figured by a formula that weakens the effect. The formula is:

Useful Life	Investment Credit Percentage
Less than 3 years	0
3 to 5 years	3⅓
5 to 7 years	6⅔
more than 7 years	10

HOME DEPRECIATION

When you purchased your home, you most likely paid a single lump sum for your lot, buildings (house and garage), and other improvements like built-in pools or terraces. When you go about taking a depreciation deduction for your home business, you cannot include the land underneath and around your house. The law says land does not automatically depreciate with time, and, therefore, is not deductible.

Your first step, then, is to obtain a value for the land on your lot and subtract that from the purchase price of the entire package. For example, if you paid $50,000 for your house and a good-sized lot, and the lot alone has a value of $10,000, start out by subtracting out the separate value of your house— $40,000.

Now, you must differentiate between an old home and a newly-built home to estimate its future useful life. If your home was already 50 years old when you bought it, you might estimate its useful life at another 25 years. To calculate one year's depreciation on the home, divide the purchase price by 25. Then multiply the result by your HB/TH ratio. For the $40,000, 50-year-old house, divide the house investment by 25 for a first-year depreciation of $1,600. If your home business takes up 25 percent of your house in space, multiply $1,600 × 25 percent for a deductible amount of $400. You will find in this straight-line method of depreciation that your annual deductions do not change. Having depreciated by $1,600, your home, in the next year, is worth just $38,400. Its useful life will be down to 24 years, which, divided into $38,400, yields the same $1,600, providing you with an identical second-year home business deduction of $400.

The arithmetic can change, however, for a brand new home. The law allows accelerated depreciation for facilities that are purchased brand new, meaning that in the early years you will be able to deduct more than with the standard formula. However, you will also have to increase the estimated useful life of a new home. They may last 50 years, although you might find this arguable when you discover the thinness of the drywall and softness of the wood. You might never find a new home, either, for $50,000, but we can use that figure again for simplicity. Remove the hypothetical land value of $10,000, and you have the $40,000 value of the house itself, but spread over 50 years of useful life. In the first year, $40,000 divided by 50 yields depreciation of $800 for the entire house, and, using the same 25 percent HB/TH ratio, $200 of depreciation deductible for your home business.

Accelerated depreciation, however, allows you to take 200 percent of the normal schedule. This pumps your total home depreciation back up to $1,600, and your home business deduction back to $400. This time, in the next year, your home will have declined again in value to $38,400, which you must divide by 49 years of remaining useful life. The second-year depreciation for the entire house will be about $784, accelerated by 200 percent to $1,567, and multiplied by your HB/TH ratio for a business depreciation of $392. With this method, your deduction will decline a bit each year.

You may find calculations such as these bothersome. In point of fact, however, there is no getting around some of the tax preparation and bookkeeping complexities of a home business, and the deductions described above are easy compared with the accounting required for the corporate business structure.

If you choose to use a professional for taxes and accounting, you will almost surely find it a wise expenditure. Don't pick just any accountant, though. As with lawyers and doctors, accountants and tax preparers often specialize in certain fields only—international finance, special industries, small businesses, or personal tax returns. Be aggressive in quizzing a prospective accountant about the nature of the rest of his practice. An accountant who understands what you do, and the financial scope of enterprises like yours, can save you more money year after year than he charges for his services. He can give you record-keeping and business practice suggestions as well. Experienced home businesspeople, asked what advice they would give to beginners, seldom leave out a recommendation in favor of professional tax services. Number one on anybody's list of chores to start a home business, says Mary Scoggins, a home-based stenographer in Washington, DC, ought to be: "Get yourself a good accountant." If nothing else, tax preparation uses up time, and you are likely to be busy enough making and selling the goods or services that will give your accountant some numbers to work with.

CHAPTER SIX

Home-based Marketing

To the inexperienced, marketing is one of the least understood and most underrated words in business. It is the entire process of selling—a process that only reaches its climax when a customer lays down his money for a product or service. That moment is really the ultimate goal of all businesses, and when the transaction occurs at the right price, at the right cost, and with the right frequency, it means the success of all the work of every employee from corporate chief executive to production worker.

Long before the moment of sale happens, marketing has taken place, and it continues even afterwards. Marketing must be an integrated part of the business experience from day one. Most business theorists consider the very selection of a product or service—the usual first step in beginning a home business— to be an early function of marketing. From that point on, the drive to make the sale under profitable conditions colors every other decision.

As the home entrepreneur goes into business, he or she has certain advantages: reduced overhead costs, instant access to the office, freedom in scheduling, and the ability to build an enterprise personally, from the ground up, Yet all will be for naught if the moment of sale is elusive. The way to seize that moment is to recognize marketing as a system which has to be a part of the very birth of the business.

For some, it takes months or years to realize this need. Good ideas rise and fall before some businesspeople integrate marketing into all else that they are doing. Other good ideas merely languish as marketing lessons are slowly learned, and then business perks up. A young toymaker in Santa Barbara, California, whose case we will examine, nearly gave up his lifetime goal of making a living from creative work, until some of the functions of marketing were hammered home in the nick of time.

It was 1971, and the toymaker had come up with a fine,

salable product. It was unique and creative, yet inexpensive to produce. Using hand tools and paints, he had devised a way to make beautiful and durable toy soldiers out of spent bullet shells, which he got for nothing. He found he could turn these out by the dozens every day. Not knowing exactly what to do next, he approached the owner of a large boutique store, divided up into little shops run by individual entrepreneurs—a weaver, a potter, a leather worker, and others. It took only a glance at the obvious quality of these colorful little armies for the store's owner (also the potter) to lease a healthy chunk of space to the toymaker.

Now, the toymaker figured it was time to employ a little arithmetic. He added up his cost of goods, which was small, and his lease expense. He knew how many soldiers he could produce in a day, and he guessed that if he sold only half, it would be enough to make a nice living at a price of about 50 cents per soldier.

Sales were rotten. Customers handled and gawked at the officers and infantrymen, but put them right back on the display table. The weeks dragged on. Extremely discouraged, the toymaker finally went to his landlord for advice. That changed everything. "People relate price to value," said the potter. "They just aren't used to seeing handmade things selling for less than a dollar. Try charging more." The toymaker doubled his prices, and his sales jumped by about the same amount. That was marketing lesson number one.

Lesson two came shortly thereafter. Another fellow worked part time for the store as a promotion specialist. With a flair for the extravagant, the promoter sent a news release to the local television station announcing there would be a war of toy soldiers, complete with explosions and fire, inside the store in two days. Always looking for a good feature story, a television news crew showed up and dutifully recorded the event, during which 30 or 40 of the soldiers were, tragically, destroyed (War is hell!). It hit the news at six and eleven. Afterwards, sales improved even more.

Finally, after a couple more weeks, in walked a customer who had seen the broadcast. It was a visit that changed the toymaker's career. The customer was a wholesale buyer for a large retailing chain, and he wanted to order the soldiers by the thousands per month. With that, the toymaker folded his shop, transferred production to his apartment, hired some help, and set up a home-based manufacturing company. This new means of distribution at a fair price and in guaranteed quantity made the business a success. The toymaker had finally learned how a good product, the right price, promotion, and distribution techniques must work as a smooth, single system to bring a business to full bloom. All of these things are marketing.

Successful selling takes a combination of skills: ability to do research, to manufacture efficiently, to communicate well with a desired customer group, and, above all, to have thought of a product or service that truly fulfills a need of the marketplace. The need, or desire, can exist before the new venture begins, or it can be created by the venture, as the invention of the instant camera created desire among many consumers. The function of the salesman who makes direct contact with customers (sometimes misunderstood to represent the whole marketing system) is only one part of the process. There is no reason to despair if you have found it hard to sell things to other people face-to-face in the past. If you perform all the other marketing skills well enough, making the sale will become easier. Some of the greatest intellects and inventors couldn't sell umbrellas during a thunderstorm face-to-face, yet they came up with products and ideas of value that others could sell, and in so doing they contributed greatly to marketing.

What really enabled our toymaker to eventually succeed was the fact that his product was good, unique, and filled a consumer demand. He was successful in the first stage of marketing without really knowing it. Product quality and uniqueness are especially important to home businesspeople, whose budget for promotion and whose geographical product distribution may be modest. A local community cannot be fooled by a bad product for long, and even in the mail order business, repeat purchases will only come from customers satisfied the first time around. Even Procter & Gamble Co., the giant of consumer household products and the mightiest advertiser in the nation, attributes its success to product quality more than it does to its immense promotion and distribution clout. At P&G the brand manager for a particular kind of detergent may spend 5 percent of all the advertising dollars spent by the entire detergent industry. But his superiors expect him to garner more than 5 percent in market share, because of the qualities built into his product by hundreds of research scientists and production engineers.

Marketing connects customers with goods, and, thus, its first step is the creation of a decent product. In *Business Today,* authors David J. Rachman and Michael H. Mescon reduce all of marketing to the "four Ps"—product, price, promotion, and placement (or distribution). New business managers have decisions to make in all these areas, and they must also keep open minds about changing their decisions as time wears on, to fine-tune the selling aparatus.

Home-based businesses must pay special attention in several respects. Typically, the product line or range of service will be more limited than with outside businesses, so quality is usually more important. In distribution, the out-of-home business can choose between retailing, wholesaling, and direct mail. So can home businesses, yet special care must be taken with retailing right out of the home, because neighbors and city zoning officials will be most sensitive to heavy traffic.

PRODUCT

This first step in marketing is of prime importance. Too often, beginning home entrepreneurs concentrate at first on ideas for distribution instead. There is a tendency to visualize the entire business in terms of how the product will reach the customer, and mail order is a perfect example. It is a technique that has become popular, and, viewed simply, the appeal is clear: Stuff boxes in the afternoon, and pick up the checks in the morning mail. The apparent ease of this system leads may down the primrose path, and only later do they scan their minds to come up with some product—any product—that can fit inside a paper box. Still others become fixated on wholesaling. They see the fast buck and a steady income ahead by selling to one of the big retailing chains. The scramble for a product, again, comes as a secondary thought.

These are serious mistakes in logic. What is it that Sears will buy? What is there of marketable value to be sold by mail? Probably nothing for a business that did not start out with a good idea for a basic product or service. Product has to come before distribution, even though there is nothing wrong with making alterations in the product later to fit with a placement method that makes sense.

In choosing products and services, home businesspeople tend to pick the ones in which they have knowledge, experience, or skill. Professionals and tradesmen transfer their careers home. Hobbyists make the jump to professional in the same fields. Homemakers frequently structure their businesses around one of many learned skills: garments, food, child care, crafts, or in a profession in which they have had prior training. Without question, this built-in expertise is helpful; it gives a head start to the attainment of quality. The danger lies in picking a business only because it is known to you, without first getting a clear reading of the likelihood of market acceptance.

The need to gauge customer acceptance calls for market research well before the business is started. But even before market research, individuals who plan to own and operate small businesses at home should make an internal examination of all the ramifications there could be to making and selling the chosen product or service. The smaller the business, the more important it becomes to do this "product research." Here are ten questions to which you should have answers:

PRODUCT RESEARCH

1. Have you picked a product or service where performance will rest solely on you? If no one else has the talent or knowledge to step in and pinch-hit for you when needed, consider what a single long illness might do to your business. Vacations might be hard to arrange, too.
2. Will raw materials for the product be in ample supply indefinitely?
3. Will raw-material prices be relatively stable?
4. Is there more than one potential supplier of raw materials for the product? If not, the health of your business will depend on the health of your sole supplier. General Motors, among many corporations, seeks assiduously to maintain multiple suppliers for every raw material and fabricated product it buys, all to avoid a dangerous overdependence.
5. Can the product or service be easily modified? Can it be made at lower cost, reformulated, or sold at a higher price, in case market conditions or your personal goals require it?
6. Is there any conceivable way that the product could cause physical injury to a customer? If so, you should be aware

that in recent years, juries have been granting huge cash awards to plaintiffs injured by manufactured products, sometimes even when the consumer purposely misuses the product! These awards have caused premiums to soar for product-liability insurance, but you should talk to an insurance agent nevertheless. This certainly goes for all food businesses, and for any manufactured product designed for children. If your product or service is potentially hazardous, the profits should be fat enough to compensate for the risk of suit from the occasional unhappy, injured, or simply litigious customer. Those who off-handedly decide to do things like selling a few jars of home-canned foods each week for an extra few dollars in spending money, without insurance protection, are taking a big risk that may backfire.

7. Is there any way that the product or service could cause financial or other damage to a customer? Appliance repair work and auto parts distribution are obvious businesses with the potential to cause financial damage if products or work are defective. Even information services have this potential; stock brokerage houses have been sued by clients for offering allegedly misleading advice that causes financial loss. For home-based writers, printers, and publishers, libel is a danger. False information about people, especially if published with malice, can bring suits alleging a resultant financial loss or damage to the reputation.

8. Can you control quality? This is a key question, especially when the business will involve more than one employee. Long-lasting success comes only with products and services whose quality can be controlled steadily, regularly, indefinitely. In the fast food industry, even its competitors admit that McDonald's Corp. has won top rank partly because of its quality control. Rather than merely lecturing your employees about quality and uniformity, you would do well to design the product so that the margin for deviation is small. Quality control applies even to such personal services as child care. If you have overloaded yourself with kids, will you be so frazzled that you won't be at your best by 5 P.M. on Friday? If so, your customers will have the weekend to listen to their children's complaints, and the results could be disastrous.

9. Is there anything about the product or service that could

cause you to lose control of how much time you devote to the business? This is problem that often hits professionals who try to set up part-time home businesses. Accountants, for example, take on clients without prior knowledge of how complex the clients' financial problems might become. Mail order businesses can be at the mercy of the postman in terms of schedule control. The buying and selling of antiques can eat up increasing chunks of time; to increase your sales volume, more and more buying trips to flea markets or auctions may be required.

10. Does the business have the potential to be sold? Eventually, you may want to put an end to your business for any number of reasons. If that day should come, will you find yourself with a business that must be shut down, or one that can be sold to someone else at a profit? The answer will depend partly on the product or service you perform. If it is something that only you can do, it will not be salable. This is a strong argument in favor of choosing a product that others can be taught to make, or a service that others can be trained to perform. For salability, you will also have to build certain assets: a valuable list of customers or mailing lists, and a good reputation, to go along with such tangible assets as inventory and equipment.

MARKET RESEARCH

If you are satisfied with the results of an inward look at your product, it is time for market research. Market research can be done in a number of ways, and can be designed to answer a number of questions. What it boils down to, however, is an attempt, in advance, to guess at the answer to one prime question. You've decided to produce something, perform some service, sell a product: Will anybody else care?

Obtaining the answer to this question is a matter of external examination. The new business operator must gather information, and the more that is gathered, the more clear the answer will become. To home in on the central question, a number of separate issues must be addressed. Among them are:

1. How much competition already exists among producers of

products or services similar to the one you envision, within the geographical area in which you plan to operate? Can the market bear another competitor?

2. What exactly is the market (customer community) for your product? What are its demographic characteristics (age of sought-after customers, sex, income level, educational level, geographical boundaries, consumer or commercial customers)?

3. Will the product or service satisfy an existing need of the market, or can it create a need?

4. How much money is the product or service worth to the market? Can it be sold at that price and still yield an adequate profit?

5. What prices do the competitors charge? Can you charge the same, or less, and still obtain an adequate profit?

6. What is the quality of competing products or services? Is there a marketplace need for something of higher quality, or a niche for something of lower quality that can be sold at a lower price?

7. What form, shape, color, or size would customers want in a product of this sort? What exact capabilities would customers want to see in a service of this kind?

8. What form and appearance should product packaging have?

9. What distribution technique would work best?

10. What advertising message, in what media, would best push along the sale?

11. What is the durability of public taste for the product? Will it be a fad?

12. What are the growth characteristics of the market? A home-based furniture builder, for example, will be able to worry less about competition if his city's population is increasing rapidly.

GATHERING SENSE FOR CENTS

The aim of market research is to develop information about all the subjects mentioned above. It is a detective game of critical importance, and, therefore, big businesses spend hundreds of thousands of dollars—and often millions—to get the job done.

The ideal goal is to reduce the risk of failure to zero before full-scale production begins. Zero risk may never be attained, but there are a number of techniques that do cut risk significantly.

Fortunately for low-budget businesses, there are some research techniques that are free, and others that are quite inexpensive. They are not as scientific as those that cost huge sums of cash, but they can be surprisingly valuable. They can, in fact, prevent the common nightmare of all operators of new ventures: an investment of money and time in the production of something that nobody buys.

Big corporations typically launch full-blown economic studies of the growth patterns of an industry, and of the demographics of a market, before moving into them. They hire people trained in scientific samplings to survey potential customers about interest in a new product. They may take the additional step of arranging for "focus groups" of consumers to examine a sample new product in depth, under company supervision. Focus groups are small groups of ordinary customers brought in by a company to participate in intensive studies of all aspects of a new item, from taste to wrappings.

Of course, before any of this has happened, teams of research scientists and engineers have developed the product itself with marketing in mind. They may try to introduce a new generation of quality into an otherwise mundane line, or they may try to develop something that can be sold at a surprisingly low price compared with the competition. Engineers at Owens–Illinois Inc., for example, have tried to produce a glass bottle for soft drinks that will replace cans by selling at a lower price. Their method was to mass produce standard-shaped bottles for all soft drink brands, and because O–I is the largest of the glass companies, its effort began to show up in most grocery stores in the early 1980s. Gone from the shelves of many stores are the once-distinctively-shaped bottles of Coke and Pepsi, among other brands.

Test marketing is the ultimate form of research for the bigger companies. It is also the final leg in the risk-reduction cycle. In test marketing, companies sell a finished new product in a small number of cities to gauge acceptance in a real environment. Advertising campaigns are test marketed simultaneously. Given the amount of market research that occurs before test marketing, it is amazing that a number of products do fail in tests. It does happen, however, even to the biggest concerns. Procter

& Gamble, for instance, recently saw two of its thoroughly researched new products fail in tests—a new frozen dessert mix called Cold Snap, and a lotion-impregnated toilet tissue called Certain, which failed to please the residents of Fort Wayne, Indiana. Both were removed for possible reformulation in the future.

HOME-BASED RESEARCH: DIRECT TECHNIQUES

Smaller businesses can scarcely afford such costly failures. In fact, for most home businesses, techniques such as focus groups and test marketing will be out of reach. Luckily, there are other ways of gathering information about the nature of the market and its likelihood of accepting your product or service. Some can be performed directly by you.

First, if you intend to make a product, buy and use some of the products that are offered by your soon-to-be competitors. Shop the marketplace for products similar to yours and write down prices, names of manufacturers, names of retail outlets. Interpret the word "product" broadly in this exercise. For example, if your "product" is going to be registered puppies in a dog-breeding business, shop the newspaper ads for price range. Examine competitors' quality of products carefully (the dog breeder would gather information from vets and other experts about what qualities to look for, and might examine animals in kennels, comparing quality and price). Keep your eyes and ears open in a search to gauge the scope of competition. Mail order sellers should spend a few days in a public library scanning periodicals for ads for products similar to those they envision.

There are ways for prospective service businesses to look at the competition, too. A hopeful home-based stenographer looking for small business clients can combine a search for competitive information with a direct sales appeal. Call on the kinds of businesses you hope to serve, ask them if they already use such a service, and explain that you might be offering one if they don't already have one. If they do have one, explain that you are trying to find out the going rates in the business and the kinds of services expected. You might gather important information. And always—always—leave a business card. You may parlay your research calls into future sales.

There are also ways to conduct surveys, though the samplings may not be entirely scientific. Instead of a hired focus group, give samples of your product to some distant acquaintances (never to friends or relatives who may want to spare your feelings). *Do not* ask these acquaintances if the product is good; that just might force them to choose between honesty and tactfulness. Instead, tell them the product is experimental, and that you are seeking outside opinions about what would make it a good finished product. The idea is to make the group understand it is being asked to contribute recommendations, not to pass judgment. You should interview, taking notes, each of the people in the group, gathering suggestions about product quality, price, packaging, distribution methods, and even ideas about the viability of the market. Ask them to compare the product to others that they have seen or purchased. As you choose the members of your in-depth survey group, try to pick those whose personal characteristics are most similar to the market you have identified, in terms of sex, income level, family status, age, and so on.

You can also conduct a direct-mail survey that can double as an advertising solicitation. Do the best you can to identify the right target market in making up your mailing list. For example, a home dressmaker can use a crisscross-type telephone directory to get names and addresses in the better neighborhoods in town, where residents would tend to have the income level to purchase garments priced high enough to make the business lucrative. Always include a stamped, self-addressed envelope for survey form returns. This will increase your cost per letter to more than 50 cents, but without the stamped envelope inside, your response rate is likely to be thin indeed. Putting the survey on post cards would cut costs, but also restrict the scope of what you want to say. On the other hand, your survey should be kept to about one side of paper so that recipients won't find the form tiresome. A professional-looking printing job is important.

Your survey letter should:
— name the business.
— identify in a phrase or sentence what the business is.
— explain that this is a survey to determine whether there is interest in the community for your product or service.
— not insist that the recipient list his or her name. You might include a name line marked "optional." But for

your own records, seek to use a code on each form that will identify who sent it back to you. And, though you leave the name line optional or exclude it, do ask about the recipient's age, sex, and occupation.

— avoid asking at first if the recipient has any need for such a product. Design your questions instead so that the recipient begins to describe the ideal form and price range for your type of product. Allow the potential customer to build his or her own interest through this self-description as each survey question is filled out.

— suggest to the recipient that the survey results will aid in the design of the product, and then ask if the person (in your last question) believes that there might be a market for such a product in your town.

— tell the date when your new business will start.

— include a business card. Otherwise, once your survey form is returned, the person who filled it out will have no record of your business name and phone number or address.

Use your survey results in good faith to help design the product or service, and to determine the general level of market interest. But also separate the enthusiastic replies into a pile that will become the core of your first concrete sales calls, or that will form an improved mailing list of potential customers who are most likely to buy.

USING THE GOVERNMENT

If nothing else, the federal bureaucracy has been effective in gathering information. It is usually free, and you can use it to help determine the potential size of markets, consumer characteristics, population growth patterns city by city, age characteristics of the population, growth tendencies in particular industries, and much more. Government publications on these subjects are usually held in public libraries, or may be obtained directly from federal offices near where you live.

A good first stop is the Small Business Administration, which not only offers advice about how to do market research, but about all aspects of marketing. Seek out the nearest SBA branch office, and ask for lists of free management assistance publications, for-sale booklets, and advocacy publications. All together, there are more than 200 topics covered by pamphlets or books on these lists. Once you have the lists, you can order from them using attached order forms and mailing instructions.

The SBA's free publications are separated into series on management aids, small marketers' aids, and small business bibliographies. One of the bibliographies is itself entitled *Home Businesses,* and it lists books written about occupations including animals and pets, crafts, catering, collecting, writing, and many more. Interestingly, the SBA reports it often finds itself sold out of this bibliography because of its popularity. The small marketers' aids and management aids also include pertinent titles, such as: *Plan Your Advertising Budget*; *Learning About Your Market*; and *Selling Products on Consignment.* For a recent price of just $1.50, you can order *Decision Points in Developing New Products,* a 64-page book. For $3.75, the SBA recently was selling the 133-page book, *Selecting Advertising Media—A Guide for Small Business.*

There are other government agencies that can be helpful as well. From the U.S. Department of Commerce, you can obtain the latest annual issue of the *U.S. Industrial Outlook,* a fat book that projects trends for the current year in scores of industries, and even looks at how each industry might do during the next several years. If your home enterprise will provide business services, you might use this book to pick out healthy industries to focus on in your search for customers. The U.S. Department of Labor issues plenty of statistics as well about trends in occupational groups, employment levels, and inflation rates broken down into cost increases in each of many areas of consumer expense.

Some states, too, issue labor statistics that identify such things as occupations within the state in which there are shortages or surpluses of labor. From all of this information, you may be able to glean much that is useful in your research. For example, if your local area is experiencing a shortage of construction workers, you can bet that is because the building companies are booming; demand for workers is outstripping supply. That would bode well for a home-based furniture maker, whose business prospects are enhanced by an active home construction industry. It would also identify a local industry so busy that it might need certain business services from your home—stenographic work, printing, computer services.

The Census Bureau, too, can be a prime contributor to your research. It can clue you into demographics, the science of vital and social statistics. Major public libraries usually have complete books of census data, and these can tell all about population and living pattern trends across the country and in your city or metropolitan area. This data can be extraordinarily handy. If, for example, your target market happens to be elderly people in your city, the census information may be able to show you quickly how big the market is, and whether it is growing or declining.

Even more helpful can be the Bureau's census of business, taken once every five years (in those years ending in the numbers 2 and 7). This tells how many there are of each kind of business in each large city in the nation; in other words, it may tell you directly how many competitors you will have. And, it can help in many other ways. If you plan a home craft-making business, for instance, it would be nice to know that your city happens to be loaded with taverns. That information could lead you to design bar ornaments. A home based toymaker interested in selling wholesale or on consignment could quickly see how many retail toy stores are in each of several surrounding cities. That information would help the toymaker focus on a particular town for sales calls.

USING COMMERCIAL INFORMATION

The two most useful sources of commercial information for low-cost market research are also the most common publications found in every home: the telephone book and the daily newspaper.

The phone book is a great source of competitor information. The *Yellow Pages* may well list others in the same small business you are thinking about starting. Call some of them and find out exactly what they do, and at what price. Don't be afraid to be a little sneaky in identifying yourself; it is not a great sin to pose as a customer. Try to find out not only what the competitors offer in products and services, and their prices, but also what geographical areas they cover. For service businesses, ask about speed of delivery of service, and hours during which services are provided. You may find some interesting opportunities in the holes in their answers. A local catering service, for example, might work daytime and evening parties and gatherings, but not at night. How about catering to the lunch crowd on the graveyard shift at a small factory?

Newspaper classified ads are another source of competitor information. Pets and antiques, among other items, are described and priced. Pet breeders should look for the ads that repeat day after day, showing there may be a surplus of a certain type of dog or cat in town. Call the advertisers who don't include prices, and ask for them. While you are looking at the paper, start reading all the display ads as well. The good ones will help give you ideas about how to write effective ad copy. If you plan a business service, pay attention to the newspaper's business section, too. It will tell you which local companies are doing well financially and might be likely sales targets.

Trade magazines are a further source of fine information about events and trends in individual industries, occupations, hobbies, and leisure pursuits. The public library is likely to carry plenty of them. The trade "books" and specialized magazines are, of course, necessary reading for prospective mail order entrepreneurs, who may need to advertise in them. These publications have increasingly become the prime source of certain kinds of statistical information in particular industries. *Modern Tire Dealer,* for example, publishes its own, independently gathered figures each year on which of the big tire companies commands what percentage of the market for original equipment tires. You may want to use trade magazines to dig out data of that sort. Rather than leafing through one issue after another, use your library's *Business Periodicals Index,* or the *Reader's Guide to Periodical Literature,* which include articles printed in hundreds of magazines, and list the stories alphabetically by subjects and names.

BUSINESS ORGANIZATIONS

A variety of business organizations can also help you size up your market and your product. For a home business with local marketing aspirations, drop by the nearest office of the Chamber of Commerce.

The information services provided by local Chambers of

Commerce vary widely from city to city. Yet, most Chambers are good sources, for more reasons than one. They may or may not have demographic information that the Census Bureau does not have. But all Chambers are comprised of members who are local businesspeople, and a Chamber's professional staff is usually well aquainted with many of the small- and medium-sized companies in the region. Chamber officials are in a solid position to critique your business idea, to offer suggestions, and to help you develop your marketing program. Bankers can fill the same role. You should get to know the manager of your branch bank; he and his colleagues are in a position to have more intimate knowledge of local small businesspeople than almost anyone. Bankers and members of the Chamber of Commerce may well know about schemes similar to yours that have worked or failed, and why. They may have good ideas about pricing and promotion (not to mention finance).

Other business organizations can provide a national view, and may have some immensely helpful information for you— though possibly at a price. These are the trade associations. Many are based in New York City and Washington, D.C., but others fan out across the country, and there are thousands of them. There are trade associations devoted to specific industries (such as the Institute of Scrap Iron and Steel Inc.); organizations devoted to the promotion of specific products (how about the California Dried Fig Advisory Board); clubs and guilds representing occupations (the Knifemakers Guild, the National Needlework Association, the International Creative Writers League), and even groups formed to advocate causes and support ideas. Seemingly endless pages of names of these organizations fill the *Encyclopedia of Associations,* a volume that also gives locations, services provided, phone numbers, membership size, and the scope of the professional staff. The *Encyclopedia* is available in most libraries.

In the United States, it is almost literally true that there is an association for everything and everybody. What other country would host the headquarters of the Cowboys Turtle Association, the Covered Button and Buckle Association of New York, and the Associated Country Women of the World? Fortunately, many of the business associations are quite solid and valuable, and there seems to be one in existence to cover almost every kind of home-based business enterprise. The American Kennel Club has a professional staff of more than 400, keeps pedigree records of some 22 million dogs, publishes books and a magazine, and offers a breeder-information service. And there are many, many more groups tailored to home businesses: The American Crafts Council, the National Woodcarvers Association, and the Handweavers Guild of America, to name just three. Outside of the American Kennel Club, there are about 130 additional clubs and associations devoted to specific dog breeds, dog handling, and care. A number of other groups cater to cat owners.

Many of these organizations require dues or membership fees, a clear expense (but often tax deductible). But some provide a limited amount of free information on a subject, and others sell information at reasonable rates without requiring membership. For example, a nonmember can purchase enough information from the Direct Mail Marketing Association (discussed at more length later in this chapter) to obtain a working knowledge of how to operate a mail order business from home. Full-fledged members get an even wider array of service. At the very least, it is worthwhile to look up the associations that might be helpful to the home business you plan, and to call or write to ask about the services offered, and the advantages of joining. Many associations have already done some of the research you must scramble to do on your marketplace, and, thus, can save you days of tedious labor.

FOLLOW-UP RESEARCH

Once your business has begun, you can get an even better handle on your market by keeping careful records of your customers. Be certain to ask them how they heard about your business. The answers will help you direct your advertising to the right media for best results. You can also hand small survey cards to customers, asking if they were satisfied with your product or service. Leave room for a sentence or two of comments. The feedback may cause you to want to modify the product, and the cards can make customers feel involved in your business, too. Get some vital statistics as well. If most of your customers are coming from a cohesive group of neighborhoods, you can target advertising to the local newspaper strongest in those neighborhoods. Once you find your business has appeal to a certain customer group, you should seek to exploit that group fully before turning to another. Product packaging can substitute for a survey card. Procter & Gamble, for instance, now includes an address or toll-free phone number on the packaging materials of many of its products, so that customers with compliments or complaints can make them known.

SETTING THE PRICE

Two big obstacles get in the way of setting a proper price for any product or service, and both can be awesome in a home business where management is usually a one-person show. The obstacles are ego and naïveté.

There are people who think too highly, or too poorly, of their own personal human worth, and this kind of personality problem at the top can cause an illogical set of business practices in home enterprises. This is the ego problem, and it can result in overpricing or underpricing. Overpricing seldom works for long. And, in home businesses, underpricing not only eliminates profits, but often fails to stimulate sales volume as well. The use of "loss leaders" in supermarkets—an underpricing tactic—does increase sales volume because most customers firmly know the normal value of products. But as the Santa Barbara toymaker had to learn, underpricing when customers do not know the inherent or typical value of the product can simply appear to demean it. The same can happen in many other home businesses—garments, catering, collecting and trading, and more. "Underpricing yourself is a risk," notes Stephen Lyon Crohn, a home-based artist in Los Angeles. "If your work becomes too accessible because the price is low, people won't pay attention to it, much less buy it." If you believe in the worth and value of what you are going to do (and you should not begin if you don't), stand up and charge what the market will bear.

Naïveté comes into play when one begins to set prices without having done solid market research. This often leads to overpricing, which is self-defeating in most businesses. Customers will be too savvy to buy, unless what you are offering is extraordinarily unique. If it is unique, and you are making unconscionable profits, the mechanisms of the free market will eventually

introduce competition against you. Others will notice the money
to be made, and will attempt to steal away the business with
a slightly lower price. Sooner or later, the general pricing for
the merchandise or service will be brought down to reasonable
levels.

What price will the market bear for a prolonged period?
That all depends on how badly your product or service is needed.
If you can *sustain* a business with unique features, it will allow
you to build in a higher level of profit than would otherwise be
attainable. For home businesses, that often means you can
charge much more if your personal skills and talents are strong.
The very talented home furniture maker who can build a superior product can charge more, and he should. The mail order
seller whose talent is for finding bargain-priced wholesale merchandise to resell through the mail stands to benefit handsomely from a more modest retail price. Your price must cover
your cost components per product, but from that point onward,
a number of features (product quality, speed of delivery, uniqueness, and marketplace demand) will allow your price to float
up.

These differentiating features function widely in the corporate world. Rates of profit differ vastly from company to company and industry to industry. Basic manufacturing companies
typically earn after-tax profits that are 5 to 6 percent of sales
volume. But supermarkets are in a tough business where very
little differentiates one store from another, and competition is
fierce. Thus, the grocery stores are lucky to earn much more
than 1 percent of sales.

The contrast is drastic between a supermarket and a company that has something both essential and unique to sell. Consider Schlumberger Ltd., the dominant company in the business
of measuring how much oil or gas lies within a well. Schlumberger performs sophisticated, computerized measuring services that oil companies find absolutely necessary. Only a
handful of other companies in the world even know how to
perform this service. Naturally, Schlumberger's managers set
their prices well above their costs of doing business. They charge
what the market will bear, and walk away with profits of 18
percent of sales or more!

Home businesses may be smaller in scale, but pricing has
the same relationship to profit. Unless you plan to start your
business to become a philanthropist, this means you must in-

tegrate a pricing strategy right into the earliest stages of business planning, in fact, right into the selection of what product or service you will offer. Pick a product with high-price potential in mind. Miscalculations in pricing are common, and if you have set yours too high, you can reduce it. But the closer the reduced price comes to really squeezing profits, the more you ought to consider changing the product, adding value to it to support a higher price, or scrapping it entirely in favor of another.

If you can land big customers who will buy in volume, you may not have to take such an aggressive pricing stance. Long production runs for a single big customer tend to reduce production costs per unit, and sales calls on the big customers need not take up much more time than sales calls to smaller customers. One retired electronics engineer in Portland, Oregon, has taken this philosophy to heart in a home-based specialty advertising business. He sells the little items on which companies like to print their names for publicity: match books, pens, yardsticks. "It takes just as much effort to write up an order for one hundred pens as it does to write up an order for ten thousand yardsticks," he declares.

STRETCHING THE DOLLAR FOR PROMOTION

Promotion is the business of informing potential customers about what you have to sell. That definition is important, especially because of what it doesn't say. Promotion does not require any set expenditure of money. For some kinds of home businesses, promotion can happen for free. News about small-scale businesses geared to local markets can spread by word of mouth. This happens frequently in a host of home business categories: hair dressing, child care, collecting and trading, furniture restoration, catering, and plenty of others. If our early customers like your product or service, promotion by word of mouth becomes an extremely successful and effective means of advertising. When a potential new customer hears about your business from a friend, the credibility of the message goes way beyond what can be accomplished with the slickest 30-second television commercial. As long as your business aims only at serving a limited geographic area, you should give word of mouth a chance to work its magic. Or, you can supplement this technique with other free kinds of advertising, including signs posted in laundromats or on community bulletin boards.

Many businesses, however, will require something more. Those that seek to sell beyond the local area will need a way to get the word out. And, paid advertising may even become essential to neighborhood home businesses that start out using word of mouth. If your first batch of products, or your first couple of months of service performance, were not of the highest quality, then the stories told by word of mouth will not be so favorable, and advertising might have to come to the rescue.

Your market research should point the way to the best medium for your message. If you know the habits of your target market population, then you know what these people are reading, seeing, and hearing. The ad delivery can occur through any one, or any combination, of several media and methods: newspapers, general circulation or specialty magazines, radio, television, the *Yellow Pages* of the phone book, direct mail, and, of course, personal contact (telephone, door-to-door, office visits, or solicitation in public places). Special advertising media such as drive-in movies, buses, or billboards, are often expensive and a scattergun approach for home businesses. To get the most for the promotional dollar, you must home in as closely as possible on the exact audience you want to reach.

For some home businesses, the correct medium will be obvious. Pet breeders naturally should choose the newspaper classified ads, since that is where the buyers look. But be careful if your business is even a shade different from the one whose medium is clear. Providers of pet services, for example, aim at a customer group that already owns animals rather than at the pet buyers. This business calls for classified ads near the pet section of the newspaper, supplemented with personal visits to pet shops and kennels, where pet owners may return to buy supplies. You might be able to pay for the shop owner to allow you to post an advertising sign about your grooming or training service, or to display a stock of your business cards or flyers.

The objective to keep in mind is to target in, ever closer, on your potential customers and no one else. Consider how this would work in a child-care business. The operator might well want to serve children who all live in the same neighborhood. That would make it easy for parents to car pool—no small consideration for a business whose clients are usually very busy. The best advertising medium might be a flyer hand-delivered to the doors of homes in the target neighborhood. An alternative would be an ad in a suburban or neighborhood newspaper. For home-based business services, personal calls on a select list of possible customers work best. Home manufacturing operations that seek wholesale distribution will need to make personal contacts as well.

Advertising placement decisions should fit in as an integrated package with all other goals of the business. Many home businesses need to appeal to a well-heeled customer who can afford prices high enough to maintain profitability. The home dressmaker who has wisely decided to make expensive garments with fat profit margins should also tailor her advertising to those who can afford to buy. A citywide daily newspaper would be a waste of ad dollars for such a business, compared with direct mail ads sent to expensive homes, or an ad in a suburban newspaper that serves a chic residential area.

Writing ad copy is a science in itself. There is no sure formula to get results. Sometimes a single catchy phrase in the right spot will do the trick in a particular market. Thirty-five years ago, for instance, Marge M. McKenzie moved to Houston, Texas, from St. Louis, and she decided to start a home-based garment business. She ran a single ad in the classified section of the *Houston Chronicle,* which simply said: "Dress-Making, Designing. No pattern necessary. Work from your sketch or mine. (From the East)." She figured that last phrase might catch the eye in Texas, and within a week McKenzie had 125 customers. Ever since, she has gotten along on word-of-mouth promotion, except for a small, boxed ad she maintains in the *Yellow Pages.*

It is impossible to suggest the right ad copy for every business, but there are writing tips and placement tips helpful for most home business:

— It is usually smart to stretch the ad budget with many small ads, rather than one big one.
— Use a headline in a display ad that announces something, promises something, describes a benefit, or simply draws the reader in through its oddity. Or, cry out to your market with the first couple words: "Gardeners. . .", "Getting Married? . . ."
— Advertising words cost money; don't try to impress by using excess language to show off your writing ability.

— Forget full sentences; write in phrases and stand-alone words.

— If you can back it up, use the word "guaranteed."

— If appropriate, use some ads to offer free brochures, catalogues, or other printed information about your business. Response rates to anything that is free are pretty high, and the calls and letters you receive will help you build a solid list of names and addresses for direct-mail selling in the future.

— Tailor ad language to the medium and its typical audience. Try not to run the same ad in different media. Throw words like "power" and "strong" into the ad that appears in the muscle magazine, but not into the *Ladies' Home Journal.*

With all advertising, keep careful track of the response rate and dollar volume of business that can be attributed to any particular ad whenever possible. There is no other way to tell which ads, in which media, work best. You can do this in print by "keying" an ad. That is, have a customer use a code number or word when he responds that will tell you which ad he saw. To do this, make the code part of the name or address to which the customer must write or call. Jane Doe, for example, places four ads in four suburban newspapers to sell homemade pottery. In one ad, customers are asked to respond to Jane Doe, Dept. A, 200 Fourth St. In the next, have customers write to Jane Doe, Dept. B, 200 Fourth St. If phone calls are solicited, have one ad tell customers to call J.D.; in the next, have them "ask for Jane," and so on.

MAIL ORDER: DREAMS AND PIPE DREAMS

A business directory published in 1981 listed no fewer than 1,000 mail order companies operating in the United States, each with sales of $1 million per year or more. The Direct Mail Marketing Association (DMMA) has estimated that in 1980, companies doing business directly through the mail had total sales of a staggering $110 billion! Without question, mail order distribution is booming.

As a selling technique, mail order has proven itself ideal for many home businesses for a number of reasons. First and foremost, it opens regional, national, and international markets for your products. It also eliminates retail traffic from the home, which otherwise might bother neighbors or antagonize city zoning officials. And mail order is growing more appealing to shoppers all the time. The increase in the number of women who work means that more people have less time to shop on weekdays, and this underscores the handiness of ordering goods by mail. Higher prices for gasoline, and periodic fuel shortages, also help.

In the coming high-technology society, the traditional mail order business will take on an added dimension: direct selling by electronic order. In some cities, such as Columbus, Ohio, experiments are already underway in television. Viewers can use electronic devices on their sets to talk back to showmen and advertisers by pressing buttons. In May 1981, the nation's largest retailer—Sears, Roebuck & Co.—took a big step toward electronic direct selling by converting its 236-page summer catalogue into a television program captured on videodiscs. Sears is testing the discs on players in some of its stores, but also in 1,000 ordinary homes. Not far off is the day when most consumers will be able to order products with messages sent directly from their television sets. Already, direct selling is being enhanced greatly by the growing availability of "800" toll-free phone numbers set up by businesses that advertise on television and radio or sometimes in print.

All of this makes direct selling the stuff of dreams. But mail order can also be a pipe dream for those who lurch into it blindly. Just to begin with, it is essential to keep in mind that mail order is an advertising/distribution system. By itself, it has nothing to do with the fundamental objective of marketing, which is to produce and sell a product that can satisfy an existing or created need in the marketplace. In addition, mail order is not as easy as it appears. It can be expensive and risky. The money you lay out in ads may or may not produce enough orders to pay back your investment and production costs. Skill in writing and placing ad copy becomes essential.

Inflation is a problem, too. Your costs of doing business, especially for purchases of raw materials or finished products you want to resell, may increase suddenly in an inflationary environment. But your mail order ad, offering products at prices you set when your costs were lower, is still out in circulation. You could end up selling products for less than your cost to buy them. Finance can become really tricky when the mail order business engages in international trade as Nelson Antosh discovered with a home-based mail order business he started. Antosh is a Texan who, in the early 1970s, began selling specialized tools made in Germany for repairing Volkswagen autos. Inflation alone made it hard for him to produce a catalogue that listed prices to which he could stick for more than a few months. In addition, there were times right after mailing out catalogues that the U.S. dollar fell in value against the German Deutschmark, really making his prices obsolete. When that happened, Antosh says, "You just hope it's a slow-moving item that is affected. I sold quite a bit of stuff for less than what I paid for it."

On top of everything else, mail order is closely regulated by the government. There are Federal Trade Commission (FTC) rules to follow, some state and city regulations, postal regulations, and interstate complications in paying sales and other taxes.

Mail order sellers must not only learn the rules, but keep abreast of changes in them. New regulations seem to pop up with some frequency. Just one example is the FTC's "30-day delayed delivery rule," promulgated on February 2, 1976. This rule applies to most mail order sellers, and it changed the industry significantly. It gives operators a choice: They must ship out all goods within 30 days of the date of order, or else state clearly in the ad solicitation that the customer must allow a longer period of time for delivery. The rule eliminated the use of ads that promised delivery "as soon as possible."

Other mail order rules seek to discourage deceptive advertising; to regulate warranties; to set rules for the use of endorsements and testimonials in ads; to regulate credit and billing procedures, and to limit the possiblity of fast dealing in sellers' "negative option plans." These plans are the ones often used by record and book clubs, wherein a new member, after joining, is automatically sent merchandise and billed for it unless the member specifically asks in writing not to be sent the goods. Some states and cities have their own mail order regulations that go even further. One law in New York City, for instance, requires that mail order sellers who use post office boxes also state the company's name and its real street address in an ad.

Fortunately, through the DMMA, a beginning mail order seller can learn current regulations, keep up with the changes, and at the same time pick up tips on useful mail order practices. One of the more active trade associations, the DMMA provides special services to its 4,000 members, but it also sells information to the general public. Nonmembers can purchase any of four information packages:

1. A mail order beginners package, including the book, *How to Start and Operate a Mail Order Business,* plus DMMA reports on advertising techniques and on legal, ethical, and regulatory matters. Recent price: $49.95, plus postage and handling.
2. Principles of mail order math and fulfillment, including profit and loss analysis methods, catalogue analysis, and information about customer service, inventory control, order processing, and other subjects. Recent price: $19.95.
3. A direct mail marketing manual, discussing creativity, mailing lists, media selection, production tips, etc. Recent price: $29.95.
4. A direct response copywriting manual, helpful in choosing advertising language that works. Recent price: $24.95.

Full membership in the DMMA recently cost $295 per year. For more information about membership, nonmember literature, and updated prices, one can write to the DMMA, Information Central Dept., 6 East 43 St., New York, NY 10017.

Before starting out in mail order, the new entrepreneur should also be aware of certain customer buying habits through the mail. It helps to know some basic mail order economics, too.

Studies show that most consumers do make purchases through the mail from time to time. Those with less education seem to make slightly more mail order purchases than those with more education. Three leading kinds of media through which purchases are made are mail order catalogues (in first place by far), magazines, and Sunday newspaper supplements.

Once your product exceeds $100 in price, chances are your mail order response rates will drop quite a bit. Most buyers simply won't pay so much for products they cannot examine in person. Some well-established, big-name companies do sell high-priced goods by mail, as the swank department store chains do with their catalogues. And oil companies, among others, solicit to sell luggage, electrical appliances, and other expensive items with ads included in bills to credit-card customers. But remember that these sellers are working with proven mailing lists of high-response buyers, and that they are companies of such size and fame that they encourage consumer trust. A home-based mail order businessperson should sell high-priced merchandise only if the security of a fat profit margin is built in.

Among the most common products sold by mail order are books, magazines, crafts and hobby products, garden equipment, plants, needlework and sewing kits, and related products. In surveys, consumers have cited a number of features in an ad solicitation as being crucial to their decision to buy. Prime among these is the money-back guarantee. A fine way to see how the well-established mail order marketers word their guarantees, and use other copywriting strategies, is to do plenty of reading of sample ads in the print media, and to obtain copies of catalogues. The catalogues from Sears and other big retailers will show you some of the most sophisticated appeals. Send away, too, for the catalogues of smaller mail order houses, which you may find advertised in magazines that you can go through at the public library.

Unlike most home businesses, advertising expense will be a big cost component in mail order. How much can you afford to spend on advertising? The only way to find out is to pin down your other costs of doing business, set forth the level of profit you seek, and subtract these figures from your proposed selling price to see how much is left for promotion. It is best to do this on a per-unit-of-product basis.

To use an example, assume that you have picked out a particular product for mail order sale—a wrought iron belt buckle with a fancy design for the "urban cowboy" look. After checking with several metal fabricating companies, you have located one that can sell the buckles to you for $1.50 each. You figure you will need a profit of 75 cents per buckle to meet your personal income goals.

You should assume that roughly 10 percent of your customers will be dissatisfied and will return their buckles for a refund. So figure your cost of goods at $1.50 plus 10 percent, or $1.65. See if you can estimate your costs for order processing, shipping, handling returns, and customer service. This will include labor costs for your employees, and postage. Say these costs come to 75 cents per buckle; your new total costs become $1.65 plus 75 cents, or $2.40. Now add in your overhead costs for operating the business (not much at home)—20 cents—for total costs of $2.60.

There are three remaining figures to juggle: selling price, loss to bad checks (a tough estimate to make), and your final calculation of the spread between price and all expenses that can be used for advertising.

Let's say you set a selling price of $5, plus 50 cents postage and handling. Figure your bad check costs at about 6 percent of sales, or 33 cents. Subtract the 33 cents and your $2.60 cost of goods from the $5.50 price, and you will be left with $2.57. Subtract your 75-cent profit. You are left with $1.82 to spend on advertising for each buckle sold. But in fact, you should again deduct the 10 percent loss for returned goods, leaving available ad dollars per unit at $1.64.

Now the key is to run ads in which your rate of purchase responses is frequent enough to meet your goal of spending $1.64 on promotion per buckle sold. Assume you spend $100 on an ad in a periodical with a circulation of 100,000. That means your cost of advertising is one tenth of one cent per household reached by the ad, or, expressed more typically, $1 per thousand of circulation. To hit your goal of spending no more than $1.64 per sale, you must get a purchase order from $\dfrac{\$1/\text{thousand}}{\$1.64}$, or 0.61 of every thousand households that receive the ad.

This should be easily within striking distance; you need purchases from fewer than one out of each thousand subscribers. However, if you had chosen to advertise in a more expensive publication, the numbers would have worked out differently. If you find yourself requiring a response rate of five or more per thousand reached, you should consider raising your selling price for safety. Of course, it is especially important in mail order to keep track of which ads in which media bring in what kind of response.

The fact that you might have to refigure pricing, or ad budgets, or even profits, underscores the fact that marketing is not an exact science. Market research will cut down risks, but never eliminate them. Marketing plans, thus, have to be kept forever in a fluid state. Managers must be as agile as any athlete, ready to reformulate a product or reconstruct a service, reset a price, throw away a poor-performing ad campaign, or change distribution systems whenever the targeted marketplace appears to demand it. The good marketers—at home or elsewhere—are those who are smart at the outset but also know how to react when the chips are down.

CHAPTER SEVEN

Surviving Growth

A small business entrepreneur rarely leads a boring life. He wrestles with day-to-day problems—old ones that stubbornly hang on, and new ones presented by the solutions to some of the old ones. He may ultimately face failure, and the need to liquidate, which can be a crushing personal blow. Or, he may face a dilemma that is quite different—one of the great challenges in business—consummate success right off the bat.

How do you cope with sudden success? In business, that's a serious question. In home-based business, it is especially serious, and a common cause of bewilderment. Fast growth is like a rose; the business blooms as beautifully as you could have hoped, but there are dangers in the handling. Dazzled by new prospects for wealth, the home entrepreneur is tempted to take on more risk, and to alter the business substantially. Whole new areas of decision making are forced to the fore:

—Should the operation be kept at home or moved outside?
—Should the sole proprietor take on partners?
—Is it smart to hire full-time employees? How many?
—Should more growth be subsidized with borrowed money?
—Is now the time to incorporate?
—Is more money worth a commitment to working longer hours?

These are merely the questions that come up. Typically, there are a host of new problems to solve as well. Sudden growth can leave you swamped with orders for your products or services at a time when you are still awaiting payment for prior shipments or work. How do you finance your expenses before your accounts receivable turn into real cash?

In addition, a bigger business will be more closely regulated by the government. Your home business might not have been covered by minimum-wage and fair-employment laws when it was tiny, to name just two of the rules. Now, it might fall under federal jurisdiction. And, of course, a bigger business may force you, as owner, to become a full-time manager instead of a producer of goods or services. Is that what you want?

THE BIGGEST DECISION

The questions and the problems that growth can bring suggest that there is a very important point to be considered while the new enterprise is still young: Do you really want a bigger business?

There is a split of opinion about this among home business people today. Part of the answer will lie in your original, written statement of your goals suggested in Chapter 4. Part of the answer, too, will come from your recognition of the consequences of growth. If your objectives are mainly financial, a bigger and more profitable business should represent fulfillment. The obstacles that bigness brings about should not dissuade you. These hurdles can be jumped.

However, if your home business was originally designed as a way to make some spare cash during your free time, think long and hard before allowing success to lure you into a change of purpose. A big, full-time home business probably will take much more time than you expect, and once you adjust your living standards upward because of the extra income, you will find yourself under pressure to keep the business growing. A lot of practitioners are keenly aware of these probabilities. "Over my dead body would this become full time," says Kay Schachtel, a designer of children's clothing in Highland Park, Illinois. She adds: "There is definitely potential for more money, but I would have to sacrifice my sanity and my nerves. I would be trading off enjoyment for pressure."

Many home businesses reach a growth limit because of space. Even with added-on rooms and workshops, there may not be enough square footage for the enterprise to prosper beyond a certain level. In metropolitan Washington, D.C., for example, Peter Fitzmaurice and his wife recently opened their own antique shop after dealing from their home for six years. The Fitzmorris couple had finally concluded that a home location would forever stifle progress. "Our profit was really in our goods," says Mrs. Fitzmaurice. "And at home, we couldn't buy as much inventory, because we couldn't store it. That hurt us."

Others tell similar stories. Caterer Susan B. Goldman in Chicago has seen her business grow from a 20-hour-per-week operation to 60 hours, all within a 12 by 15-foot home-based kitchen. "If it gets much bigger," she sighs, "I may have to move out of the house. You can't run a General Foods from your home."

For many entrepreneurs, the whole idea of launching the home business is to keep overhead costs low until there is enough volume of sales to justify moving to a store or plant. When the home location is temporary to begin with, the only question is at what point to make the switch. But this is a critical decision that bears careful financial study.

Before moving, your business should very clearly show the potential to become much larger in both sales and profits. Your expenses will be significantly higher on the outside, and, therefore, must be spread over more products sold or services rendered. There will be two attacks on your profit margins: First, the new overhead costs of outside office purchase or rental, new real estate taxes if you buy space, new utility costs, and a host of hidden expenses (restaurant lunches and dressier clothing may be two of them). Second, you will lose the chance to deduct expenses of using your home from your income—or rent, mortgage interest, utilities at home, and all the other incidentals mentioned in Chapter 5.

These considerations have led a number of home business-people to rethink their original plans to move out. Marjorie Maxfield, the home-based public relations agent in Houston, notes thoughtfully: "When I started the business, I thought it would be easiest to run it out of the home for a while, but eventually pick another spot to move into. But once I started, I saw the problems I was avoiding, how much I enjoyed it, and how much real estate rates were going up in this town. It made the decision to stay put very easy."

In or out of the house, business growth will force changes in your family life. Your spouse and children may have been understanding enough, after a period of adjustment, to give you peace in the home workplace for a very small business. How will they feel about you being home but inaccessible, or outside and inaccessible, for 40, 50, or 60 hours a week? Will you feel role-related guilt about your new relationship with them?

When you ask, your family members will probably give you a fairly honest answer about their feelings. It might be trickier to get an objective answer out of yourself. Intellectually, you may have perfectly legitimate justifications for spending more time on business and less with the family, but you cannot deny the presence—or importance—of emotional turmoil if you feel it. This may be a problem that you can put aside temporarily, but it could come back to haunt you and your marital or family ties later on. There are few things more time-consuming than managing a small business in a stage of fast growth. Even 60 hours a week might not be enough.

Meanwhile, within your company, growth is liable to change your function. As owner, your prime task is to manage. Some enjoy that role, and, as the business grows, it can be a pleasure to leave production-type work to others. Delegating responsibility to employees, in fact, is the only way to hold down the length of time you must spend operating a larger business. In Tucson, home-based food processor "Sugar" Cane Birdsall enjoys concentrating on marketing and new product development while others produce, package, and ship. But other entrepreneurs, especially in such fields as creative products, animals and plants, and repairing and restoring, love the nuts-and-bolts work more than management.

The biggest mistake is to suppose that you can continue to do both indefinitely in a growing business. And even if you are a willing manager, do you have the capacity to trust others with the responsibility for production? The chief executive who tries to run everything often fails to succeed, and almost always sees his best employees leave for other jobs where they will be entrusted with greater authority. This kind of problem has been a black mark on the records of some of the biggest companies in the United States, including Occidental Petroleum, CBS, and Polaroid.

Do you really want a bigger business? If the answer is yes, it ought to be a resounding yes. You will need that kind of mindset to survive growth.

COPING WITH THE CASH-FLOW CRISIS

In Portland, Oregon, a retired electronics engineer found a ready market for the products of his new home business: advertising specialties, such as matchbooks and pens, with the names of business customers printed on them. In fact, the market was all too ready. He purchased the items from manufacturers, shipped them to his customers, and awaited payment. What he discovered is that he was expected to pay his bills within 30 days, and no excuse was a good excuse. "Vendors are merciless. If you fall behind, they'll cut you off like that," he says. But his customers paid him in 60 days. He found he needed $2,500 in capital to finance the gap.

In a small business whose growth is mushrooming, this cash-flow crisis becomes even worse. A gap may exist between accounts paid and accounts receivable even when there is no growth. The mud gets deeper when the checks coming in are payments for last month's shipments of 1,000 widgets, but your fast-growth business has just received orders for 3,000. If your selling price is $5, and your production cost per widget is $3.50, then today is the day that you take $5,000 to the bank while you face the need to fill orders that will cost $10,500.

This is a very common dilemma for small businesses, and one that is not easily solved. It does not go away quickly. As long as the business keeps growing rapidly, the cash-flow crisis can deepen. The faster the growth, the bigger the gap becomes between money flowing in and money flowing out.

The biggest step one can take to minimize this problem is to set up a business that can demand payment on delivery. That is possible in many home businesses, especially those that sell services. A home day-nursery operator, for example, will typically ask for payment weekly. But for manufacturers, and some providers of service, cash on delivery is impractical, impossible, or a detriment to marketing. If you sell to big retail stores, for instance, you must live with standard policies they establish for payment of vendors.

Unless your product or service is in very hot demand, you'll get no exception to the rule. One of the early producers of personal computers, Ohio Scientific, had a product to offer at such a good price, and with such impressive capabilities for the money, that its young owners were able to get away with a cash-on-delivery policy. But such cases are fairly rare. And, since most people don't like to pay bills rapidly, a business that demands immediate cash payment can stymie its own growth. Casual customers will turn away. That is why so many advertising pitches for magazines and housewares include the statement that the customer can buy now but pay later.

So, if cash on delivery is possible and advisable, any new businessperson is wise to use it. If not, there are other steps that can be taken to cope with the cash-flow crisis. If the problem is serious, you can bite the bullet for a while on your ultimate dreams for a huge business, and try to purposely slow down the rate of growth by reducing ad placements a bit or postponing publication of the next mail order catalogue. You can also make personal visits to your large customers, if you sell wholesale, to explain your problem, and put a maximum limit on the number of products you will send them. Retailing home businesses can most easily manage growth: Cut walk-in traffic by reducing the hours that the at-home shop is open. With a little thought, the methods to manage growth in your business should become apparent; they probably will involve doing something in a manner opposite from the aggressive way you did it before.

Managing growth is especially important for those who want to retain full ownership of the business, and for those who want to avoid debt. The reason is that if growth is uncontrolled (or only modestly controlled), the cash-flow crisis can only be solved with fresh capital to finance your purchases. That capital can come from three sources: your own personal savings (which by now are probably invested in the business already), a loan, or a sale of part ownership in the business to someone else.

If your business has reached the point where it is having these kinds of problems, it probably should be incorporated, if that step has not yet been taken. Among other things, incorporation can make it easier to sell partial interests in the business by issuing new stock or selling part of the stock you own. Help from an attorney knowledgeable in small-business transactions is absolutely necessary for a stock sale.

You may have relished the idea of owning your own business outright, and there is nothing wrong with keeping it that way if you can. But if the opportunity is there to own 60 percent of a $1 million company through an infusion of new cash, instead of 100 percent of a $100,000 company, then selling part-ownership is a viable way to go. It is important to carefully consider who you want your new partner in ownership to be. A good venture capital company may not only become a provider of cash, but an able assistant in financial management. A respected corporate official in your city may be of similar help as a partner. But friends and relatives usually make poor co-owners. Personal relationships can get in the way of business decisions.

If you are looking for money, there are other avenues to explore as well. Now is the time when friendly relationships with suppliers and bankers can pay off. A well-heeled supplier of your raw materials or products may understand your cash-flow problem, and be willing to change his terms for payment. The supplier might even help finance your purchases if you can convince him of your eventual success—which will be mutually profitable sooner or later. Your banker will want to pore over your financial records of course, and he may find your profits are low or nonexistant in a period of fast growth. But if you have a good relationship with him, you may convince him to pitch your case to his loan committee at its next meeting.

As your cash-flow crisis comes on, rely on your accountant or bookkeeper for advice. He should be able to evaluate where the cheapest source of money is to be found. Interest rates on bank loans are much higher than before virulent inflation began, but keep in mind that a sale of stock will cost money, too. The new stockholders will expect dividend payments, and there will be legal fees to pay.

The greatest danger in a cash crunch is to underestimate its importance. An unexpected flood of orders for your products can make you giddy, and blind to the danger. With careful and conservative management, however, you can put out the fuse before the powder blows. Fast, if not runaway, growth can still be achieved.

HIRING AND MANAGING PEOPLE

As your business grows, you will almost certainly have to hire new employees. You may also have to begin to treat your incumbent employees differently than you have in the past. Your business may fall under the jurisdiction of federal, state, or even local labor regulations, which do not cover some of the tiniest of companies. In addition, as you relinquish more and more operating responsibility to subordinates, you'll have to hire more carefully, pay more, and make the work environment pleasant enough to keep your best workers from moving to another job.

Hiring is where government regulation begins. When the work force of a private employer reaches 15, the operation falls under the jurisdiction of Title VII of the Civil Rights Act of 1964. But it is a mistake to assume that with fewer than 15 employees, your business is unregulated. Some states and cities have their own labor laws to prevent discrimination in hiring, for example, and some of them cover companies with far fewer than 15 employees. You must check the local rules with city and state agencies.

Under Title VII, it is illegal to discriminate (to deny a job or fair treatment on the job) because of an individual's race, sex, color, religion, or national origin. The ban on discrimination starts with the wording of classified newspaper ads soliciting employees, and carries right through to the terms of employees' retirement plans.

Title VII is enforced by the U.S. Equal Employment Opportunity Commission, which also handles other federal legislation. Under the Age Discrimination in Employment Act, it is illegal to discriminate against persons aged 40 to 70 in hiring, discharge, pay, promotion, fringe benefits, and other aspects of employment. Under the Equal Pay Act, it is illegal to pay different wages based on sex to employees performing equal work on jobs requiring equal skill, effort, and responsibility, under similar working conditions.

These are broad statements, and even the most well-intentioned employers can use more specific information. In hiring, for instance, you must be sensitive to certain questions you might ask a job candidate, but which might be judged discriminatory. To get some direction, call the nearest office of the EEOC to request a copy of the brochure, *Pre-Employment Inquiries and Equal Employment Opportunity Law*. This publication is based largely on case histories of discrimination charges brought against employers for particular employee screening practices.

To stay out of trouble, it's wise to simply avoid asking job applicants questions that might be interpreted as discriminatory. Questions about race, religion, color, national origin, and even age should be stricken from both written job application forms and from verbal interview routines. The sex of the applicant should be fairly apparent without asking, but it could be a violation of law to go beyond sex identification and ask about marital status, pregnancy, future child-bearing plans, child-care arrangements, or the age or number of children an applicant has. The Commission or courts have also found to be unlawful, in certain circumstances, some questions about applicants' credit ratings, English-language skills, arrest records, conviction records, citizenship, military discharge status, and even height and weight (to protect minority groups whose average size is smaller than that of the majority).

In addition to laws against discrimination, there are the standard federal rules to consider about pay and hours of work. Most U.S. businesses are covered by the Fair Labor Standards Act, which sets the minimum wage, overtime pay rules, record-keeping requirements, and child labor standards.

A fast-growing home business may well fall under the jurisdiction of this act. In fact, it might have been covered in the past. Almost all enterprises that somehow engage in interstate commerce are covered. So are retail and service businesses conducted totally inside one state, but having annual sales of at least $325,000 ($362,500 beginning January 1, 1982). Other companies within a state are covered if sales exceed $250,000. There are other details in the law. The Wage and Hour Division of your local office of the Department of Labor can explain them.

As of January 1, 1981, the minimum wage was $3.35. Overtime payments are required at one and a half times straight pay for hours worked in excess of 40 per week. However, the laws do not require vacation pay; holiday, severance, or sick pay; time off for holidays or vacations; premium pay for holiday or weekend work; pay raises or fringe benefits; or discharge notices or reasons for discharge. These are matters to be resolved privately between employers and employees or unions. Of course, in this day and age, employers who want to keep good workers will grant most or all of the benefits listed above.

Once you become acquainted with the labor laws, it should not be difficult to stay within them. The real challenge in hiring is to pick people with the right qualifications, work habits, and attitudes toward your business. It's a serious error to rely too much on the verbal, pre-employment interview. Some people are better at talking than working. Before hiring a person, you ought to have hard evidence in hand about that candidate's work history and his or her ability to do the specific work you'll require.

Ask any candidate to provide, in writing, a complete work and educational history. Ask for names and telephone numbers of prior employers you can contact, and for other personal references. Of course, you'll never get the name of a reference who the candidate knows will speak ill of him, but the written history will be valuable anyway. Be wary of a history of many job changes in short periods of time, and of job changes where the candidate seems to have made little progress in pay or career advancement. If you are hiring a youngster fresh out of school, ask for high school or college transcripts. Also ask about part-time jobs held, if any, during schooling years. A young woman or man who has worked during school years and achieved reasonably good grades at the same time is probably a very good risk. Those who did not work during their teenage years, but who immersed themselves in extracurricular school or community activities, will likely be good bets as well.

After you hire someone, there are a lot of ways to stimulate his or her interest and productivity. The employer-employee relationship should start on a happy note automatically; after all, you have told the new employee that you trust him by selecting him for the job. Don't renege on that message by overmanaging. Allow a new worker the courtesy to make some mistakes on his own. As long as he understands why and how he made them, he deserves your continuing trust until he proves himself unworthy of it.

Any employee will work harder and better if he sees good reasons to do so. A quick raise in pay after a short trial period carries a clear message from employer to employee that his work is valued. Handing out more responsibility has a similar effect, and makes an employee feel he is important to the business. Naturally, most employees work for money, not love. You can give financial incentives through piece-work payments, profit-sharing plans, or bonuses tied to the company's financial performance. Remember that with piece-work, you are still required to pay the minimum wage to low-volume producers. Many workers, however, will produce more to earn more, and paying by the piece also will enable you to have more precise knowledge of your labor cost per product.

As you get ready to hire employees, it's a good time to recheck your local zoning laws. Quite a few of them allow people to work at their own homes, but not to hire others to work in the home. If that is the case, then the time has come to consider moving the business to outside headquarters. A home business-person may be tempted to hire at home anyway, with the idea that, if caught, the business can always be moved. The trouble is, zoning officials might insist that the move be made very promptly or the business be shut down. Being forced to rush into an out-of-home location can put you in jeopardy. You might easily get stuck with whatever location you can find, and that can mean unnecessarily high rents or poor proximity to markets or transportation. The right way to move the business out of the house is to spend whatever time it takes to shop for the right spot.

There is one alternative to moving when zoning laws prohibit at-home employees. You can hire others to work out of their own homes. But this can have mixed results, and is obviously inappropriate for home businesses such as child care, where the work must be done on-site. By hiring others who work where you cannot supervise them, you can be left with such problems as poor product quality without knowing why. It could also become bothersome to transport raw materials and finished goods back and forth. On the other hand, if you know that your employees can do the job right in their own homes, this solution can be the least expensive one to a zoning problem.

MOVING OUT

When you are certain that you want to—or that you must—move the business to an outside location, you'll enter a very busy period in the history of your operation. Above all, don't go too fast.

There will be decisions to make about costs, location, and whether to rent or buy outside facilities. Circumstances within any of these three areas can help build or tear down a going business. They merit careful attention, and if that means you'll be working double time for a while, it is a penalty you must pay. Like leading a virtuous life, the work you do on moving will be rewarded later.

The first evaluation to make is how much you can afford to spend on a new level of business overhead. If you have ever purchased a house, you might recall the old principle that you should never try to make monthly payments that exceed one fourth of your monthly gross income. You must be even more thrifty when shopping for office or production space. For instance, large corporations pay only a tiny fraction of their revenues for administrative offices. It is true that total overhead costs are often higher, as a percentage of sales, in small businesses than in big operations. There is no standard formula. But if your monthly payments for total business space and utilities look as though they will exceed 10 percent of your monthly sales, it is certainly time to be concerned. Remember that your costs for raw materials and labor may be beyond your firm control. You do have a chance to exert some control on overhead, and that starts with a modest leased space or building. Heating and cooling systems should be efficient at the time you move.

Beyond the amount you choose to spend, there are plenty of other things to consider. Here are some of them:

1. If it comes cheap, buy lots more space than you need at your current level of activity, so that the business will have room to grow. Chances are, however, that space will not be cheap. So, buy enough to accommodate a couple of years of projected growth if you can, but seek a balance between initial cost and your own optimism. If things are going so well after a couple of years, you may be able to move again to a bigger place. Give serious consideration to any location where you will own a big lot on which your building can be expanded, or where you will have the chance to lease additional space later without moving.

2. Buy or lease with transportation in mind. For one thing, you'll want a place easily accessible to you and your employees. But a more serious consideration for manufacturers is nearness to commercial transport for products.

3. Owning a business property, rather than leasing, can be a risky proposition. Small businesses are not always the most enduring, and you'll want to make sure that if your plans for the business go awry, you are not stuck with a building that you must sell at a loss. Picture your business, too, in the midst of a fast-growth cash-flow crisis on the day that the roof begins to leak or the plumbing breaks down. If you have the cash to make a downpayment on commercial property, is that the best way to invest it? What effect would that same cash have if invested in new advertising, inventories, or machinery?

4. Before signing a lease, get to know the landlord. Make some discreet inquiries with other tenants. What is the landlord's track record for building maintenance? No matter how good the space looks, renting from a landlord who will not provide good service will be a mistake.

5. Have a lawyer look over the lease before signing. It is mighty handy to have the right to sublet, in case your business does not work out. You should also try to get as much control over utilities as possible; certainly, you should have the right to control temperatures in your space with thermostats installed by the building owner.

6. Keep security in mind. Make a personal visit to the police station nearest the location you are considering, and ask about crime rates in the area. Set aside some money for extra locks and alarms. Your own and your employees' safety is at stake, together with whatever valuables are kept at work.

7. If your out-of-home space will be used for retail selling, you'll want heavy auto and pedestrian traffic at the new location. Look for the right kind of traffic as well. Space in the better neighborhoods may cost more, but a more monied class of customers will allow a higher price structure for your products.

Clearly, these points only touch on the start-up problems and possibilities for out-of-home businesses. They are mentioned in short fashion because readers of this book will be predominantly interested in home-based ventures. There are other books—lots of them—that offer more advice on small-business site selection; a trip to the library or bookstore will be worth the effort. For all the glories a home business can provide, small businesses outside can be glorious, too. When a home business grows so large that it spills beyond the four walls into quarters of its own, it is a mark of success and a moment of pride that the owner will never forget.

Part 2

The Practitioners

CHAPTER EIGHT

Food and Feeding

In the typical household kitchen today, most of the housewares that fill the shelves, closets, and counters are factory-made, thank goodness. General Electric, Rubbermaid, and all the other corporations that spend millions on efficient production do come up with products of good quality at much lower cost than most "cottage" industries could manufacture. But inside the kitchen pantry lies an exception to the rule.

The exception is food itself. A single good cook or caterer can make and serve a meal whose quality exceeds industrially-processed foods, or the offerings of the average restaurant. With a home base to cut overhead costs, the prices in a home food processing or catering business can be competitive as well. With a superior product at the right price, a home food business can be ideal, and those who try them usually find that marketplace demand is strong.

Even so, a home-based food operation is not all a bowl of cherries. To begin with, financial management can be tricky. Fast-rising wholesale costs of food mean that business managers must keep a sharp eye on purchases and their own price-setting. And, perhaps more disconcerting than anything else, government regulation of home food processors and caterers can be very tough.

More than any other standard type of home business, food preparation is closely watched by a number of levels of government. The U.S. Food & Drug Administration is charged with ensuring the purity of foods in all processing operations, and the federal laws give no breaks to home businesses merely because they are small. State and county health departments regulate sanitation in food processing and retailing establishments. These local rules tend to be harder on home-based operations than they are on out-of-home businesses, and some states and counties have chosen to practically ban commercial food processing at home.

The regulatory scheme is reminiscent in some ways of zoning laws. There are logical reasons to have some regulations, certainly, but others seem to stretch the bounds of good sense. At the turn of the century, the conditions in meat and other food processing plants were often abhorrent. Muckraking newspaper stories and novels, such as *The Jungle*, by Upton Sinclair, galvanized the public to act. Ever since, the government, at every level, has assumed the responsibility for policing the food industry. As a result, foods and eating places are generally cleaner and safer today.

Like the zoning laws, however, some of the food-related rules appear to go too far. In California, state regulations on food retailing and marketing establishments include this provision: "No food prepared or stored in a private home shall be offered for sale, sold, or given away, in an establishment operating under the provisions of this chapter, without the written approval of the local health officer." One health officer in Los Angeles County says that such written approvals are seldom given. In Texas, the law is a little less restrictive. It says that no food can be prepared for sale to the public in a kitchen that is also used as the kitchen of a private residence. The business kitchen, in Texas, can be attached to the home, but must have a separate entrance and no connecting doorways with the rest of the home. Laws in others states and counties vary widely.

One is tempted to note that even state and county legislators were raised by parents who cooked at home but didn't poison them. And it wasn't the home kitchen that invented the nitrate, nitrite, and certain red dye food additives that some people believe are dangerous, not to mention saccharin. It is true that the home-based preparation of canned and processed foods for commercial use requires a different kind of expertise than cooking fresh foods. But undoubtedly, one unstated reason for restrictive local laws on home food businesses is simply that they would be bothersome to police. Otherwise, the harsher laws seem to assume that home kitchens are guilty of unsafe or unsanitary conditions without ever having been inspected.

Since tough laws do exist in some places regardless of their fairness, it is essential to check with county health authorities in your area before investing a penny in a home food business. There is no reason to be discouraged before checking, and in many places home kitchens can be used if they are modified. In addition, you may be able to devise a food business run partly from home and partly outside the home. Your house can become the business office, recipe idea center, and marketing headquarters, while production and shipping can be done off-premise—even contracted out to a private company.

Still, aside from health regulations, there is another point of legal concern. No one should begin a home food business without product liability insurance, which gives financial coverage against suits brought for allegedly causing physical harm to the consumer. The tensions of modern life seem to have made U.S. society increasingly litigious. Food companies can, and are, sued for all kinds of reasons—supposed poisonings, assorted bellyaches, cuts from sharp lids or broken jars, and so on.

Some consumers are legitimate victims; others are not. One Ohio attorney likes to tell the story of a visit from a married couple, one of whom thought a bottle of soda had a "funny taste." The regional bottling plant was right down the street, and the twosome wondered if they could make some spare cash by filing a lawsuit. The attorney refused, but says he was visited again by the couple a few days later. They just wanted to let him know that they had walked over to the plant by themselves, acted outraged, threatened a suit in conversation with the plant manager, and walked away with $250 in cash as a settlement.

Consumers, or even retailers who buy from home food processors, can also misuse a product. One home-based cake baker worries that a retailer might leave her cheesecake on a shelf until it spoils, but sell it anyway. The consumer always has the right to sue the manufacturer, and with any lawsuit, victory by the party in the right is never 100 percent certain.

All of this makes product liability insurance a necessity to reduce risk. The implications of this are powerful. The premium payments may be pretty steep, at least high enough to discourage a truly small-scale home food business from getting started. Your premiums will depend on a number of variables, so it is impossible to know what they will be without shopping for a policy. Look up the insurance agents and companies that offer commercial lines in your city and surrounding cities. The more you check, the better your chance of finding the lowest rates. It is certainly advisable to buy no less than $250,000 of coverage. Jacque Hertz, a cake baker in Denver, reports that she has purchased $500,000 of coverage at a premium cost of $126 for six months. But the rates can be much higher—$1,000 per year or even more, depending on your scope of business, type of product, and your agent.

You'll have to make some contacts, too, to find out about the health regulations. County authorities should be able to apprise you of local and state regulations. The federal rules covering food production are somewhat longwinded, but once you get them you should be able to read through the pertinent parts over a weekend. The regulations administered by the FDA are listed in Title 21 of the Code of Federal Regulations. Home food business operators will need two sections:

— Part 1 to 99, including general regulations for the enforcement of the Federal Food, Drug, and Cosmetic Act and the Fair Packaging and Labeling Act, plus laws on color additives. Recent price: $5.50.
— Part 100 to 199, covering food standards, food additives, good manufacturing practices for food, low-acid canned foods, and food labeling. Recent price: $7.50.

Both of these sections can be purchased by sending a check or money order to: Superintendent of Documents, Government Printing Office, Washington, DC 20402. To make certain the prices have not changed, make a quick phone call to your nearest FDA office.

The regulations and the legal risks may seem burdensome, and even scary at first glance. They are, indeed, a complicating factor for an ordinary person who has a knack for baking a good apple pie, and a yen to make some extra money selling some at neighborhood stores. But part of any business involves overcoming complex obstacles, and many home entrepreneurs have done so in the food business. Catering has become a hot area within the home business movement, and some home manufacturers of their own processed food recipes have succeeded neatly. To demonstrate that even tough local food laws, such as California's, can be accommodated, consider the tale of a Santa Monica woman who has become a full-scale manufacturer:

HERBED VINEGARS

"I started this business because I grew herbs in my own garden and wanted to do something with them," says Paula

Fishman, who lives in a five-bedroom Santa Monica home. "It was never designed to make money," she adds. "It was just an accident that it was such a success."

Fishman grew three herbs in her garden: rosemary, mint, and oregano. It was her idea to mix these, in combination with purchased amounts of tarragon, dill, garlic, and shallots, into bottles of vinegar. The herbs added flavor and visual appeal, making something special out of an ordinary bottle of vinegar for use on salads and other foods. At first, Fishman's only idea was to give the bottles to friends as gifts. But they suggested to her that her products (she made several formulations) could just as easily be sold commercially.

So the business began. At the start, she experimented at home. Fishman invested just $25 to buy 12 bottles, some store-bought vinegar, and labels. She perfected her recipes. Then, she planned how to cope with the state's tough home food rules. Fishman was able to employ a bottler in downtown Los Angeles, making it easier as well to obtain product liability insurance. The bottler not only accepted her business, he also offered space in his shop for Fishman and some friends to gather, fill the bottles with herbs, seal them, and apply labels.

That split the operations of Sweet Adelaide, the company name, between home, where Fishman coordinated her marketing and office chores, and the plant. With personal sales contacts, Fishman was able to line up accounts at specialty gourmet shops in the Los Angeles area. In one nine-month period, she moved 3,600 bottles. She says she is able to gross about twice the cost of her raw materials, though Fishman also laments: "The only trouble with spending $1,500 to make $3,000 is that most of the profit goes toward the liability insurance." Recently, Fishman allowed the business to slack off while she attended to some home remodeling. But this is temporary, and she hopes not only to revitalize the business but to develop more companion products.

With a business of your own, she notes, "You are doing it because you love it. It's a passion." She finds this in marked contrast to the typical out-of-home, nine-to-five job. The vinegar business, she adds, seems to require no special training, although there can be embarrassing moments in learning on the job. Fishman recalls her first attempt at learning the art of properly packing a box to be shipped by United Parcel Service. "UPS said I had to test the breakage of the box. They made me pick it up and drop it from waist height. UPS will never smell the same."

Adding ingredients to an already-prepared food like vinegar is, of course, just one avenue for home food processing. Other entrepreneurs work more from scratch. Although it is rare, there are even those who produce raw foods for commercial sale other than by farming. One of them is Rob Stewart, who gave up a landscaping business in Southern California to work at home full-time in Oregon.

$100 PER HIVE

Rob Stewart and his wife, Anne, started with a dream: Both wanted to make a living and reside in the country. It was in 1973 that Stewart, then a landscaper in Laguna Beach, struck on an idea to make the dream come true. He decided to try beekeeping.

He started with two hives, right in Laguna Beach. Within 18 months, the hives grew to 15, and Stewart had harvested 3,000 pounds of honey, which he had no trouble selling to local stores at $1 per pound. Since it took just $75 of investment to build each hive, and since each purportedly had a life span of 15 to 20 years, Stewart decided that the honey business "looked pretty attractive."

In the fall of 1980, Stewart made his biggest decision: to go into the honey venture full time and move, with his wife and son, to Sutherlin, Oregon, a rural community of 4,500. Still, he found he could handle the business on just two acres, a space not much bigger than some city-sized lots outside the crowded eastern seaboard. In short order, Stewart had built a total of 70 hives, invested $10,000 in honey processing equipment, and bought a used, two-ton truck for hauling. He found wholesaling an adequate distribution method, and sold his honey to a number of small retailers and to Fred Meyer Inc., one of the Pacific Northwest's largest retail chains. Stewart's target is to build a total of 500 hives within two years, and to average an annual income of $100 per hive—a seemingly conservative goal given his past performance.

By keeping the business at home, Stewart says, he is able to fulfill his hope to live in the country even without a big farm, to maximize time spent with his family, and to "minimize overhead." At times, the hours are exceedingly long; 80-hour weeks can be the norm. But Anne helps with marketing a couple of hours a day, and she has worked outside the home as well while Stewart expanded his business.

With the 70 hives, Stewart was able to wholesale nearly 1,000 pounds of honey a month at $3 a quart. Jars and labels cost just 33 cents a quart. Stewart recently was preparing to build a 1,000-square-foot honey house for bottling and storing, and he says he hopes that when his production quadruples to 4,000 pounds a month, he will have fully achieved his goal to support his family comfortably in a life-style he and his wife have long desired.

Stewart's business demonstrates, among many other things, that for a home-based food business to grow large, it takes capital. His big expenses were for outdoor processing equipment, but more typical food processing operations can face similarly high costs for indoor cooking and processing facilities. When there is a need as well to remodel a house to meet state or city health regulations, the costs can shoot much higher. But a good product with a substantial profit margin can more than compensate.

SUGAR'S KITCHEN

"Sugar" Cane Birdsall, the home-based producer of Arizona Champagne Sauces mentioned in Chapter 1, ran up against local health regulations early on. She lives in Tucson, one of a number of local jurisdictions in Arizona that requires commercial food products to be manufactured in facilities separate from the family kitchen. She could see that the conversion would be costly, but she had confidence in her products and decided to forge ahead.

Birdsall spent $10,000 on remodeling and equipment. She converted the laundry room of her spacious home into the business kitchen, equipped with four microwave ovens. New lighting and electrical work was done, and special venting was built for five refrigerators. Luckily a separate bathroom and entrance to the business space were already available through the maid's quarters, part of which also became a cold storage room. In addition, the local rules called for a three-compartment sink, so Birdsall had one of them installed to meet that requirement.

The work was done in 1978. Three years later, the value of having gone ahead was evident. "I remember when a two- or three-case order was heaven," Birdsall reminisced. Those days were long gone. She had just received a $3,000 order from Saks Fifth Avenue of New York.

A former Manhattan real estate seller, Birdsall had started out by inventing a mustard sauce to serve at a New Year's Eve party. Her guests proclaimed that she ought to bottle and sell it, and she decided to try. She took on the Sugar's Kitchen business name, and branded her products, "Arizona Champagne Sauces." The line quickly grew to four products, and Birdsall sought out retail customers through personal sales calls. At her very first meeting with a major Arizona department store retailer, another costly reality of the food business came up. He asked if she was insured for product liability. Birdsall quickly purchased the requisite policy.

But the quality of her products helped make up for all the costs. As she lined up more and more prestigious retailers as customers, a snowballing effect took place. Gourmet food writers began to take notice, and Birdsall won plaudits in national magazines and *The New York Times*. That pushed sales even more, and Bloomingdale's, Macy's, and Saks became three of many gold stars on a list that grew to 200 accounts. She also sold by mail order. Her products were retailing for $3 to $4 for a half-pint jar—a high price made possible only by Birdsall's careful marketing strategy to sell her sauces as gourmet items and stick to high quality.

At first, Birdsall did the marketing and cooking herself. Later, she was able to hire another woman to work a six-hour shift turning out 50 12-jar cases a day. Neighborhood kids dropped by to help out on an hourly basis, labeling and packing, and Birdsall's husband, a Tucson realtor, pitched in to man the business office. Birdsall herself was able to concentrate on marketing and new product development. She offers a one-sentence piece of advice to home food business newcomers, and it is a thought that certainly has guided her from concept to production, and through periods of high investment in the business: "You've got to be aggressive."

Food processing is a huge business nationally. In fact, from production to retail sale, food is by far the biggest U.S. industry. It is marked by such billion-dollar names as General Foods, Nabisco Brands, General Mills, and Kellogg. Yet even most of these companies play only one part of the game. A lot of the action is in "food service," the expression generally used to refer to restaurants, institutional feeding, machine vending, catering, and related enterprises. It is in these areas that an increasing number of home workers have found opportunity. Some who live in properly-zoned neighborhoods have converted their houses into restaurants. But one of the hottest spots for new home businesses is catering. People who can learn the eating habits of their local communities can often find a niche to fill with catered meals.

FROM BOXES TO DINNER PARTIES

Fresh out of college in May 1978, Susan B. Goldman of Chicago studied her market. "I felt there was an inadequate availability of good lunch places in the Loop [Chicago's financial district], and on the catering side there was nothing in between a major production and deli food." Goldman conceived an idea to fill the gap: fancy boxed lunches priced at about $5 and sold to corporate offices in the Loop area.

Little did she realize how much demand there was for all kinds of catering service in that district. She began promotion with some direct mail and door-to-door visits. The response was so great, and called for such a range of services, that before the boxed lunch idea could really get going, Goldman was being called on to cater elaborate corporate luncheons and full-blown dinner parties.

Sugar & Spice Catering, her business name, had started out as a basic knife-and-fork operation that soaked up 20 hours of Goldman's time per week. Within a couple of years, it took 60 hours of work, and Goldman needed to hire temporary staffs of waitresses and bartenders for the big parties. Her initial costs had been limited to printing flyers and stationary, and buying a station wagon to haul food. Later, food purchases and lesser expenses grew to about $1,500 per month. But she was able to cover her costs and pull in enough cash to build a business capable of earning $30,00 per year. By 1981, she says she felt she had reached a decision point about whether to try to hold the business to mainly a one-person operation, or to expand it significantly and become one of Chicago's larger caterers.

Food service is usually limited in terms of growth, compared with processing. Even the revenues of McDonald's, the restaurant industry leader, cannot compare with General Foods. But Goldman found she also had a cost advantage over home processing. She didn't need to purchase the elaborate cooking and storage machinery that processors need, so up-front costs were much less. She also was able to concentrate her attention on efficient and careful purchasing of raw foods.

At first, Goldman bought food at retail markets. She switched to wholesalers pretty quickly, but not only because of price. "The reason was not so much price as the problem of quantity. If you needed 50 boned chicken breasts, a store butcher would tell you to get lost." Furthermore, she finds that by personally visiting the food wholesaler, she can obtain better-quality products, which are more important to a catering business than low purchase prices. "You're not an A&P, " she notes. "There's no reason to haggle for price. You haggle for quality. As a relatively small caterer, you also learn not to be a hassle for the wholesaler. You try to come down and buy when it is convenient for them." As a rule of thumb, Goldman tried to charge three times her cost of ingredients to customers. She adds a charge for her staff at dinner parties, and finds she usually charges a total of about $20 per person served.

The business is not without drawbacks. "Customers can drive you crazy calling all the time asking questions, worrying about their parties," she says. "Because I'm not a restaurant," Goldman adds, "I can't get deliveries made to me. And when you are up to your elbows in potato salad, you often wish you had a regular job." On the other hand, Goldman is able to provide herself with a social life by controlling her own schedule. She may refuse some weekend party business, or work weekends and take time off during the week. The overwhelming response of customers right off the bat to a business of her own has also been a source of personal gratification. "The boxed lunch idea never took off," she laughs, "because I was so filled up with other orders."

VEGETARIAN SERVICE

When Emily Schurr and her partner, Ann Robare, began thinking about establishing a catering business, they sought, like Goldman, to fill a special need in the market. They wanted to stick to natural foods, and to avoid red meats, deep-fried foods, white flour, and sugar. In Norton, Ohio, and its surrounding metropolitan area of more than 500,000, there was little competition in vegetarian and natural foods cooking, and they sensed a significant demand.

The two started with just $150 in kitchen equipment, and they have come up with some interesting cost reduction techniques. When customers need catering at home or in buildings with kitchens, Schurr and Robare try to arrange to cook and prepare food on-premise. Both have strong ties with a food purchasing co-op near their homes, and they use the co-op's wholesale buying power to supply foods for their larger affairs. For smaller gatherings, they merely deliver the food, and do not serve.

The business, Any Thyme Catering, specializes in stir-fry cooking with lots of fresh vegetables and tofu, salads with sesame dressings, whole wheat pastry with honey, carrot cakes, spinach dip with raw vegetables, homemade sesame wheat crackers, and herb and poppyseed rolls. Any Thyme avoids canned and frozen foods, and in meats, the business restricts itself to fish and chicken. Recently, their prices ranged from $4 to $8 for lunch, $6 to $8 for dinner, and $25 to $50 for party trays. They like to set a $50 minimum price.

The business is still young. Schurr says it grossed just $1,500 in 1980, and the two entrepreneurs are just arranging for business telephone service, business cards, and other standard paraphernalia. They plan a newspaper advertising campaign to expand the operation, which has been part time. So far, they've been especially pleased by market acceptance among younger adults, who seem most interested in natural and vegetarian foods. Schurr and Robare have even supplied family meals at the behest of flustered parents who have no experience cooking vegetarian foods for their grown children. "I am not so nervous any more when my kids come over to eat, because they are all into this vegetarian food," one customer recently remarked. "The catering has shown me it is a delicious way to eat."

PROFIT POTENTIAL

A food processing business, operated fully or partly from the home, has unlimited earnings potential through wholesale and direct mail distribution. Sugar's Kitchen reported sales topping $100,000 on an annualized basis, to name just one. Growing food processors can make a natural transition to out-of-home space if desired. Profits in home food service are more limited. More than $5,000 per year can be earned on a part-time basis, and an upper- middle-income salary for an individual can be achieved full time.

RISK

The risk can be high or low, depending on steps taken to meet local and federal regulations. Buy adequate insurance, carefully control food purchases, and adjust pricing on short notice. Ignoring government regulations can cause immediate closure if discovered and can also be a point in a plaintiff's favor in any lawsuit against the business. Without insurance, risk far exceeds potential gain.

ENJOYMENT

Because food businesses involve creativity, they can be extremely gratifying. Food processing, after the fun of initial product research and development, stays enjoyable if the entrepreneur also likes marketing, production, and business management. Time consumption can be a problem, especially in food service, which also requires a substantial ability to get along with people.

CHAPTER NINE

Caring for People

A century ago, self-sufficiency was a hallmark of the American family. Except for the occasional visit at home by the doctor, and the growing recognition that the children ought to get a few years of schooling from a professional teacher, there just wasn't too much need for a "human services" sector of the economy. Families were large. Child care and grooming services were handled at home. People literally "took care of their own" and took care of themselves.

For better or worse—and it is probably worse—self-sufficiency is now rare in our society. Americans today need, demand, and pay for personal services on a vast scale. With their time stretched by outside work and commuting, and with few (or zero) adult family members to handle chores at home, many individuals find that their list of "can't dos" is growing very long indeed: child care, grooming, housekeeping, grocery shopping, laundry, transportation, and more. The free market, of course, has responded. There are now more workers in the United States service sector than in manufacturing. Even so, they are not enough. Demand exceeds supply for many personal services, and consumers are often unhappy with the quality of services from outside companies, agencies, and shops. Home-based businesses can fill in the holes.

Personal service businesses at home seldom find a lack of customers. Child care, grooming services, and related activities may never make the home entrepreneur rich, yet they will rarely fail to provide a steady income. Operated part time, personal services are a ready source of supplemental cash.

Demand for personal services is burgeoning mainly because of the dramatic changes in the structure of families. The dynamic increase in the number of families that now require outside child care demonstrates this change. The Census Bureau reports that between 1970 and 1979, the total number of families with one or more children at home increased by 1.6 million, or 5 percent. But the number of families with two parents decreased by one million, or 4 percent. The result: The number of one-parent families jumped 79 percent during the decade. By 1979, an astonishing 19 percent—nearly one out of five—U.S. families had only one parent, up from 11 percent in 1970. Divorces and separations were the main causes of this change; the proportion of single-parent families because of a death of one parent declined.

The 1980 census is almost certain to show a continuation of this trend. Before the numbers were tallied, there were already 5,857,000 single-parent families in the country. The market for child-care services created by this phenomenon was huge. By the spring of 1979, there were 11,529,000 children under 18 years old living with only one parent. Of these children, fully 5,472,000 were under the age of nine, and, therefore, in need of adult supervision all of the time, an impossibility for a working single parent. And for the same reasons that household units are shrinking in size (see Chapter 2), there are fewer and fewer unpaid relatives around willing and able to help care for these children. Outside services care for most, plus many of the children of two-parent families when both parents work.

What the statistics show, of course, is that child care is the hottest of the personal services today. Caring for children can be a fine at-home business. Outside child-care centers are sometimes overcrowded, impersonal, or inconvenient. Among other things, they usually have strict opening and closing hours that impose tough limitations on parents whose work schedules must be somewhat flexible. Home workers in child care do not need extensive training or education, and start-up costs are relatively low. They do need to enjoy the presence of children, and to have some knowledge of a proper way to care for them. Parents who can pick between depositing their children in a day-care center or a warm and loving home will usually make the obvious choice.

Hair care is a second big category of personal service available to home workers. The forces of the marketplace are different, however. There are no cataclysmic changes in demographics to boost demand, as with child care. Customers of at-home hairdressers and barbers are usually seeking something specific: a slighly lower price, a more private setting, quicker service, or the special skills or friendship of a certain person. Start-up costs for at-home hair care operations can be high, but lower than at an outside shop. Overhead expenses are much lower, making it easy to price one's service competitively.

The growth of families where both marriage partners or unmarried adults have jobs has created additional business opportunities for service workers. There is an increased demand for laundry services, grocery pickup, and other shopping services, and certainly for housekeeping. Only some of these kinds of services, however, can be performed from the home of the worker, and, therefore, they do not get much attention in this volume. These businesses do represent money-making opportunities, though, for entrepreneurs who are interested.

Like so many home businesses, child care and hair care are government-regulated. Most of the regulations are state and local rules regarding licensing, and, with child care, safety equipment, such as the placement of fire extinguishers. Many states and municipalities have specific agencies that regulate child-care and hair-care industries. If you cannot find the right one, your city, borough, or county law office should be able to direct you to the proper source of information about what the regulations are. Since the personal care businesses will put customers inside your home, you should also check with your insurance agent about increasing your liability coverage for at-home injuries or accidents. Your policy may have to be changed significantly.

The added insurance coverage, however, will be a tax-deductible cost of doing business. It is also important to note that child-care operations, which are almost certain to fail the "exclusive use" test for home office-type tax deductions, need not worry about that problem. As noted in Chapter 5, the IRS requires taxpayers to meet a number of tests to deduct overhead expenses of running a business at home, and among them is exclusive use: Business space must be used strictly for business, and not for personal living. But this rule specifically exempts home day-care centers, as long as they are licensed or certified by the state, if the state requires it. The regulations in your state should tell you whether your child-care operation will need to be licensed. Occasional babysitting, of course, needs no license, so the state or local rules should define where babysitting ends and a regular business begins.

The real challenge in personal services will not involve licensing and taxes. Instead, the operator's ability to get along with people will be most critical. Without a pleasant and conversational atmosphere, the home hairdresser will be without customers. In child-care operations, the manager must be able to impose discipline and yet have the youngsters leave the house with a generally good feeling about the day-care experience.

Sometimes, income and service must be juggled to find a happy medium. Taking on too many customers to boost income is a certain way to degrade the quality of service, by lessening the amount of individual attention one can give. The homeowner's less-crowded environment, conducive to more personal attention than a commercial facility can provide, will be the biggest single draw to customers. You should investigate every possibility to charge a premium price for this extra feature of your service.

Unfortunately, with child care in particular, hot competition puts a lid on pricing in most areas. On the other hand, steadiness in the volume of clients, made possible by the new levels of demand for personal services, can help make up for a lack of price elasticity. Market research on pricing is extremely important. Fees charged by at-home child-care and hair-care operators typically follow rates in local communities, but these vary widely around the U.S.

A WHOLE-HOUSE BUSINESS

When Madeline Wangler talks on the phone, her voice is often barely audible above the din of eight children. Her home business office, she jokes, is every square inch of her three-bedroom apartment in Chicago.

Wangler had recently left her job as manager of a retail clothing store when she and her husband parted, leaving her with a year-old daughter. "I wanted to spend my time with my daughter," she says. "Taking care of kids in my home seemed to be a natural way to integrate that with making a living." She marketed aggressively. Wangler placed ads in a local newspaper, put up notices in grocery stores, and told "everyone I knew about my business. I even went up to strangers on the street and told them about myself," she says.

Within two months, she had two children full time in addition to her own daughter. Wangler quickly built the business to eight paid-for kids, which is the maximum for which she was licensed under Illinois law. After minimal start-up costs, her expenses grew rapidly with each new client. "As more money came in, more went out," she recalls. "I had to buy more food, more toys, etc. I scouted out garage sales and flea markets for toys. It took me a year before I could buy cots for all the kids." Wangler also paid $80 per year for extra home insurance coverage, and has hired two part-time helpers.

Her fees range from $60 per week for older children to $75 per week for infants. To make her income secure, she has an understanding with clients that they will pay the weekly fee even if the child does not show up for some reason.

Handling eight children plus her own is more ambitious than most. Wangler notes that "the burnout rate in this business is high. You have to be able to tune out the constant chatter. You also have to be extremely patient. Sometimes you want to tie their shoes for them because it would be so much easier, but you just have to let them try it. But I love it. I love sitting down with the two year olds with glue all over their faces."

Most of Wangler's children have been with her from her early days in the business in the late 1970s. As they have aged, she has happily become more mobile, and Wangler takes the children out frequently to the zoo, aquarium, and to a gym for daily exercise. So far, only one child has been even modestly hurt; he needed stitches when he jumped off the ladder of a sliding board. Wangler's earliest arrival comes at 7 A.M., and the last to leave goes at 6 P.M. She admits the long hours are tough, but she is adjusting her personal life to fit in. "In fact," Wangler notes happily, "I'm even taking a vacation next month. I can't believe it!"

COMPANY AT HOME

As a young married woman in 1967, Mary R. Martinez of Lakewood, Colorado didn't relish the idea of being home alone while her husband worked. She began babysitting for neighbors, and eventually set up a regular child-care service. Recently, she was caring for five children for a weekly fee of $35 per child. Martinez also has three children of her own, but they, and her husband, seem to enjoy the congestion. "The kids call my husband 'Dad' and wait for him at the door when he gets home from work so they can sit on his lap," she says.

Martinez has run into some significant start-up costs since she moved to Lakewood from Denver. Her property was already fenced-in, but she has bought a play pen, swing set, extra toys, fire extinguishers, and safety locks. She pays $10 a year for a license, but she and all members of her family also are required to have annual medical checkups for the business. These kinds of expenses are similar to those reported by other home child-care businesses. Isabelle Connelly, owner of Connie's Nursery in northwest Houston, spent $400 for fencing, and another $400 for playground equipment after she set up shop in 1976. The hardware would cost more today. Connelly also bought a special heating system, a smoke detector and a fire alarm, and such standard equipment as cribs, bottles, and toys.

Martinez's on-going expenses include $50 per week for lunches and snacks. Coloring books and similar supplies cost just $25 a year; she buys them on sale. But general wear and tear on the house can be expensive. Martinez finds there is some painting to do inside every year. Usually, marketing costs are minimal. Martinez simply maintains a listing in the *Yellow Pages*. Bigger operations, such as Connie's Nursery, sometimes have to do a bit more promotion to keep vacancies filled. Connelly runs ads in a local newspaper, and says she sends out cards soliciting business to parents of newborn children. She gets the names from newspaper birth announcements.

More serious than expenses is dealing with children with behavior or emotional problems, especially if the parents are not understanding and helpful. Martinez recalls one child who was supposed to walk to her home for care after school, but sometimes wouldn't show up. In another case, a mother complained about bruises on her son after he spent a day of hard playing in Martinez's care. "I told her it's going to happen when he's with other kids," says Martinez. Though she has cared for infants in the past, Martinez now requires that children be toilet trained before she will accept them.

PASSING ALONG EXPENSES

There are a number of ways to set prices in home child-care businesses. Some set flat fees and put the burden on themselves to make ends meet when buying food and supplies. Others bill for food and supplies. Dhur Narayan of Santa Monica, California asks parents to send food and diapers along with their children. Mary Ann Stang of Springfield, Virginia, charges $1 per meal for children on top of her hourly care rate of between $1 and $1.50.

Without food to worry about, Narayan charges $45 per week for each of about five children whom she usually cares for in her three-bedroom home. Narayan and her husband are natives of the Fiji Islands, where Narayan also did babysitting at home. In Santa Monica, she has spent about $1,000 on equipment and some extra eating utensils. Her home insurance premiums, with a rider to cover possible accidents, come to $200 per year.

She wisely insists that parents provide phone numbers that would allow her to reach them at any time in case of emergency, and she keeps the names of family physicians for each child as well. As most child-care people already know, it also has become increasingly important to keep on hand parental permission slips that authorize the manager to administer first aid or to sign for professional medical care. Worried about legal entanglements, doctors and hospitals now frown on giving medical attention to children without a parent present, or without a babysitter who has a parental authorization note.

Narayan's brood is a young one; the ages typically run from two months to three years. The purpose of her business is to supplement her husband's income as a maintenance worker. The Narayans seem satisfied that that purpose has been fulfilled, and they have no plans for expansion. "Five children is the maximum number that Dhur can handle," Narayan's husband says. "Any more children than that and we would probably have to open an agency and hire more people to help out, and we don't want to do that."

PROMOTION BY "HEAD OF HAIR"

Jan White traveled a long, hard road, but she has ended up with an at-home beauty shop in the Houston area that is so busy she has to turn some customers away. She doesn't advertise. "Quality of service will bring you customers," she maintains. "My business just grew by word of mouth, or head of hair."

Things weren't so rosy at the beginning of White's career. When she was divorced, she had three young daughters, a large suburban home to care for, and no college degree. White says she "always had a real interest in hairdressing," but no formal training. She needed 1,500 hours in cosmetology school to get a license, so she attended classes, worked weekends at a veterinary clinic, and simply persevered through tough times until she could get into the business. Her first job was at a salon that was part of a chain of haircut shops. But some customers who were also White's friends suggested she could make good use of her big, five-bedroom home by opening her own shop.

White investigated that possibility, and found that to meet state licensing requirements, she would need a room sealed off from the rest of the house, and at least 200 square feet in size. Her master bedroom had 230 square feet, so with a $2,400 personal bank loan she began remodeling. She added a new wall, turned a window into a door, and added the necessary plumbing and electrical supply for sinks and dryers. She got a license and started her own business in 1977.

Aside from the quality of her work, there are two additional draws to White's shop. She is willing to work a more flexible schedule than most out-of-home shops, including some nights and weekends. Some of her customers with busy weekday schedules appreciate this. She also finds she can do well financially without charging high fees. She says she does haircuts for $12 and permanents for $30, about half of what some salons charge. "I have very little overhead," White says. "That's one of the beauties of a home shop. Too many services in America today are overpriced, and when people get ripped off, they don't come back." Despite her low prices, White estimates that her take is about 70 percent of what she charges. Chemicals and solutions are the biggest cost factors. She takes depreciation tax deductions for her salon and the equipment in it, and deducts her electricity costs, too. White pays only $18 per year for her personal license, and $25 per year for a salon license.

Even though there were lean times at the beginning, White says she would do it all over again the same way, especially because the business has allowed her to stay near the children. "They come over as soon as they get home from school, and they bring their friends. Then it's play time, and I get to be around them. That way I can have both a career and a family life."

TWENTY YEARS AT VEL-JEAN'S

Like Jan White, Jean Canfora of Barberton, Ohio, wanted to combine working with child-raising—not an easy task since Canfora had five children. But in 1960, Canfora's husband remodeled her sunporch and living room into a beauty shop, and ever since she has been able to stay at home and make money with her own operation, Vel-Jean's.

Canfora works between 30 and 50 hours a week, and charges very low prices. Recently, she was asking $5 for a shampoo and set; $8 for shampoo, cut, and blow dry; $6 for a cut only; $25 and up for permanents; $6 for tinting; and $15 for a bleach. Still, she says she averages $200 to $300 per week. Canfora's cost of doing business is lessened by the fact that her equipment, including three dryers and two wet sinks, was purchased before inflation became rampant. She says that it would cost about $3,000 to replace her equipment today. Hydraulic chairs are running between $300 and $500, hair dryers at $200 each, and wet sinks $350 to $450.

Canfora worked just one year at an outside shop before launching her own. She concedes she misses chatting with others in her profession, but says that when she thinks about battling the snow to get to work during the cold northern Ohio winter, she is glad she is at home. A more serious concern, Canfora says, is the possibility of falling into the category of "an old-fashioned hair dresser." To prevent this, she goes back to school on a regular basis to learn new styles and methods.

She counts on about 30 regular patrons each week. One of the frustrations common in hair care is the occasional difficult customer, but Canfora says she has relatively few. "There was," Canfora winces, "the little brat I did last Tuesday night." She does her own bookkeeping and office work, but uses a CPA for taxes.

GOOP AND PRIVACY

After six years of operating a home beauty salon in Denver, Angie Valdez says she has a pretty good idea why her customers like her shop. "They love to come to a home," she says. "It's more personal. They don't have to sit around with goop on their hair in front of a bunch of people. They say other places are so cold. When I go on vacation, some of them go without getting their hair done until I come back."

That sort of customer loyalty has nearly backfired. Valdez set up her business to be a part-time operation only. When her daughter, Jackie, was a baby, Valdez, then a beauty salon worker in a Denver department store, wanted to split her time between her child and business. She and her husband spent $2,000 renovating the basement for an at-home shop, and they bought used equipment. Valdez recommends that novices today avoid the used equipment, which she bought only because the family did not want to borrow money.

Valdez passed out fliers advertising the business once, but mainly she has succeeded through word of mouth. Some customers followed her from the department store to her home. Her work week recently was about four days, five to six hours a day. To hold down the hours and control her schedule, she has had "to be firm with customers. You have to put your foot down, or they will want to come on Saturday or Sunday." Despite her less than full-time schedule, Valdez says she makes twice the money she did in the department store. "Even with low prices, it's all mine," she notes.

Denver law does not permit Valdez to hire others in her home. This limits expansion, but a big business was never her interest in first place for the home shop. She named the salon "Jackie's," for her daughter, and finds she has enough time for the business, the child, and other activities besides. Valdez has been active in girl scouts, and is taking piano lessons as well.

Child and hair care are certainly two of the biggest personal services adaptable to the home, but they are not all. A number of personal services are run part from home, and part outside. One of the most innovative of these is Everett Airport Service Enterprises, a transportation service in Everett, Washington, created to fill a hole in a big service market.

A FLEET IN THE FRONT YARD

In 1971, Diane J. Coombs was a travel agent in Everett, some 30 miles north of Seattle. The Northwest was beginning a growth spurt, and air traffic was increasing at Seattle–Tacoma International Airport (SEATAC), about 45 miles from Everett. For those without private transportation, getting from Everett to SEATAC was a major problem. One day, Coombs packed a suitcase, and, with one of her five children in tow, tried using public buses to get to the airport. The round trip took an astonishing number of hours, she says.

Since Coombs and her husband had a five-acre farm southeast of Everett, she proposed that the family set up a commuter service to SEATAC based at home. It sounded simple. But 14 months of hearings and legal work ensued. As a new public utility, Everett Airport Service Enterprises (EASE, as in "ride with ease"), was closely scrutinized by the state's Utility and Transportation Commission. The bus companies protested, and the Coombs' legal fees alone topped $1,800. But the family stuck it out, and eventually won approval. Recently, EASE was making 15 round trips a day, employed nine drivers, and owned ten vans, some of which were used for spare parts.

The fleet clutters the Coombs' front yard, but Diane notes: "You have to give up something. Our front yard looks like a [vehicle] graveyard." Paperwork spills into nearly every room of the house, from the roll-top desk in the den to the dining room table and the living room floor. But the Coombs' have made a truly family business out of EASE. The children take turns answering phones, helping with mailings, and working on the books. They are paid for their work. In the beginning, Coombs and her husband also worked as drivers, though now they mainly manage the business from home. They have added a number of midway stops between Everett and Seattle, though the new routes have involved further legal hearings and costs.

This business, of course, required a major investment. There were, for example, two brand-new Chevrolet 12-passenger vans, costing about $4,200 each. One was purchased for cash; the other was 50 percent-financed. Coombs now regrets not having financed more, since the cash outlay left the couple "too strapped to do the advertising we needed at first."

Coombs finds the business at harmony with a rural lifestyle. "For the kids," she says, "it's no different than living on a farm. There are always chores to do, and everyone pitches in." In fact, Coombs declares, "I'd never do anything that wasn't home-based." She and her husband, in their forties, are considering additional home businesses, perhaps a tour company, or a handmade quilt business. As for EASE, one of the best aspects is that there is real value in the equipment and the regulatory approvals that the Coombs's fought so hard to win. Recently, Coombs says, outsiders have offered as much as $90,000 to buy their little "baby," as she calls it.

PROFIT POTENTIAL

Child-care businesses at home can supply a high enough income to support a family, but to do so the hours must be very long and the number of children cared for must be high. As supplements to the income of a spouse, however, these businesses can add more than $8000 per year without much hardship. At-home hair-care businesses can be more lucrative than doing the same work at an outside shop owned by someone else. The earning potential of other home-based personal services varies widely. Shopping services are good for spare cash, while such large-scale services as the transportation company set up by the Coombs family of Washington can provide better than middle-class incomes.

RISK

With any child-related business, risks are high. Liability insurance with a high level of coverage is an absolute necessity, and any real tragedy could cost even more than the insurance company will pay. These are good businesses to incorporate, so that the owner will have limited personal liability. Risks are much lower in hair care, although up-front costs of $2,000 or more mean that operators should be certain they will garner enough business to pay off investments. Working first at an outside shop is helpful in establishing a reputation.

ENJOYMENT

The degree of happiness one will find in caring for people depends on the personality of the manager. Generally, patience ought to be a natural quality; otherwise, children or tough customers in hair care will leave the operator gritting his or her teeth most of the day. Extroverts who love children, or enjoy the personal contact in a beauty shop, are best-suited.

CHAPTER 10

Creative Products

Most people enjoy making things with their hands. Not everyone is good at it, of course, as this author can readily attest. The memory is still painful of the day my son's cub scout den, after my long instruction, showed off a sleek fleet of paper airplanes to the rest of the troop. Another boy's father quickly stepped into the spotlight. In half a minute, this fellow folded an unbelievably intricate craft that outdistanced, outsped, and outmaneuvered all else in the sky. It finally did a loop-the-loop just to rub salt in the wound.

Guys like that probably have some money waiting to jump into their wallets. People are impressed by and enamored with the good handiwork of others, and that suggests some marketplace demand. In fact, public interest in homemade creative products has seldom been stronger. This is much in keeping with the social movement toward old values—natural foods, country living, and such. Further, in an inflationary era, big manufacturers of consumer goods are strongly tempted to keep profits up by reducing the quality, or selection, of their product lines. As some store-bought goods deteriorate in quality, the market opens more to home-designed products. Because a home location cuts overhead costs, producers of creative products at home can better afford to keep quality high.

Opportunities for profit in home creative products strongly depend on how aggressively the entrepreneur approaches manufacturing and selling. Those who, in their spare time, make a few small items by hand to sell at periodic craft shows or flea markets will earn a little money, and they may find this fun and gratifyng. Others, however, can streamline and at least partly mechanize production, and then seek wholesale outlets or mail order sales. Using these techniques, a home craftsperson can build a multimillion dollar business, big enough to warrant an out-of-home location if desired. Wholesaling can succeed through individual agreements with big retail stores, or by other means, such as using a manufacturer's representative.

146

Good creative products may require the capabilities of the old-fashioned tradesman or craftsman. They do not require (as some home home enterprises do) any formal education. The importance of the trades and crafts is being increasingly recognized today. The fast growth of vocational public schools, many of which give instruction in wood working, metal working, and other crafts together with occupational teaching, are strong evidence of a new level of public appreciation. Adult educational systems are expanding nationwide as well, and seldom does the curriculum exclude the crafts. With awareness of hand-designed creative products surging upward, the chance to build a solid home business making them is enhanced.

WINDSOCKS FROM WASHINGTON

In 1977, Lance and Laurie Haslund were none too happy about moving. The lean economics of small-scale farming had been unavoidable, and the Haslund family moved from a spread in northeastern Washington to a house on Bainbridge Island, near Seattle. Laurie took a job as cultural director of the Bainbridge Parks and Recreation Department. Lance, a carpenter, established his own drywall operation. But they still dreamed of producing income from a base on their own property.

In the fall of 1980, they took a major step in that direction. They founded Toroda Enterprises, a home business that makes nylon "spinnaker" cloth windsocks, the decorative items that resemble Japanese kites and are often hung on patios. A few months earlier, Laurie, who had long enjoyed crafts, had agreed to handle a booth at a local Bainbridge Island craft show. She made four windsocks out of brightly colored nylon just to decorate the booth, but before the show had even begun, two of them were sold. The other two—priced at $15—sold within two hours of opening. Laurie started taking orders for more.

With that, the couple began traveling to craft shows around the northwest. They concluded that retail selling might not be their strongest suit. To expand the business, and put selling into the hands of a professional, they sought out manufacturer's representatives. One in Seattle that specializes in high-fashion lines signed them up.

The wholesale dealer was somewhat skeptical, though, at

first. "There was a lot of concern over whether we could really pull off the product out of our living room. Convincing our rep was a major hurdle," says Lance. But Toroda met its shipment schedules. Lance halted his construction business and began putting in 30 hours a week at home on Toroda. Laurie adds 10 to 15 hours a week. Together they produce some 30 windsocks per week, and planned in early 1981 to double weekly production within a year. At a wholesale price of $16.50, that would bring weekly gross receipts to an impressive $990 per week. With the business well established, the Haslunds planned a move back to their farm, where they hoped to get a net profit from the business of $1,000 per month.

The Haslunds say they do not want the business to grow too large. Running a really big operation would conflict with the life-style they are seeking. "I've always hated making money to pay taxes," says Lance, who wants to farm at least enough to supply the family with its own needs. He wants to keep the business strictly at home, and notes that if the living room isn't big enough, he can spruce up the barn and fit it out with electricity. The Haslunds' initial capital investment of $1,400, he says, was enough to cover materials, a heat cutter, marketing brochures, and supplies—all that was needed to get Toroda started.

THE WOODEN TOYMAKER

"People who believe in plastic couldn't care less about what we make. But there are plenty of parents who want sturdy toys not run by batteries, but by imagination," declares Jan Koellner, operator of a home based toy manufacturing company she calls The Wooden Toymaker.

Located in Copley, Ohio, Koellner found her inspiration in a 120-year-old box of wooden blocks that had been handed down in the family. They were vastly different from today's store-bought blocks. Made of sturdy hard wood instead of pine, cut into varying shapes that fit together as tightly as a puzzle, the antique set made bridges, castles, or just about anything else a child wanted. Koellner already had a hobby—antique furniture repairing—so a table saw, band saw, radial arm saw, and some woodworking tools were in place. With some help from her husband, Fred, she set up shop in the garage. Her product line grew to 30 items, which she calls Appalachia Folk Toys.

These sell for a wide range of prices. A whirly bird propeller on a stick goes for $1; a wagon with blocks for $85. Full-time operation for Koellner began in 1980. She found that a $55 rocking horse, whose material costs were $20, was a huge suc-'cess at Christmastime. Koellner sold 120 of them. The standard, prime quality set of blocks also sells for $55. One of its unique features is that the blocks come in a wooden box with a sliding lid, into which the pieces fit like a puzzle when playtime is over. Putting the toys away becomes part of the challenge of playing with them—a part that parents enjoy. "I have yet to master the feat of putting them in the box. But my kids can do it," notes one customer.

So far, Koellner has acted as her own retail salesperson. In northeastern Ohio, where the family lives, craft shows are plentiful in shopping malls, museums, and flea markets that dot the Cleveland and Akron areas. Koellner's cost to be in a show ranges from $35 to $260. She sometimes has to pay a fee of $85 to set up wares. Other than her appearances, she has used no external advertising so far.

The wood comes from a producer in Arkansas, and it is carefully finished with Danish oil and stain. Profits were meager in 1980, mainly because Koellner had to buy the wood already planed. But she has now purchased a $2,000 machine to do this work herself, so costs will drop. She fully expects fast growth. With the business well established at home, Koellner says she will be prepared to move into an outside building, hire a work force, and expand.

REELS FOR RECORD-SETTING

The Florida coast has a lot of attractions, from swimming to nightclubs. One of the best is sport fishing. Within that recreation, one local entrepreneur saw an opportunity for profit in a handmade product. The serious fishermen go out not merely to catch fish, but to pursue sport fishing records. Some will pay quite a bit for a reel capable of handling light lines and heavy strain. Our entrepreneur has been making custom-designed reels that the pros want to get an edge over their competitors.

The manufacturer is one of several contacted for this book who keeps his business quiet because of uncertainty about whether local zoning laws permit his home operation. We'll have to call him John. He is an avid fisherman himself, and also has long had a well-supplied home metal shop in his garage as a hobby. The reels were first suggested to him by a friend, who asked if he could use his metal working machines to come up with a better reel than could be found in stores. The business, says John, "found me."

Businesses that involve bending and shaping metals can require heavy start-up costs. John bought his machinery, used, in the early 1970s for $8,000, but he estimates that the replacement value would approach $40,000 to $45,000. Once in place, other operating costs are a lesser concern. John's major expenses are marine alloy metals, electricity, and machine maintenance. Working 10 to 12 hours per week, he made $7,000 in 1980, of which $3,500 was profit. It was enough, he smiles, to finance the fishing excursions that he and his sons go on.

John sells to tackle shops, and his reels are now in demand among Wyoming and Montana sport fishermen, as well as those in Florida. "These guys are competing against each other in their fishing clubs. They're all looking for something that will give them an edge, and they're willing to pay for it. Personally, I wouldn't spend as much as they do," says John.

Top-flight reels designed for special purposes are not always widely available. Right now, John believes, there is market demand for fly fishing reels to take big saltwater fish. Some models made by bigger manufacturers are selling for whopping prices of $250 and $300. "Everybody is after me to make fly reels," an extension of his current line of products, John says. He feels that leaves him at a key decision-making point in the business. "I have a choice. I can make reels and become a workaholic, or I can go fishing. I have no doubt in my mind that I can make a living making reels." He views the business, operated at whatever level he chooses, as a future source of supplemental income when he retires from his full-time job.

CERAMICS THROUGH THE MAIL

A number of home businesses in creative products go beyond self-manufacture of every part of an item. Carle Dwight, for example, started a mail order business in 1978 as a distribution method for figurines he had designed for Valentine's Day. Afterwards, however, Dwight expanded his product line, including purchased figurines from an outside manufacturer. The purchased pieces, which include figurines of human hands, are sometimes painted by Dwight or otherwise processed by him. He packages them and operates the business from his four-bedroom home in the Los Angeles area. Dwight launched the enterprise with $10,000, which included money supplied by four private investors.

"I was looking for a very large market," says Dwight, "especially of young girls who seemed to like my 'Don't Forget I Love You' figurines." Dwight spent a few hundred dollars for professional help in designing ads, and then placed them in *Seventeen* magazine and *National Enquirer*. He says he spent $2,400 on the first round of ads. "The initial response was good. I got one thousand orders, which sold for $6.99 plus $1.75 for postage and handling. But I made a mistake in not repeating the ads in those magazines, and orders fell off after that."

Dwight has learned his lessons in mail order on the job. He recommends "placing an ad four or five times consecutively when you begin to offer a new product, because people tend to shy away from first ads. They get more confident if they see the ad more than once. That gives them a chance to grasp an idea and hang onto it and eventually buy." Dwight also learned to "key" his ads—to write them so that customers respond to a name and address that includes a code word or number. This identifies which ad in which publication is drawing the best response. He picked United Parcel Service to deliver his products because he says he found the private company less expensive, more reliable, and better at record keeping than the U.S. mail. UPS also makes pickups at his home.

Although the mail order system has brought in some good orders, Dwight says he also is considering trying to sell on a wholesale basis to retail chains.

GLASS OF FASHION

By 1980, John W. Plessinger, Jr. and his wife, Pat, found that the utility bills at their stained glass shop in Denver were approaching the rent payment. When the city closed down the street the shop was on for construction, it was the final straw. The Plessingers moved their business, Glass of Fashion, to the basement of their home.

For a purely retail business, such a move doesn't always work out. But Glass of Fashion does not rely much on passersby. About 95 percent of the Plessingers' business is custom work—repairs, lamps, and windows—done for a mix of individual and commercial customers. Pat makes some ornaments that are sold at church fairs. The windows sell in a wide range of prices, $100 to $2,000, and the higher-priced pieces often go to restaurants.

Plessinger is a former real estate salesman. In 1977, he took a class in making stained glass, and liked it so much he decided to try making a nearly full-time business of it. He recently was working two hours a day at a neighborhood bar owned by his family, and eight hours or more in the home business. Pat works one day a week as a bookkeeper, and the rest at home.

Plessinger has spent $2,000 remodeling his basement to accommodate the business. But he notes that the money has also generally improved the property, whereas a similar investment made in his rented shop netted nothing to the couple when they moved out of it. Since working at home, he says he has increased his repair business by landing some antique shops as customers. When Plessinger had his own shop, the antique dealers probably would have viewed him as a competitor. The total volume of Plessinger's business, in fact, has increased. Another reason for that, he says, is that he no longer has to stop production of glass to take care of shoppers who used to wander into the store. "Downtime because of people is greatly decreased," he declares.

Even so, Plessigner concedes that making stained glass at home—a time-consuming and exacting craft—does have its financial limitations. "The only way we could get larger is to have so much business we would have to hire employees to fabricate, and then we would have to get a shop. You physically can't make a whole bunch of money making something for someone yourself." But he also points out that making money is not his only goal. Because of his new life-style, Plessinger says he is "happier than most people living in the city today."

MACRAMÉ, BY APPOINTMENT

Customers can help design the macramé wall hangings and planters they order from Sue Rogers of Aspen Hill, Maryland. Rogers' sales technique is a little different than most, and seems to work well. She places ads in local weekly newspapers for $20 or $30 per month. Interested customers then typically stop by her home, where they help pick out the yarn, beads, pots, and sometimes plexiglass or formica (for hanging shelves) to be used in their made-to-order products. Rogers collects a 50 percent deposit, and then goes to work.

Like many home crafts makers, Rogers has loved working with her hands for many years, and developed her skill gradually. She started selling her macramé products in the mid-1970s, while living in Oklahoma. "I really enjoy it," she says. "It's like a piece of me hung in someone else's house." In the beginning, she wanted to keep the business at home so she could stay with her three young children.

Rogers charges $10 to $20 for a wall hanging or planter. Hanging shelves go for $40 to $100. Profit per item averages between $10 and $30. In the past, Rogers says, she has pulled down $100 to $200 a week, and sometimes more, for 40 hours or more of work. Some of Rogers' pieces do sell from a store on consignment, but the store owner adds one-third to each item's price so that Rogers nets the same amount as if she sold it herself.

While she clearly has a talent for macramé, Rogers' story also demonstrates that many home crafts businesses can be launched without extensive formal training. She never took macramé classes, nor worked as apprentice to a professional. "I just looked at a book, went home, and did it," Rogers says. The personal contact she keeps with her customers helps keep the work from becoming too isolating, and has provided some memorable moments, too. One female customer, she recalls, "asked me to make her a husband-hanger."

Rogers does hope to expand her business into an outside shop eventually. "My dream is to be really successful at what I do. I know my stuff is good."

DOUGH TO PAY THE BILLS

The motivation that started Judy A. Eyrich's business in bread dough crafts was her annual auto insurance bill. It came near the Christmas season, the very time when Eyrich once made the ornaments as gifts for relatives and friends. "I needed some extra money to pay my car insurance which is due just about that time of year," she says. "I found that if I entered one or two art fairs and sold to a few stores, I could make about $1,000 during the holidays, which was enough."

Eyrich's business is similar to many, perhaps most, home crafts enterprises. She uses it to make a little spare cash when she needs it. Eyrich has a full-time job outside, working with children with developmental problems near her home in San Raphael, a community in northern California.

Raw material costs are minimal. She needs flour, water, salt, wire, paints, and polyurethane sealer. For about $40 of these ingredients, Eyrich and a partner, working out of Eyrich's three-bedroom house, can make between 200 and 300 ornaments and figurines. These, she says, can be sold for $3 and $3.50 each. The bread-dough items must be baked in the oven, but Eyrich says the cost to do so runs just $5 or so per month. Entry fees for art fairs can be one of the biggest expenses— anywhere from $5 to $60.

To expand production and income, Eyrich makes some items that can be mass produced. These are bread dough pins and magnets, which she can make at the rate of 50 per hour versus only 20 ornaments per hour. "The ornaments are more fun to do because they are more creative," she says. "The pins and magnets are not as rewarding, but I can make more money in less time and can do them while watching television or talking to somebody."

Selling the crafts at fairs and shows may not open up national markets, but Eyrich finds her style of marketing enjoyable. "This business gets to be a social thing," she says. "You go to fairs and people tell you how much they love your work, that you are terrific. It's a real ego boost. Although there seems to be more and more people making these things, everybody makes them a little differently. I never have problems selling my figurines, and I usually have requests for more from people who have bought them before."

PROFIT POTENTIAL

Mail order and wholesale distribution can lead to huge businesses in crafts, as Annie's Attic, the needlecraft pattern and kit business mentioned in Chapter 1, demonstrates. Creative products made by hand by the entrepreneur only, and sold at shows or from home, are likely to be tough businesses in which to make a full-time living. As part-time businesses designed for some extra income, creative products can be good. They often are hobbies that can be turned into profitable enterprises without overhead costs of an out-of-home production facility.

RISK

Generally, the risk is quite low. There are some exceptions, however. Those who make toys or other products to be used by children should always obtain product liability insurance. Products with moving parts that are sharp or exposed fall into the same group. Decorative home items pose little risk of injury. Financial risks in creative products are typically low because of small investment requirements.

ENJOYMENT

The smaller home businesses in creative products seem to be set up as much for enjoyment as extra income. Big mail order or wholesaling operations, however, will eventually separate the founder from hand-making of all his products, a possible drawback. Crafts are among the best home businesses to operate around children, who often can help in production and feel a sense of contribution to the family which is otherwise unattainable.

CHAPTER 11

Information Processing

Nothing in the world of business has undergone so radical a change as information processing. The term itself is a function of technological revolution. Companies once employed big and separate staffs of personnel to type letters, collate documents, perform computations for accounting and billing, and do research about products, markets, and securities. All of these jobs involve working with, or finding out, information, and processing it. But only in the last decade have computers grown so powerful, and so much less expensive, that the average business could afford one to help perform many of these chores. Today, the capabilities of electronic machinery are so broad that information processing can be thought of as the field of activities that is adaptable to the computer.

Most people have yet to realize what the new machines can do, let alone the more powerful devices still being developed. Technology has run past imagination in many cases. Therein lies the opportunity for a home business.

Once limited, the kinds of home-based businesses that can fall within information processing are now without boundaires. The older opportunities still exist—typing and stenographic services, printing, telephone answering services, and business and scientific research, for example. But the new tools have opened the way for an individual at home to perform services and manufacture information products for sale nationwide to consumer or commercial customers. Costs are much lower in the traditional, low-technology information jobs. But computer systems, once purchased, multiply one's working power many times over, and earning power can follow suit.

Most applications of home, or personal, computers to make money are yet to be invented. Even so, now is the time to get thinking. Competition is starting to show up. By mid-1981, more than 500,000 home computers were in use in the United States, and though most of the owners did not use them to launch entirely new businesses, others have done so.

What kinds of new businesses can home computers provide? The answer depends on the creativity of the owner, and his understanding of the capabilities of his equipment. A consumer-oriented home computer business might, for example, find a fertile market in family nutrition. Here is how such a business might work:

More and more people are becoming concerned with nutritional values of foods, and with calories taken in by themselves and their families. Imagine, then, the potential of a home-based Family Nutrition Service that would offer personalized nutrition and diet analysis. Using pencil and paper, the calculations such a business would face would be so monumental that the service would be priced out of reach. Not so with a home computer.

Step 1 would be for the computer operator to punch into his machine's memory the exact nutritive values and calories of perhaps 1,000 packaged foods. Food labels now provide this information on a per-serving basis for protein, carbohydrates, fats, specific vitamins, and minerals. Additional information about raw foods, whose nutritive values are published in a variety of books, could be punched in as well. Once accomplished, this stored information could be used to generate cash almost indefinitely.

With ads in national publications, one would ask customers to send in itemized supermarket receipts from, say, four weeks of shopping trips. The increasing use of supermarket scanners, which produce itemized receipts automatically, would make this task easy for many customers. With the receipts in hand, the computer operator would punch in the names of the purchased products, and, taking into account the number of members of the customer's family and the number of days' worth of eating, come up with a quick printout. The printout could tell if the customer's diet is sufficient or deficient in any vitamin or mineral. It could show the average level of caloric intake per day. It could also analyze grocery spending habits.

Related services would fall into place. People trying to lose weight, but frustrated by unappetizing, suggested diets, could send the nutrition service a list of favorite foods in each of the basic food groups. The computer could then fashion a weekly diet plan tailored to the individual's palate, and his desired level of caloric intake. For the computer operator, the service could be performed speedily, but command a healthy price.

The nutrition service is just one idea, developed in casual

conversation with people who understand a computer's power. Computer retail stores are springing up all over the country, and their managers can tell real stories of how customers have profited from their purchases of home computers. "We've sold a lot of computers to people who want one for reasons of greed and avarice," smiles Dick Brown, president of The Computer Store Inc., recently the largest independent chain of computer retail stores in the United States. "Some of our customers ask how to start a business with one. I tell them to open the Yellow Pages and pick a spot. That's how open the market is for the application of computers to new businesses."

Plenty of personal computers are already in use by professionals for accounting, real estate management, and other businesses performed either at home or on the outside. But, as Brown notes: "There are thousands of even mundane applications for personal computers that have never been done. Mailing lists are one of them. Phone directories could be entered on discettes (computer memory storage discs costing $5 to $7 each), and sold as mailing lists. You could make lists of all the restaurants in a city from the phone book, add specific data on each, and sell that as a mailing list. You could become a specialist on all hotels and inns in Majorca, Spain, enter the characteristics and prices of all of them on discettes, and sell them to every travel agent in New York City, provided you keep the information updated. Two years ago, I even sold a computer to a guy who claimed he could use it to make money by handicapping greyhound races."

To many people, computers are scary. They represent some fantasized notion of electronic brains and robots taking precedence over humanity. And the intricacies of their construction and operation are imagined to be far beyond the understanding of the average individual. Most of this thinking, of course, is ludicrous, but it is terrific for the home entrepreneur. As long as the general population attributes magical qualities to the computer, and as long as most people assume computers are far beyond their own ability to understand and operate, more business opportunities will exist for those who know the truth. A computerized business service will warrant a high price.

A lot of computer retail stores not only sell products, but offer short courses to customers about how to use them. Officials at The Computer Store insist that it takes only a week or so to learn computer language and operation, and that a lot of customers without college or even high school credentials have been able to master the machine in that period of time. Many clerical employees of companies have already been trained to do so.

A home computer business is not without financial risk, however. It has bigger up-front costs than most home businesses, and higher maintenance expenses, too. You can check out the latest prices at many electronics products shops, including the Radio Shack chain, a big seller of personal computers under its own brand names. At The Computer Store, Brown estimated that at the end of 1980, the investment required initially to buy a modest but complete system ranged from $4,000 to $7,000—comparable to buying a car. For that money, one could get the computer, its keyboard, video display terminal, disc system, and a printer to produce results on paper. Personal computers can use regular household current, and Brown maintains they use less electricity than color televisions. But some breakdowns are inevitable, and repairs and maintenance can average $200 to $300 a year, also similar to the automobile. Computer paper for the printer costs $20 to $25 for a box of 1,000 sheets.

With this kind of start-up and continuing expense, it is wise to plan the business very carefully so that what you offer is unique enough to be sold at a high price. Along with equipment and maintenance expenses, it is vital to recognize that any employees you might need for computer operation will probably have to be well paid.

Labor costs are especially high in sophisticated home computer businesses such as those that design programs and software (the instructions that tell a computer how to do a job) for commercial customers. Gary Hartzler, operator of home-based Systems Unlimited in Maryland, employs four full-timers and as many as a dozen part-time consultants, who design complex software for federal agencies in Washington, D.C. He must pay the least skilled of his professional workers $15 an hour, and others a great deal more. Hartzler pays himself a salary of $36,000 per year, plus roughly $9,000 worth of fringe benefits.

Most personal computers fall into either of two basic categories: those that are best for word processing, and those that are superior at working with numbers. Both can provide marketable home businesses.

A COMPUTER SERVICE SUPERMARKET

Roger Clark of Stamford, Connecticut was once the owner of his own computer retail store. He later became a merchandising executive for an electronics corporation, but held onto the entrepreneurial world of computers through a part-time home business that his wife, Mary Lou, helps to run. He now offers a wide variety of products through the home business, ranging from production of mailing lists and letters to more complex software programs. His purpose: "Extra income, and to pay for the machine, which I love."

In his prior retailing career, Clark got to know a number of fledgling home computer businesspeople. One of the most interesting, he says, is a woman who operates a computerized pet-finding service. She stores a central record of clients whose pets have identifying numbers on their collars, together with a message asking to call a certain phone number if the pet appears to be lost. The phone number connects to the pet-finding service, which promptly notifies the owner of the whereabouts of his lost animal.

Clark himself has some offbeat uses for his computer, a Digital Equipment Corp. (DEC) machine that is best at word processing. Without charge, he uses his machine to keep a mailing list, send letters, allocate playing fields, and make schedules for teams in the Stamford Youth Soccer League, which has 1,600 members. Clark also volunteers to keep the books for the Northeast Elementary School PTA, of which he is treasurer.

For profit, Clark and his wife offer a sort of supermarket of computer services. He handles mailing lists, and produces mailing labels, for the National Organization of Women. Another customer is a local orchestra, for which he does mailing list work and personalized letters. Using the DEC, Clark can instruct his computer to do a form letter, but automatically put different names and addresses on each. The letters spew forth from his printer. He can even make each letter appear to be personally typed—a service for which he charges extra. Clark spends about 20 hours per week using his computer to do consulting work on computer language for other computer users, and he has even assisted a book author who wanted to make corrections in his manuscript on the machine to save time. Clark has 13 regular customers, and says they are "as many as we want."

In 1976, Clark bought his equipment for $16,000. It included a printer of high quality to produce neat letters. Even so, by 1980, the prices for the same kinds of equipment had dropped to $9,000, he reports. Although they are still expensive for middle-income families, computers do happen to be one of the only products whose prices have fallen consistently, despite inflation in other sectors of the economy. Breakthroughs in technology have caused this.

Clark had to cope with the higher price, and also had to finance his DEC through a bank loan at a time when "banks didn't understand these devices." Now, he reports, most do, and loans are easier to arrange.

His prime opportunity, Clark says, is to be "a supplement to the internal clerical service" of an organization or a business. His charges to customers are made through a formula of separate prices per line for putting information into his machine, taking it back out for use, and for the letters or other media used. But he estimates that on average, he can easily make $16 an hour. His supply costs (often billed to customers, too) come to no more than $100 per month, but Clark does pay $150 per month for a maintenance contract with DEC. With high fixed costs, Clark warns, "The serious risk is not getting enough business. The machine has got to be working. You've got to actively seek out new business."

TECHNICAL WRITING ON A SCREEN

In southern Florida, Sam Jones (a fictitious name; the real man's employer frowns on moonlighting) has duplicated what he does as a corporate employee with a computerized sideline at home. In the daytime, he is a full-time technical manual writer for an engineering company. In the evenings at home, he likes to spend two to four hours writing technical manuals as a free-lancer under contract to others. He uses the computer to produce the documents, which can be printed camera-ready for a publisher on Jones's home equipment.

It is a rigorous schedule, but one that pays off. Jones can charge between $25,000 and $30,000 for one of his home-produced manuals, which takes three to six months to prepare. Technical manuals are documents that describe in detail how to use, or repair a piece of machinery or equipment.

Jones has had to gradually assemble some $50,000 worth of gear over three years in order to get the capabilities he wants. He has a small computer, two kinds of memory storage, two printers, and a "plotter." Indeed, most of his home business earnings have been plowed back into the system. But he says the endeavor has been worthwhile because he is building a home enterprise with the potential to "make three times my salary." As Jones has built his home system, he has had to devise his own programming instructions, and he now sells his programs to other personal computer buffs to make additional income. He does this by sending his programs to a clearing house, which markets them and pays Jones royalties. The only trouble with this, he notes, is that the selling prices for programs must be kept low, because high prices can cause illegal program counterfeiters to step in, copy his programs, and market them at cut rates.

Quite a few computer experts such as Jones have quit out-of-home employment and become private contractors working from home. Two persons at his company recently did so, and Jones says he might. One of the difficulties, though, would be that he would miss rubbing shoulders with other computer workers on the job. This is more than a social consideration; group contact involves sharing information about the latest technological changes, and Jones says that without it he would "have to spend more time reading to keep up with the industry."

But working at home exclusively would also cut the time wasted when Jones has to wait in the office for his turn to use the hardware. "It's easier to work at home," he adds. "I can leave something laying (on his computer), and it's still there when I come back. Computing is an excellent home business."

BUYING AND SELLING INFORMATION

As information itself has become a definable business, it has taken on the characteristics of other businesses. There are companies that seek out raw knowledge and are front-line manufacturers of information products (daily newspapers, for example). There are information wholesalers, and information retailers, and those who sell information by direct mail. With the advent and proliferation of computers, many information gathering companies have put their words and numbers "on line"—an expression in computerese that means the data have been set in electronic storage. Now, many companies charge a fee for computer owners to tap into their electronicized information banks, a procedure usually done by telephone connection between the computers of the sellers and the buyers. A number of information buyers, working at home, have devised ways to repackage and resell the raw data to consumers and businessmen.

Fred Bellomy of Santa Barbara, California and John Nisbet of Houston both started home businesses of this sort. Bellomy works full time from his two-bedroom apartment in sunny Santa Barbara. Basically, he sells bibliographic, statistical, and demographic data to companies. Nisbet is a long-time home computer consultant who recently launched Futures Computing Co., a home business designed to provide information about commodities trading.

Both men pay to tap into on-line sources of information set up by gatherers of raw data. Bellomy's customers often call on him when they have a specific subject, about which they need complete information fast. For example, a multinational corporation might want to start a business in Germany, and might need quick information about the history of the value of German currency. Bellomy can tap into electronic information banks set up by *The New York Times,* by periodical indexing services such as the *Reader's Guide,* and into the data banks of other publishers and companies that produce statistics. He pays for that privilege, but comes up with a guide for his clients that they can use to learn all that they need to know. Nisbet pays $150 to tap his computer into a commodities "chart service," and he buys data which give him the ability to act as a paid consultant to clients who want to invest in the commodities markets.

These are some of the highest expense and highest revenue home businesses. Aside from the cost of buying or leasing computer hardware (leasing is worth looking into, especially since the expense of it can be fully tax deductible), the fees charged by the raw information banks can be high. To tap *The New York Times,* for instance, Bellomy must pay $110 per hour, plus the cost of his telephone connection. The key is to charge enough to clients to compensate. Bellomy charges $450 for a comprehensive search, $175 for a basic search, and $50 per hour for consulting work. Nisbet says he plans to ask $25 per hour as a tuned-in commodities consultant. He hopes to make additional income by investing in the market himself.

The buying and selling of computerized information takes some expertise. It takes time to learn how and where to tap into other data banks, how to do so at lowest cost, and how to get and maintain an adequate list of customers. The pace of the work can be irregular, too. "You may have nothing for a month, and in one week get ten jobs that all need to be done immediately," remarks Bellomy. But these businesses also can be fascinating and high in growth potential. Bellomy recently was called upon to use his system to locate a missing person. He did it by tapping into certain business computers until he found an office, which had maintained contact with the person. "I had never done that before," Bellomy says. "Customers tend to think of information in the broadest sense and come up with requests that you never thought of before."

Information processing is an umbrella over many occupations. Some of them still have no connection to the computer. Ordinary stenographic and related services may or may not use word processors. Despite the new realms of business opened up at home by electronics, there is still marketplace demand for plain, old-fashioned clerical work. The money-making potential for these businesses may be lower than some computer businesses, but start-up costs and risks are lower as well.

TYPING AND TELEPHONES

In the Chicago suburb of Lincolnwood, Darlene R. Hauesen believes her home stenographic and phone answering service is profiting directly from the trend toward working at home. "As the economy gets worse, my business gets better. People are working more and more out of their homes, saving office expenses." Many of Hauesen's customers are professionals— doctors, lawyers, and engineers. These people can often work from their homes, as long as they have someone available to answer the phone and handle secretarial work as an outside contractor, rather than a full-time employee. Hauesen's business fits that need.

Building the business was not easy at first. Hauesen had left the work force for eight years while her children were growing up, and, in 1979, she had a yen to return. But Hauesen didn't relish the idea of a full-time job outside her home, and she found even part-time work in an accountant's office kept her away from home longer than she wanted. On one momentous night, her idea was born. "A couple neighbors, who were independent businessmen, were over at the house. They were complaining about incompetent answering services and the high rates for typing. I began thinking that I could do all of that for them." With a fully paneled basement that made good office space, Hauesen decided to take a crack at her own business.

Start-up costs were about $500 for stationery, and to mail letters to some 300 companies in the Chicago area, soliciting business. She also leased a typewriter. The early results were poor. She garnered only enough clients to keep her busy two hours a day, and she barely met monthly expenses of $100 for the typewriter, office supplies, and telephones. Slowly, however, her list of clients increased, especially through word-of-mouth advertising from her first group. After 1½ years, her income, after expenses, had hit $900 per month, and she was spending 50 hours a week on the job. She had 13 separate phones, each with a slightly different ring, paid for by clients and installed in her basement. She began hiring friends at times to help answer them.

"I was advised by a lot of people not to bother answering phones. They said that business would tie me down. But I found that every phone client always used secretarial service," Hauesen says. By combining the two, she concedes that she finds herself working about 15 hours per week more than she had hoped, even with the occasional hired help. But it is a hassle Havesen says is outweighed by other advantages.

"I'm providing a service and building something on my own. It's my own business, and if I want it to grow, I'm willing to work more than I anticipated. I have learned that nothing is impossible. If you want to start your own business and make it grow, and if there's a need, you can make it go. There aren't ten to twelve days at a stretch that I don't get a referral, which may be more gratifying than even the money."

A STENOGRAPHIC ACQUISITION

Lane Page found a short-cut to business start-up problems when she decided to start a home secretarial service in Miami. In 1974, she paid $400 to buy Busy Owl Secretarial Services of Miami. Her predecessor had felt that eight years of running Busy Owl was enough. In addition to the cash, Page agreed to give 20 percent of her revenues in the first two years to the seller. For that, she got a used IBM typewriter, and a clientele she has since shaped to her liking.

Page has transcribed legal briefs, television and movie scripts, and letters, but her biggest business segment by far is medical work. Out of 20 steady clients, almost all are doctors. To make her business especially appealing, Page uses a delivery service, which costs $100 a month. Another strong selling point: her 24-hour dictation service, in which customers can call anytime and dictate to a machine in Page's home for later transcription. Sticking to a carefully selected customer group that is relatively affluent and well established in town, Page has had little trouble with slow payments, bad checks, or credit risks.

There is competition. Page is aware of four other women in her area who do the same kind of work at home. But the competition "isn't the killer type," she says. In fact, the other women have sometimes referred work to her, especially work involving medical records, Page's forte. She, in turn, has referred some clients with copyediting needs to her competitors. Page says that in 1980, the business grossed a little more than $28,000. Subtracting expenses and taxes, she reports, net income fell between $16,000 and $17,000. Her expenses include the occasional hiring of temporary help.

Page says she finds the work enjoyable because "Every time I do something for a client, I learn from the work they are doing." This kind of sentiment is heard frequently among operators of home business stenographic and secretarial services, which, to the unacquainted, might seem to be deadly repetitive work. Mary Scoggins, home-based operator of Letter Perfect, a secretarial service in New Carrollton, Maryland, says encounters with a number of unusual clients have spiced up her workdays. One was a Arabic man who wanted her to type a document that was hand-written and scarcely legible. It turned out to be a quasi-legal statement accusing the customer's mailman of kidnapping his daughter. Scoggins later discovered that the mailman and the daughter had indeed run off—because they were married! Some time later, the same man, pleased with her work, dropped by with a similarly unintelligible piece. It was a flyer advertising English classes for Arabic-speaking people.

SHARON PRINTING

It takes experience, and a lot of capital, but printing and publishing can be at-home businesses at the finished-product end of the information processing spectrum. Jerry Weaver of Medina, Ohio runs the Sharon Printing Co. out of his spacious basement. In the daytime, Weaver works at a B. F. Goodrich Co. plant's print shop, the source of his expertise. He works part time at home, and his son, Jeff, works full time at the home business. Weaver feels that among other things, his home business has given him a chance to teach his son the trade.

Sharon Printing has impressive capabilities, and it cost plenty to provide them. Weaver has $100,000 invested in his basement business, part of the cash having come from a personal loan from relatives. The equipment includes a 19- by 25-inch single color printing press, another printer sized 11 by 17 inches, a multilith machine, a computerized typesetter, a second-hand camera, a folding machine, a plate maker, and other lesser pieces of machinery and supplies. Weaver had to rewire his home for industrial machinery, another significant expense, though he reports that his equipment is surprisingly energy efficient. "My electric bill only went up $20 to $30 after all the equipment was in," he says.

Weaver has 300 to 400 regular customers, most of whom came to him by word of mouth. He prints a wide assortment of goods: newsletters, announcements, business forms, letterhead stationery, and brochures. Many of his projects are monthly periodicals, giving him some schedule control. Weaver estimates that to perform the same business in an outside shop, he would have to raise his prices fully 30 percent to handle extra overhead costs. Recently, Weaver's prices came to about $20 to $25 an hour.

The job has its imperfections. Some customers, he says, are terrible spellers, and others expect him to second-guess at how their work should look. These, however, are difficulties in all commercial printing operations. At home, Weaver says, he and his son "can do what we want to do. We decided to keep this fun, and it has been."

PROFIT POTENTIAL

A good idea, well marketed, has unlimited profit potential in computer services and products at home. Expenses of such businesses are among the highest of any home working category, however, so the quality of the product and assertive, steady selling is the key. Home stenographic businesses typically can provide spare cash, or, if handled full time, a middle-income annual salary. Building a solid customer list, and some typing and dictation equipment, has the added value of making home stenographic businesses salable to others should the founder choose to leave the business.

RISK

Home computer businesses carry high financial risk. Machinery purchase or leasing expenses combine with unavoidable maintenance costs to push the entrepreneur to keep selling at a fast pace. The proliferation of computers also enables others to copy a good business idea, unless the idea is tied to the founder's personal expertise or special training. Home secretarial services, with low overhead and much lower equipment investment, are low-risk operations. Printing services fall in between, with a need to keep revenues steady to pay equipment costs, but also a typically strong and regular market demand.

ENJOYMENT

Computer buffs are often hooked on their machines; little else that they could do would be more pleasing. Some even create home businesses just to pay for the expense of having a personal computer for enjoyment. Home stenographic services require workers who happen to find secretarial work enjoyable. Some people don't. Many of the information processing businesses are good fields for family participation in the work, if desired.

CHAPTER 12

Writing and Art

Writing and art are two of the oldest home businesses. They merit other superlatives as well. They can be most rewarding and most frustrating. Producing stories, books, or artworks are an undeniable passion for many people. The atmosphere at home is not always perfectly conducive. This work requires concentration, and usually quiet and solitude. But for free-lance writers, book writers, and purely creative artists, home is the most common business location. This occurs by necessity, if for no other reason. These businesses can be the hardest in which to earn a living full time, so many writers and artists have other jobs outside the home. They must fit their creative work round and about outside jobs and the duties they may have as spouse, father, or mother.

This problem isn't new. Consider this account told by one well-established author, who, in one of his books, describes the difficulties of trying to write at home:

". . . My other commitments have left me less than no time to get this perfectly easy job done. I've been kept hard at work in the law courts. . . . Then, there's always someone that has to be visited, either on business, or as a matter of courtesy. I'm out practically all day, dealing with other people—the rest of the day I spend with my family—so there's no time left for me, that is, for my writing.

"You see, when I come home, I've got to talk to my wife, have a chat with my children, and discuss things with my servants. I count this as one of my commitments, because it's absolutely necessary if I'm not to be a stranger in my own home . . .

"Thus, the days, the months, the years slip by. You may ask, when *do* I write then? Well . . . in fact the only time I ever get to myself is what I steal from sleep and meals."

So wrote Sir Thomas More in his book, *Utopia*, published in 1516.

For both creative writers and artists, these kinds of problems have continued unabated. The "starving artist" (or starving writer) is the one who is trying creative work at home full time, without having yet cracked into the major leagues. The very famous artists or writers are those who, by virtue of extraordinary talent, drive, or luck, are very well off indeed. In the entire world, there can scarcely be more than a few tens of thousands of people (out of three billion or so inhabitants) who truly fit into the latter category. That makes the odds for stellar success pretty poor.

Fortunately, there are some ways to squeeze in between poverty and riches. There are hundreds of thousands of jobs in the United States for writers and artists: newspaper and magazine work, writing or editing of books and periodicals, public relations, advertising, graphic design for companies and publishers, and fashion design. These full-time, out-of-home jobs eliminate the starvation routine. They also give one credentials that will make a prospective publisher or gallery operator pay more attention to creative works produced at home in spare hours (if any can be found).

There are a number of free-lance writers and artists who do work full time at home, though they often must scramble to get ahead. Those who have grown up with the image of doing creative work only when the "inspiration" hits usually find that they must throw that concept out the window in a full-time home business. The real watchwords of such businesses are "hussle" and "grind." Relying on self-employment in writing or art to raise a family or even to pay one's own cost of living typically means churning out a steady stream of work, and at the same time marketing a steady stream of new project ideas with prospective publishers or art purchasers or show people.

As part-time businesses for extra income, however, home writing and art are often lucrative enough. Many full-time newspaper reporters, for example, also work as "stringers" on the side; that is, they do part-time reporting and writing for bigger publications, including national or international publications like *Time, Newsweek,* or the *Wall Street Journal.* Jobs like these can add several thousand dollars to annual income.

There are other ways to perform home businesses in writing and art as well. Some writers have their own mail order businesses through which they begin to sell their own pamphlets or books, and these enterprises can grow to include the works of others. One artist, Chicagoan Thomas A. Burnison, does graphic design work at home, but because of his prior experience in design in the newspaper business, he also ran across a sideline. He purchased molds for rubber suction cups that are used in newspaper folding machinery to stuff inserts. Now, together with his at-home graphic design work, he markets his rubber cups, manufactured by others, through mail order distribution.

Still others have found highly specialized niches in writing or art. In recent years, for example, the booming need for good information, especially in business, has helped create a spate of newsletters, which can be produced from home and privately printed. These can be high-priced and very profitable operations. A leader in the newsletter field is Leonard E. B. Andrews of Edgemont, Pennsylvania. When the Penn Central Railroad went bankrupt, he launched the *Stockholders & Creditors News Service Concerning Penn Central Transportation Co.*, which kept hundreds of creditors of the road informed—at a substantial price—during years of legal battles over the bankruptcy. One of Andrews' more recent newsletters has been the *Iranian Assets Litigation Reporter*.

Much of the action for writers and artists is still in New York City, where publishing houses, major art galleries, fashion design, and related industries have long been based. One can enter these industries through out-of-home jobs in the city, or try to push in as a home-based entrepreneur with products to sell.

Regardless of market location, one of the toughest decision points for any new home businessperson in writing or art has to do with skill. Do you have the raw talent to make it? It is a question that is probably a little easier for prospective artists to answer than for writers. Though the quality of artworks is a matter of subjectivity, most people, by the end of their schooling, have some idea of their real level of artistic skill. On the other hand, anyone may run into or conceive of an interesting story to tell, and may wonder if he or she has the ability to tell it on paper. Teachers, friends, and relatives may give you conflicting feedback about your level of writing skill. Sometimes the only way to find out for sure is to try selling your work.

A good first move in marketing is to stop at a bookstore or library to pick up a copy of the latest annual *Writer's Market*, a volume that lists hundreds of publishers of short fiction, nonfiction, books, and plays. It even includes publishers who buy gags, poetry, and greeting card verses, and it shows the names of corporations that publish magazines and books for their employees and customers, as the airlines do. The book tells which of these publishers accepts outside free-lance works, whom to contact, and what the rate of pay is.

Fictional short stories are a very tough market. The high-paying publishers print relatively few of them, and the supply of unsolicited manuscripts far exceeds demand.

With non-fiction, or journalistic story ideas, it is always best to send a query letter, or make a phone call, to the targeted publisher. He'll have to rely on your accuracy and training as a reporter of events, no matter how good the idea is, so your credentials must be presented. With virtually no experience in journalism or non-fiction writing, this, too, is a hard field to enter. It is advisable to try to sell some stories first to local publications—newspaper Sunday magazines, regional business publications, or city-type magazines, for example. That way you build some by-lined clippings, and some professional credentials to insert in a resume.

Book writing takes some special awareness of standard facts and procedures. Here are some tips, including ideas gleaned from a New York author who has just published his fourteenth book:

1. The best marketing entrée to the big New York publishers is through a literary agent. He will also help you settle a decent contract with a publisher. One way to find an agent is to write to the Society of Authors' Representatives, 40 East 49 St., New York, NY 10017. Agents usually charge a fee of 10 percent of the author's gross income from a work, and they may charge as well to read and critique an author's book outline.

2. For books, don't call publishers or even agents on the phone. Prepare an outline of your book idea, and write a couple of chapters. These will be what you market, either directly to publishers or through an agent. Writing entire manuscripts first gives publishers more than they want to read in making go-ahead decisions, and it can also waste many months of your time if there is no interest.

3. Remember that autobiographies hardly ever sell unless you are famous.

4. There should be some originality to your work.

5. Read *Publishers Weekly,* the magazine that tells what book publishers are looking for.
6. Examine book sub-markets for their sales potential. These include self-help books, how-to books, women's romance and gothic novels, journalistic exposé, and so on.
7. Concerning your own talent, and ability to turn out a long manuscript, ask yourself these questions: Have others recognized you as a good writer before? Have you ever written and had published anything before? When you read, are you conscious of what writing is good, and what is bad? Do you really have something to say that is new or different, and important?
8. Be ready for a slow and chancy payback. There is no telling what a publisher will offer as an advance payment against royalties on a first book; it can vary from $1,000 to $10,000, and you may get only half the advance up front, and the other half on submission of an acceptable manuscript. Commonly, royalties for hardcover books weigh in at 10 percent of the retail price for the first 5,000 or 10,000 copies sold; 12.5 percent for the next 5,000; and 15 percent thereafter. Softcover books are less lucrative. You may be offered just 7.5 percent on the first 25,000 sold, and it will be a percentage of a smaller retail price. Before you get a cent in royalties, they must accrue to equal your advance. Then, you may have to wait for checks to come at six-month intervals. How well your book sells will depend partly on the publisher's promotion of it. The degree of promotion is often beyond your control, and the number of copies that will eventually sell is truly a matter for the fortunetellers.
9. If fame is what you're after, you may find it elusive. Most people don't read very many books. Not long ago, a rendition of *East of Eden* was broadcast on television. The next day, a New York radio disc jockey remarked: "I think that this John Steinbeck is going to go very far."

PAINTING ON THE FARM

Len Chmiel is one of the country's more successful creative artists. His paintings of figures and scenes, with water colors and other media, have been widely written about in such publications as *American Artist* and *Southwest Art*. In 1976, he bought a 2½-acre farm in Lafayette, Colorado and consolidated his home and studio. Chmiel does a little light farming and hunting—for the artist, a pastime when he is not painting.

Most creative artists can set up a well-equipped and supplied studio at home for about $1,000. Chmiel, however, has spent $7,000 to convert a small dairy barn and grain storage shed into a medium-sized studio heated by a wood-burning stove and solar power. He feels this is a good way to take advantage of home work, and at the same time separate himself from the bustle of family doings. "It's psychological," he says. "It's a place to go to work. It's not like working on the kitchen table. Nobody is saying you can't do this because we've got company coming." Like many artists, Chmiel's work hours are irregular, but tend to be intense and long once begun. A former resident of Denver, he says these work habits make the home location better. "If I have to stay out until three in the morning working, I feel better than if I had to go out on the street in Denver and walk to a parking lot." Chmiel also says he doesn't miss the door-to-door salesmen who used to stop by his former studio.

He completes 40 to 65 paintings a year, and they recently were selling for $400 to $4,000. Chmiel, unlike some lesser-known creative artists, seems able to sell most everything he can produce, mostly through galleries. Some galleries try to charge artists a 50 percent commission on the retail price. Chmiel recently opined that one third is more "honest," and that for the commission the artist should expect the gallery operator to help promote and aggressively sell.

The farm location has had some influence on Chmiel's choice of paintings. He has done portraits of the farm, his garden, poppies, and cloud conditions he sees outside. He wouldn't have produced as many paintings of his surroundings from a studio in the city. "I wouldn't drag an easel out on the sidewalk in downtown Denver," he declares.

FASHIONS IN CHICAGO

"It's not that I'm a rebel," laughs Barbara K. Finn, a freelance fashion illustrator. "It's just that no matter how hard I tried, I just couldn't get to work in the mornings." Finn doesn't have to any longer. For 15 years, she has built up an at-home business illustrating fashions and other objects for retail advertisers. Advertising illustration is probably the most pervasive artwork in the nation; it is, in fact, so commonplace in the environment that many non-artists take it for granted. But every drawing in every newspaper display ad, on every cereal box, book, and magazine cover was handmade by an artist somewhere. The market is huge, and a surprising number of big companies use outside free-lance help to supplement, or replace the need for, an in-house staff.

Finn's biggest account, she says, is the Marshall Field chain, Chicago's largest full-line department store company. But she also draws for other stores. She charges $50 to $150 per drawing, and maintains that a competent artist in her field, working at home, can easily make between $40,000 and $50,000 a year. The top-rated fashion illustrators who also care to work longer hours can make more than $100,000. Finn says she works six to eight hours a day on drawings, but spends additional time picking up assignments and delivering her work. Her exact schedule is hard for her to pinpoint, since she works around the hours when she has to care for her daughter, a grade-schooler. "The business works out very well for my daughter and me," Finn says. "I can pick her up at school and take her wherever we need to go. I do a lot of my work between eight P.M. and midnight. Those hours are all yours."

Finn started her career at an out-of-home workplace, and she recommends that now for beginners. Or, she says, one might try to become an apprentice to a professional. Finn's own reasons for leaving the outside work force were more complex, of course, than a dislike for getting up early. "I wanted more time for my own interests and pursuits," she says. Free time has turned out to be a bit more limited than she bargained for, but over the years at home she has built a substantial business— one clearly more profitable than many art freelancers achieve.

She points out one risk in the art business that is in common with musicians and athletes: An injury to the drawing arm or hand puts a fast stop to the business. "Whenever I go skiing and fall, I pray it's not my drawing arm," Finn says. Artists in her field, she adds, "are subject to the whims of the advertisers and the economy." Indeed, in periods of recession, advertising is one of the first cost reduction steps many businesses make, as magazine publishers are well aware. In regular times, however, the earnings potential for good fashion illustrators is strong. And, Finn says, "I like the fact that everything I earn comes from my own energies."

AN ARTWORK COMBINATION

Like Barbara Finn, Stephen Lyon Crohn does free-lance artwork from his home in Los Angeles. But Crohn divides his time between free-lance commercial work and creative painting, which he loves. "It's a matter of economics," Crohn says. "To make painting full time, I would have to be selling more works, or be under contract to a gallery that was giving me a stipend, or be on a grant where I could be painting all of the time. I would have to sell at least one or two pieces per month to make it."

Crohn is a former New Yorker who recently moved to Los Angeles. In the East he had a studio separate from his apartment. Now he has converted one of the two bedrooms in his duplex into a studio. "I have the chance now to actually live with my work," he says.

His paintings do sell. Crohn's prices are simply more typical of the creative arts community than those of Len Chmiel. His works recently sold for $1,000 or so, and his drawings for about $200. As a part-timer, Crohn made more than $5,000 in 1980, he reports, but much of that money is still outstanding because many art purchasers pay in monthly increments. This method of payment is a common problem in the business.

"There is a potential to make more money, but it is based on reputation, publicity, and showing your work more," Crohn says. "It is difficult to get the exposure. Sometimes you can push yourself really hard to gear up for a showing, but nobody wants to show your work." Even so, he says, it is advisable to go to galleries and openings for a few reasons. One must keep in touch with what other artists are doing, see what the public wants, and what it is willing to spend. Also, he says, "It is politically advantageous to be seen at openings from time to time and talk to dealers and gallery owners, and make yourself known."

One of the pleasantries of working at home is the spontaneous reaction Crohn gets to his works from visitors. The feedback is valuable in the arts, and Crohn happily recalls one visitor who quickly snapped up $700 worth of work from his walls. Crohn also says he has much more space to work at home than in a studio, many of which are cramped.

Education and training are a matter of degree in creative art, Crohn says. He knows artists who have never had formal training, but he also believes that education of some sort in drawing and painting is important to widen the scope and ability of an artist with raw talent. It is the talent that cannot be well taught, Crohn maintains. Without it in a student, "You can't teach somebody art."

POLITICS AND ENERGY

One problem with free-lance writing is that it can be a hit-and-miss business financially. A good-selling book, or the advance money for it, can give a spurt of income. So can a story sold to a major magazine. Articles sold to newspapers, however, can be financially disappointing, and good nonfiction takes a lot of research before a single dollar slides in through the mailbox.

In Miami Beach, Florida, John Rothchild tries to mix his production of work between books, magazines, and newspaper articles. He is a former editor at *Washington Monthly* who switched to free-lancing after realizing, "I wanted to leave Washington and seek my fortune elsewhere." Recently, he was working on a book about energy for a New York publisher. His magazine stories, often about politics or energy, have appeared in national publications such as *Esquire,* and others closer to home such as the Miami *Herald's Tropic* magazine. Rothchild has an agent in New York who gets 10 percent of his pay for work she helps to market.

Experienced in this work, Rothchild seldom goes beyond sending a one-page query letter to an editor about anything, until he gets a go-ahead to proceed. Most freelancers eventually become aware that otherwise, they can waste weeks of precious time writing something no one wants to print. Extensive magazine articles can sell for $1,500 to $2,000; shorter ones perhaps for $500. But Rothchild notes that the long stories can take two or three months to complete. He says his yearly income has fluctuated between $10,000 and $30,000, and he is now spending most of his energy pursuing book contracts. Without them, he notes, "It's very hard to free-lance."

BOOKS THROUGH THE MAIL

Not far from Rothchild, in West Miami, is the home base of a writer who probably views his work more in a businessman's sense than most. Craig McTyre has sold goods through the mail since 1972. His ideas have come fast and thick, and not all have had something to do with writing. He recalls his biggest bust— the time he advertised a service in which he offered to enter sweepstakes for customers in their names, 25 contests for $5.

McTyre says that one reason he went into the bookselling business was space. After achieving a certain amount of success in mail order, he says, you can "simply run out of space at home." Books, he points out, are nice and flat, especially those printed as softcover pamphlets.

McTyre spent six to eight months writing one of his items, the *Fast Food Restaurant Diet Book.* Another title was *Addresses to the Stars.* Such works he had printed at a cost of about 30 cents each, and he sold them for $3 or less to keep them an impulse buy for his market. He advertised the books for $250 per 2- by 2-inch ad in the back of *Teen* magazine and similar publications. The magazines, he notes, want ads paid for quickly, whereas it can take three months for customers' order money to really flow in, posing a risk if the ads are poorly composed or the product just doesn't sell.

Newcomers to this business ought to target their ad appeals to women and children, McTyre suggests. It might not be true for everyone, but McTyre says be believes that statistically, women and children have more time for "reading magazines down to the want ads." He says, "Most of the orders I got were from women." The choice of media, of course, has much to do with that.

Mail order flops haven't helped, but McTyre contends that once one of his books gets rolling, "For every one hundred dollars spent you get back three hundred." His latest book idea: a how-to-do-mail order manual, sold by mail order.

COVED BEACHES AND A TELETYPE MACHINE

The talented researchers and writers who contributed interviews to this book are all part-time or full-time home workers. One of them, Marcella Rosene of Seattle, is a former full-time employee of *Business Week* magazine, who began raising a family and switched to an at-home free-lancing business years ago. Based then in Laguna Beach, California, 70 miles south of Los Angeles, Rosene contributed articles and reporting with some regularity to *Business Week,* but also to the *Reader's Digest, Venture* magazine, and other publications. Asked to interview a home-based writer for this book, Rosene decided to tell her own story—the tale of a home-based writer whose business worked well. Here it is, in Rosene's own words:

"Your subject is almost glutted with examples. I suspect that for the last eight years, I have been one of them. After three years working with *Business Week* in the LA news bureau, I moved to Laguna Beach. It was an exquisite place to roost—a seaside village of coved beaches. But then, the novelty of pushing my toddler's go-cart back and forth to the beach began to wear off, and my free-lance business began picking up. By 1979, I had a full-time-plus job at home, complete with my own teletype machine (installed by a publisher to speed communications), two telephone lines, and a heap of reporting files that filled the closet of my home office.

"It was a lovely existence in many ways. I have written many a story sprawled in the sun on the deck of that canyonside house. I have skimmed miles of wire copy (the messages and reporting from the teletype) while sitting in the grass of a nearby park or in the sand of our favorite beach—one eye on my adventuresome youngster, now eight, and one eye on the outlook of one business subject or another. I have halted in the middle of frosting a birthday cake or making gingerbread boys to interview imposing chief executives and aspiring entrepreneurs.

"Credibility (with some colleagues and business contacts) comes hard when you're doing double duty. Even when you've proven yourself dozens of times as a professional, the home worker in some ways is not on a par with those who commute to an office. In part, you are the object of limitless envy. And that's fun, like the novelty of keeping a year-around tan while your office counterparts can only manage a little color on infrequent weekend outings. You also have enviable diversity. I would never schedule interviews on Thursday mornings because that was my school volunteer time. Or, there was the year when Tuesday afternoons were crossed off the work calendar for mommie-and-me swim lessons. But all of this, while in part making you super mom and wonder woman, also dillutes your professional status. Others believe that even though your work may be nearly flawless, you are just not quite as serious as the conventional versions.

"Working at home can dilute your economic standing. There is a big savings in commuting costs, wardrobe, and so on. But then, too, there are no fringe benefits. For comparable time and performance, I was earning at best sixty percent of what I might have if I'd been on staff.

"Yet, like all those other home workers you must be reading about, I would not have given up that arrangement—at least during that period of child-rearing and homemaking— for any office job I could imagine. There is certainly an irrefutable ego rub that comes from saying I do it my way, on my own terms, on my schedule, in my own setting. And for that, I guess you give up the paid vacation and official standing."

PROFIT POTENTIAL

Skilled and trained writers in journalism can make a handy extra income from a part-time home business. They must scramble to make earnings comparable to outside work if the home business is full time. Book writers at home always have a chance to hit big money, but it is a slim chance, and payment on books is often delayed by the infrequency of royalty checks. Short fiction writers have the hardest row to hoe. Established artists, however, can sometimes make as much or more working from home as from a studio. Good markets exist for free-lance commercial art, which can pay an upper middle-class income to those well trained in the field. Strictly creative artists, working without contract and hoping to find markets after production of works, are hurt by intense competition and sometimes lack of recognition, making profits difficult at home or outside.

RISK

At-home art businesses can be almost risk-free. Writers encounter risk in libel laws. Accuracy of printed information about people is the main factor in reducing this risk. Financially, the cash and investment at risk in art is usually modest, and home-based writing businesses usually need almost no up-front investment beyond a used typewriter.

ENJOYMENT

For writers and artists, the need to express themselves through their medium can be altogether compelling, so that the quality of life is diminished only by not performing. But frustrations can be frequent and serious. There is more space, easier access to work, and comfort at home than in most offices or studios, but family distractions can disrupt concentration. Lack of financial reward for those whose talent or drive do not measure up can be very discouraging.

CHAPTER 13

Collectors and Traders

Collecting is one of the great cultural traditions of the United States. And in recent years, the collecting phenomenon has gone beyond even that description. As if they were trying to grab at some means of expressing their individuality in an impersonal and homogenized world, millions of people have taken to building the finest collections of the most obscure items—from beer bottle caps to brass buttons, and from New York Yankee baseball cards of the 1950s to toy cap pistols.

This binge of new collectors weighs in on top of a standard group of hobbyists and businessmen long established. Coins and stamps were common collections of the past. Art and antique collectors, too, have been around for centuries, usually at the higher end of finance in the collectors' subculture. These collectors have by no means diminished in numbers as the others have sprung up. There are, on the contrary, more collectors of every sort than ever before.

The collectors tend to fall into two basic categories. First, there are those who collect to accumulate. Second, there are the collectors and traders, who seek to make a profit as they buy and sell. It is the second group that has grown most notably, because the economics of collecting have undergone dynamic change. Inflation has made collecting in many fields a major financial industry, albeit fragmented among millions of small dealers. Most collectors work from home.

In brief, here is what has happened economically: As inflation ripped away at individual earnings in the 1970s, people with money to invest began to look for new outlets. Savings accounts at banks and savings and loan institutions, paying perhaps 5 percent interest per year, became nothing more than a way to lose a little less money to inflation than keeping funds stuffed in the bedroom mattress. The stock market often did not work much better. Not only were corporate profits (and, therefore, stock prices and dividend payments) suffering from inflation, but the increasing political turbulence in the world had a nagging way of hurting the stocks of U.S.-based multinational companies. Rare goods—precious metals, famous artworks, oriental carpets, antiques of high quality, and so on—began to look like the only products that might appreciate in value faster than the inflation rate.

This brought new money into the collecting and trading business on top of the old, and it happened at about the same time that collecting obscure, formerly worthless items became an American fad. Of course, as the collecting craze hit each new field, value suddenly accrued to things once thrown out with the garbage. Comic books and baseball cards that were children's playthings of the 1950s, thrown out by millions of mothers during spring cleaning, were worth money as soon as somebody, somewhere, decided he was willing to pay to have the best collection of them. "All those thousands of baseball cards," lamented one mother recently. "If only I'd have picked them up and put them in the attic."

Fortunately, it is not too late to make money despite such mistakes. Collecting has never been quite so lucrative to those who know their markets and have the cash to get started. The big money is still in the more traditional areas—coins, stamps, art, antiques. But some of the new collectibles can yield income, too.

The business of collecting and trading has become much trickier than in the past, however. The finer goods that investors rushed into during the 1970s are now undergoing what amounts to a third phase of evolution. Before inflation, the prices of these items were relatively stable, though they certainly showed some appreciation. During the 1970s, phase two took over: Rampant price increases in a superheated marketplace became the norm. The flood of cash into collectibles sent prices ever higher, and no end was in sight. Only very recently did collectibles appear to enter a third phase: one of retrenchment and uncertainty. As the U.S. government began to push interest rates higher and higher to fight inflation, money started flooding back again into cash-type investments. Banks began offering investment certificates with interest pegged to the high rates paid for U.S. Treasury bills. The stock market began to enjoy something of a comeback. The price of gold fell from a sky-high level of $875 an ounce down closer to $500. The sense of panic that once seemed to have driven profit-seekers into collectibles appeared to vanish, and some prices began to drop. Some good examples are in rare coins. High-quality three-cent nickels, minted in the United States between 1865 and 1889, sold for about $300 each in November 1979, according to the *Wall Street Journal*. Within 1½ years, the price jumped to $3,000 each, and then fell again more recently to $1,200. Those who bought at $300 were still sitting pretty; those who bought at $2,000 were in trouble.

The three-cent nickel demonstrates the riskiness of the collector's world today. Some coins, stamps, artworks, and antiques have dropped from inflated highs, like the price of gold. Others have continued to appreciate. More than ever before, collectors who seek profits have to know exactly what they are doing. Reading has become more important than ever. Annual price guides for many kinds of collectibles are available in bookstores and public libraries, but the volatility in some markets demands more updated information. There are a number of magazines and newsletters, some of them new, that give more recent price quotations and offer news articles about special collections and industry trends. Coin, stamp, antique, and art shops and galleries can direct you to the right publications, as can many libraries.

The ways to buy and sell collectibles depend on the particular market. A number of them can be sold by mail order, especially some of the newer kinds of items that are not very expensive. Antiques and artworks, however, are still bought and sold in person at auctions, private homes, flea markets, or galleries, as they have always been. Collectibles now span so huge a number of articles that there is no standard marketing technique that applies to all of them.

Regardless of how you choose to handle marketing, you will find that collecting poses a minimum of three kinds of risk. The first (and most serious) is financial. The casual collector may buy or sell at the wrong price, or may even purchase counterfeits. For financial protection, you must immerse yourself in knowledge, from the history of your type of collection to the latest price quotations. The savvy collector also will familiarize himself with the appearance, the materials, even the feel of the specimens. Interaction with other collectors should be frequent.

The second risk involves security. If your collection is the sort that will fit, it should be stored in a bank's safe deposit box. Among those most aware of the growing numbers of collectors are burglars. Most collections do have to be stored at home for want of a better place that has enough space. Collectors report that they have installed all manner of security systems and devices, and the better ones are certainly worth the investment. There are systems available now that set off audible alarms and house lights even before a burglar has penetrated a window or door.

And, aside from physical security, collectors need good insurance protection. Your home insurance agent should be made aware of the exact nature of your collection; he may want to go so far as to list individual pieces in a policy. It is advisable as well to take photographs of collection specimens to help verify losses in case of theft. Finally, if your collection is of substantial value, it is wise to pay close attention to fire prevention (not a bad idea if you value the people in the house, too). If you don't already have them, it might be time to buy a smoke detector and fire extinguisher.

The third risk is that you might not be able to take tax deductions for a home collector's business, unless you are wary. The IRS, in its audits, will try to separate out the collectors who accumulate (hobbyists) from those who conduct an on-going business designed to make a profit. In reality, the line is thin that divides some collector/hobbyists from collector/businessmen. But if you fall on the hobbyist side in the eyes of the tax auditors, the consequences can be serious. You will be taxed for any profits made in selling collectibles, but be disallowed from declaring any losses or expenses. Collectors and traders who make a living at this work should strongly consider regular or Subchapter S incorporation (see Chapter 5), which helps verify the business nature of their activity. All collectors who want to be considered businesspeople should keep careful books and records, without which the IRS is certain to disallow deductions and tax profits.

Collectibles today are so diverse that they defy a single success formula. Yet, in general, there are a couple of principles that are sure tickets to fatter profits. Rarity of specimens is the most obvious. Specialization of the collection must be a second goal. The more specialized your collection, the better its chance of being the best of its kind in your city, state, or the entire nation. With good advertising, a collection that is tops in its field will sooner or later intrigue a buyer somewhere. Since the value of collectibles is subjective, having the best will fetch top dollar in a marketplace of unpredictable, and possibly very rich, prices.

CONFEDERATE CASH

Grover Criswell was 13 years old before he moved with his parents from Chicago to St. Petersburg, Florida. Now, the more southern he appears to be, the better it is for business, Criswell jokes. "If I looked like Colonel Sanders, it would probably increase my business by 60-percent."

Actually, Criswell seems to be doing well enough. He is regarded as an international expert in Confederate currency, and is certainly one of the biggest collectors and traders in that field. Criswell is so well established, in fact, that customers call him from all over the nation, sometimes in the middle of the night, to deal. About 25 percent of the floor space in Criswell's home, now in Fort McCoy, Florida, is devoted to the business, and he employs five people. He is reluctant to say exactly how lucrative his business has been. "Let's just say," Criswell remarks casually, "that my gross income is in excess of a half-million dollars a year."

With a business of that size, Criswell maintains lock boxes in banks all over the Florida panhandle. Security is a real concern. "There are some individual Confederate notes that are worth ten or twenty thousand dollars," he says. "You don't keep them laying around the house." But the business has been enjoyable, and a life-long passion. Criswell began collecting stamps and coins at the age of eight. By the time he was twelve, he was a full-fledged mail order seller. Encouraged by his parents, Criswell recalls: "I continued in the business while I was in high school, and I continued all the way through college, and I continued in the business all the time I was in the Air Force on active duty." It was while Criswell was attending the Citadel, a military college, that he began to specialize in Confederate currency.

Like many successful collectors, Criswell's early years in the business were tough. But his reputation and skills gradually became better known, and he got some national publicity during the Civil War centennial. Criswell says personal contacts and regular correspondence over the years with other collectors have been of prime importance. He makes many of his contacts at numismatic conventions. The hotels that host these meetings generally provide special rooms with tight security to protect collections. By maintaining contacts with others, Criswell says,

"Every collector or dealer will eventually have a following that will seek him out."

Criswell warns, however, that beginning coin and currency collectors who are interested only in profits may find themselves in trouble. Without a genuine interest in the subject, there will be a tendency to skip or shortcut the development of expertise, which Criswell notes is "not acquired easily or overnight." He adds: "People should go into it with the idea that there is more to be gained than the buck. That way they'll do their homework."

ANTIQUE AMERICAN CLOCKS

In 1973, Malcolm Frouman bought a house in the borough of Queens in New York City. "When I had to furnish my home, the choice was between antiques and department store furnishings, which lose their value," Frouman notes. He bought antique furnishings, and became a hobbyist thereafter.

The hobby was a part-time venture, just as Frouman's collecting business now is. An associate art director at a New York-based magazine on weekdays, Frouman decided in 1980 to turn his hobby into a business, operated at night and on weekends. As he learned more about antiques, Frouman picked his specialty—antique American clocks. He recently had 18 of them, with an approximate value of $20,000.

When Frouman moved from Queens to an apartment in Manhattan, he took out a renter's insurance policy. His policy includes a detailed description of each of his pieces, and covers not only theft but accidental breakage. Frouman estimates his policy premiums are about double the cost of regular renter's insurance in the city.

Like many small antique collectors, Frouman often travels to buy and sell. He sells his pieces at auctions, where he puts a "reserve," or minimum price, on each item. Finding bargain-priced pieces to buy, however, is becoming more difficult, even by doing a lot of traveling to auctions and markets, Frouman explains. "It has become harder and harder to find bargains that no one else knows about. This is because of the tremendous new interest in antiques. There just aren't very many little old ladies who still have antique cars in the garage that have only three thousand miles on them."

On the other hand, Frouman enjoys his antique-hunting business trips to upstate New York, Pennsylvania, and New England—all of which are tax deductible. He also likes the "balance" between his magazine job and clock business. "As an artist, what I like is working with people and being creative— the exchange of ideas and the battles. With antiques, I like the history and the aesthetics. They are a striking change of pace. I like to go shopping in the countryside. Late at night, I like to work on my clocks. I have an old jeweler's workbench and some tools."

To keep abreast of the market, Frouman reads books on antiques but also maintains a membership in the National Association of Watch and Clock Collectors, which puts out a monthly news bulletin. "The money you make," he says, "depends entirely on how active you choose to be. Part time, you really can't get rich." To solve that problem, Frouman adds, "Making this a bigger business is something I'm considering for the future."

MISCELLANEOUS MAN

In little New Freedom, Pennsylvania, lies one of the nation's largest mail order houses for collectible vintage posters and advertising graphics. It operates out of the home of George Theofiles, a former teacher and illustrator who decided to try to market his collection of motion picture posters in 1970. Theofiles developed a mailing list, and tried to market his posters for prices of $1 to $4. He was largely unsuccessful at first.

"But I knew there was a market, and little by little, I managed to find buyers," Theofiles says. He found quite a few. Ten years later, Theofiles had 5,000 subscribers to his 64-page, biannual catalogue, which recently listed 1,100 items for sale. His prices moved up, too. "Now", he says, "none sell for one dollar, and very few for ten or twenty dollars." Among the items listed in one catalogue: old Ringling Bros. circus posters for up to $100 each, and an early and rare Michelin tire poster for $550.

Theofiles has named his business Miscellaneous Man. It has become so large that in some years he may buy 30,000 items from poster and graphics collectors to fill out his inventory. He often buys whole collections at a time, ranging from movie posters to French turn-of-the-century works to advertisements for products that have become part of America's cultural history. The boom in collecting has had a mixed effect in the last few years. Theofiles says that finding good collections to buy is harder than ever, and "getting them at good prices is becoming more difficult." But once he has a new group of products, he seldom has trouble selling them. Theofiles says he spends $5,000 to $6,000 per year on advertising in periodicals— a supplement to his direct mail catalogues.

Once something of a collector himself, Theofiles is now much more a trader in his products. Moving so many pieces per year, he explains, "the novelty wears off." In addition, Theofiles would seem to have little time to pore over a collection of his own. He runs the business almost singlehandedly despite its huge size. Because his posters are often very fragile, Theofiles worries that employees might damage them in packaging. He does hire helpers to mail out catalogues. Aside from the 5,000 regular catalogue subscribers, he gets lots of individual requests for them: 25,000 inquiries in one 18-month period. Doing most of the work himself, Theofiles says his schedule is often a long one. He may work only 20 hours in some weeks, but in others he may work more than 100 hours.

The fruits of his labor are tangible. Theofiles recently bought an 18-room house. The third floor and basement will be devoted to the business. "This business is very successful," he declares. "I make more money than I need. I don't feel I have to become a millionaire, though it may happen, frankly."

STAMPS AND "COVERS"

"Collecting," warns Barbara J. Wallace of Wilmette, Illinois, "is only a semi-rational business. You may fall in love with material as a collector that you don't want to get rid of as a dealer." Indeed, many collectors have agonizing decisions to make about long-treasured pieces if they want to turn a hobby into a business. For Wallace, however, necessity dictated her path. Widowed while she had three children to raise, she fell back in the early 1970s on one subject she knew well: stamps. She had been collecting since she was six years old, and had a fairly substantial inventory. Because of that, she says, "Stamps were about the only thing I could get going without much available capital." Wallace became a full-time stamp dealer from home.

Because she already had a good collection of stamps from the Netherlands, Wallace made herself a specialist at first in issues of that nation. She bought some additional bulk lots of Netherlands stamps to bolster her position. Wallace has since diversified into stamps of several other European countries, and those of the United States. Further, she has gone into "covers"—stamps still mounted on the envelopes on which they were originally mailed. The covers frequently have some historic value, and sometimes are worth much more than the stamps would be worth alone.

Wallace is reluctant to disclose the profits of her business, but she suggests that home-based stamp dealers ought to be able to make $30,000 to $50,000 per year. There is a need, of course, to develop some expertise, and start-up costs for those without good collections can be very high. "I don't see how anyone could start from scratch and expect to make a living at it with less than fifty thousand dollars," she says.

She advertises her wares in trade magazines and local newspapers, and she often travels to stamp shows in neighboring states, where she sets up shop in rented space that can cost several hundred dollars for a weekend. There are other ways to market stamps as well. In Delray Beach, Florida, for example, home-based collector Frank Riolo has a mail order business, and he also does business with fellow members of the big Hollywood, Florida, stamp club.

Wallace points out a number of pitfalls that merit caution. She can recall spending $300 once on a fake cover of 1870 U.S. stamps, for instance. "When I bought something I didn't know, I got burned," she says. Wallace advises collectors who want to become dealers to avoid that error, and another: "Don't be a gambler. Don't buy beyond what you can afford to throw away. The mindset in buying is crucial." Dealers, she notes, must think as everyday businesspeople would. "If you are able to keep your mind organized in the same way you would sell groceries or manufacture bricks, you should be able to get by," she says.

Because stamps can be worth so much, dealing in them attracts some unsavory characters. "It's a tough game, and some play dirty," Wallace says. But she adds that she has no regrets. "I am my own boss. I'm subject to the vicissitudes of the market, and those are very real and not arbitrary. But in other businesses, I was relegated as a woman to arbitrary inferiority."

THE EXCLUSIVE CLUB IN FINE ART

Probably more than any other collectibles, works of fine art tend to be handled by a unique group of highly knowledgeable dealers. They often know their customers keenly, know each other, and travel extensively. Many are home-based businesspeople, yet this is a "club" that will be challenging for the novice to enter. To make a business of buying and selling fine paintings and related works takes some capital to start, and a gradual building of reputation among suppliers (artists) and customers (private collectors, museums, galleries, architects, interior designers, or corporations).

Two who have succeeded are Marvin Friedman, a lawyer in Cutler Ridge, Florida, and Ron Gremillion, an art dealer, distributor, and publisher in Houston. Friedman started as a collector. "I bought a painting with the first money I made as a lawyer," he says. Gremillion is a long-time professional who moved from New York to Houston in 1980. In New York, Gremillion had been employed by an art dealing company. In Houston, he formed his own home-based enterprise, Gremillion & Co. Fine Art, and he sold more than $250,000 worth of works in his first year.

Friedman became interested early-on in modern and contemporary works of this century. He has applied himself to art dealing most diligently in the last five years, and says he has handled paintings with values ranging all the way from $1,000 to $1 million. His home—a luxurious one south of Miami—has become a stopping point for other dealers, collectors, and museum directors from around the world. Friedman advertises in art publications to indicate the kinds of works he is interested in trading. Actual sales, made mostly to private collectors, often come from word-of-mouth promotion within the tight-knit circles of the art world. To buy works, Friedman and his wife, Natasha, often travel to Europe for sales and auctions.

But buying properly is not an easy task. Inflation has provoked special interest in art works as a safe investment, and that has made the highest quality pieces scarce. "The biggest problem today," Friedman says, "is getting top-notch pictures. Even within one artist's works there are ranges of quality. Works of a first rank are difficult to get. Private collectors who own them don't like to part with them, and new ones that are on the market are in high demand." Even so, it can be risky to jump at what may appear to be a great find by an artist without a proven reputation. "I'm suspicious of the notion of the instant superstar," Friedman declares.

Many dealers are exclusive representatives of certain artists. Gremillion in Houston handles works by about 45 artists, and is the exclusive rep for several of them. Among the dealer's jobs is to get to know the artists almost as well as they know themselves. Customers are likely to ask a myriad of biographical and technical questions about the artist and his techniques, and they begin to get nervous if the dealer doesn't have the answers. Many dealers print biographies and résumés of the artists they handle, noting professional achievements, awards won, and schedules of where the artist's work will be exhibited.

Starting an art dealing home business from scratch is difficult, risky, and expensive. But it can be done, especially if one has some experience in art selling or other expertise on the subject. When Gremillion moved to Houston, he had experience, but not much capital, and he had yet to build a reputation as independent dealer. He had a hunch that there were a number of good artists in the San Francisco area who were being shown locally or regionally, but had no access to the fast-growth market of Houston and the Southwest. Gremillion, with less than $10,000 in hand ($5,000 borrowed from a bank), went to California to scout out the territory.

"I started explaining to the artists who I was, but they were leery about someone coming from Texas wanting to take their work on consignment. So I agreed to buy some, if they would also consign some to me." The ploy worked very well indeed. When it came to marketing, Gremillion found the Houston area to have just the right combination of conspicuous affluence and rapid growth, partly because of Texas oil wealth. Within a year, Gremillion was dealing in works of California artists and many others. He had a full-time salesman and a part-time secretary, and an inventory of more than $100,000 in value in his contemporary, three-story townhouse. Gremillion's living space, in fact, was whittled back to the third story only. Offices and display areas fill the rest, and he sells to customers on-premise. "It spreads around," Gremillion says. "You can't help it. But that's good. It gives people the feeling when they come in here that surely there's something here for them."

PROFIT POTENTIAL

With the right combination of skill and aggressiveness, the collector and trader can have the highest income of any home businessperson. In many collectibles, inventories worth hundreds of thousands of dollars can easily fit into extra space at home. Collectibles also conveniently make either full-time or part-time businesses. However, unlike some other home businesses, the big money in collectibles usually cannot come quickly. Inventories and reputations of traders take years to build. Even in the building years, however, dealing in collectibles can provide plenty of extra income part time, or adequate annual incomes full time. Of course, collectibles also have the advantage of invariably giving the collector and trader something of value to sell off should he desire to leave the business.

RISK

Just as the payoff can be the highest among home businesses, collectibles also pose the highest risks. As collectibles have become financial instruments like stocks and bonds, their price volatility has increased. With coins and currency, stamps, and art works in particular, the great danger is buying when prices are temporarily high, especially if one buys with borrowed money at high interest on the assumption that proceeds from selling the pieces will be used to pay back the loan. Security is also a risk that must be diminished by purchasing plenty of insurance coverage.

ENJOYMENT

There is a definite "Catch 22" in collectibles. Without a passionate interest in the subject, the collector is likely to lack the expertise to become a good seller. But a good seller is likely to be so caught up in love of his inventory that he will be torn by parting with it. The answer for most is to keep some and sell the rest, though even this can be a bittersweet solution. Notes art dealer Marvin Friedman of Florida: "The interest [in art] was there long before I got involved with the objects. I wish I had back every picture I sold in the last four years."

CHAPTER 14

Animals and Plants

A fondness for living things is such a common trait among people that it makes a near-universal business market. The creatures that strut on four legs, or sprout wings, or swim or slither, or those that sink their roots quietly into a pot of earth, are inside most U.S. homes as well as out. Producing pets for sale is a most common home-based business in a part-time sense. The furry pets have litters, and they can be worth money. But people who love animals and plants and who want to be aggressive in business have all manner of additional opportunities awaiting. Pets, houseplants, and flowers, bred or grown at home, represent one market segment. Home-based animal and plant services are another. There are even ways, at home, to produce a quantity of some kinds of game and food crops without a lot of acreage.

The variety of the biological businesses is a good reason to think twice before jumping into those that come to mind at first. Those who consider home businesses in animals and plants typically think first about breeding pedigreed dogs and cats, or growing flowers to sell at retail, just like the shops. These are, indeed, common home businesses, and the prices one can get are a natural draw. But breeding pets and growing flowers are not easy businesses; they can be laborious and risky from start to finish. Commercial pet breeding, for example, requires:

1. Skill.
2. Space.
3. Special personality characteristics for the business manager—patience above all.
4. Understanding neighbors.
5. Significant expenditures up-front and for maintenance, from vets to feed.
6. Willingness to assume clear risks—still-births and small litters, and a marketplace that may lose interest in a particular breed that the operator becomes stuck with, and to which he is emotionally attached.

Growing flowers for retail sale has difficulties of its own. Bad weather can hurt. Access to sun is needed. Inventory perishes quickly, so marketing skills must be sharp. Competition from the big commercial shops and greenhouses can be fierce.

None of these caveats is meant to suggest that breeding and flower-growing are bad businesses. Properly done, each has its rewards in money and satisfaction. *Fortune* magazine estimated in 1981 that cut flowers sold by shops, supermarkets, and street vendors have reached annual sales of $3 billion in the United States. And, some pets now command astonishing prices that cannot help but attract prospective new entrants to the business. In the Los Angeles market—one of the more active for pets—a single recent newspaper classified section listed finely bred Shih Tzu pups at $1,500 each, and a mastiff at $800. A pet store was advertising Hyacinthe Macaw birds at $6,500 each.

These, however, are top-of-the-line prices. One's horizons of thinking about the biological businesses should be broad. In breeding, growing, and service, the most successful home business will be the one that uniquely fills a need in the market. Creative ideas in plants and animals may work best, as one home entrepeneur has discovered in Florida.

THE BIRD TAMER OF FORT LAUDERDALE

Kay Gilbert found a wonderfully unique niche in animal services. A part-time waitress in Fort Lauderdale, Gilbert is a long-time pet lover who yearned for a cockatoo from the first minute she saw Fred, the bird that starred on the Baretta television series. She got one, and eventually parlayed her knowledge of exotic birds into a neat home business.

Gilbert quickly discovered what pet store owners know all too well: A lot of exotic birds are fearful of humans, and tend to bite and claw. For many owners, this becomes an especially painful dilemma, since they pay extraordinary prices for the birds. Retail prices for cockatoos can start at $1,500. But Gilbert found she had a knack for understanding and taming the birds. By closely watching a specimen's behavior, she could tailor a training program to calm its fears. She began to sell her bird-taming service to pet shops and private owners for $50 to $150 per bird.

"Just from having birds, you meet other people who have birds," she says. "People came to me with problems. I really started out helping friends.

"Most people hold their finger up to a bird, the first thing. That's the worst thing you can do. With every bird I've known, the biggest fear is the human hand, probably because they were handled when they were caught, and they were handled in quarantine, and they were handled in shipment. Everything associated with hands has been a bad experience for the bird."

Gloves are even worse, Gilbert says, so she wears none. She performs a sort of encounter session with each client's bird, lasting seven or eight hours. One lasted 19 hours. She begins by talking and moving very slowly. Morning is the best time to begin, she says, because toward evening the birds "tend to get more noisy and active, getting ready to roost." Watching for the warning signs birds give before biting, she waits until they are calm, and then carefully pets them. Eventually, she coaxes them onto her bare hand. The first hand contact isn't always a perfect success, causing one drawback that is peculiar to the bird-taming business: a parade of claw marks. "People sometimes ask, 'What do you do for a living? Hang barbed wire?' " she says.

Nonetheless, the sessions have been profitable enough to allow Gilbert to cut back on her waitressing hours. She hopes to expand into the cockatoo-breeding business as well.

Costs in the pet service business can be minute compared with those in breeding and raising. For Gilbert to breed cockatoos, she says she would need to buy another at $1,500 or more (cockatoos mate for life). That doesn't include vet or other bills, which also escalate very rapidly with dogs and cats.

"By the time you're through with the expense of vets, marketing, feeding, caring, and showing, you may not make much money breeding cats," advises Tom Dent, executive manager of the Cat Fanciers Association in New York. The list of cat-breeding and raising expenses is pretty high: stud service at $75 to $150 for a female, possible boarding pay for a cat that has to stay at a place of mating, plus veterinary and advertising expenses that can vary with geographic location and selection of media and doctor, Dent says. Litters can be registered at $4, and individuals for $5, with the Association. Shows can cost

$15 on average for entry. Some Persian kittens, Dent says, have sold for $1,000 or even $1,500, but most sell for $75 to $150, and the average litter is just four.

Cats, of course, have certain advantages over dogs in ease of care. They can more easily be left alone for short periods of time, and they eat less. One Denver cat raiser likes to note a terrific fringe benefit: he no longer has mice in the house. But the Denver man, a chemist who must travel for his regular job, has to stay home when one of his females is ready to give birth. That, he says, does pose one drawback. "I added it all up," he notes, "and realized that my calendar would be determined by the cats' pregnancies."

Many humanitarian organizations are concerned that too many dogs and cats are being bred, too. Still, there is a clear market for a certain number, and Dent agrees that the business is profitable for some.

With dogs, both expenses and income can be higher. But dogs also require more time and patience, being less self-sufficient than most pets. One New York woman who tried once to breed Dobermans gave up quickly. She says the cost to dock tails alone came to $120 for a litter of nine. "It's too much work," she adds. "I'm exhausted. And I spent more than I took in. Never again." Others, however, do tell a happier tale. "This is a business like any other business," says Norma Carbonaro of Elmont, New York. "You have to know what you're doing and be ready for anything."

DOZENS OF DOBERMANS

Carbonaro raised 16 litters of Dobermans in seven years. Profits have varied with the size and health of the litters, but she says she has never lost money. She says litters range widely: 2 to 3 puppies for some small and toy breeds to as many as eight to 14 puppies for larger breeds. Carbonaro counts on an average of eight puppies that can be sold for an average of $350, for gross income per litter of $2,800. She sells puppies at 8 to 12 weeks old.

A good female for breeding can be bought for $500 or so as a puppy, or full-grown from a kennel for $700 to $1,400. A diet for a Doberman will cost about $20 per month, she says.

She recommends beginning the dog's breeding life during the third heat, when the dog is about 1½ years old and the bones and chest are fully developed. Stud fees, according to the American Kennel Club, range from $100 to $400 for Dobermans, but a very good stud can cost $500, and a championship male $1,000 or more, according to Carbonaro. Some male dog owners will accept "pick of the litter" in exchange for service, but whatever the terms, a stud agreement should be set in writing. The heat may last for a few weeks, and it is essential to keep the dog away from other males. That means a frustrating in-home lockup, or care in a kennel, which will charge a per diem fee.

During pregnancy, three or more trips to the vet are advisable. In whelping, someone knowledgeable should be on hand, perhaps to help cut the umbilical cord if the mother is having trouble. Complicated births are a big financial risk. If a vet is needed for a Caesarean, for example, his fees may range well into the hundreds of dollars. The female, at any rate, should visit the vet after giving birth, and each puppy will soon need at least two shots at $9 to $12 per shot per pup. Carbonaro says the way to save money in breeding is to learn to dispense shots oneself, although it's wise to check state laws on the subject first. In New York, Carbonaro says she can buy distemper medicine and a syringe for $1.60, compared with a vet's fee of $15.

There are utility and other unexpected expenses, too. Puppies should be kept very warm—85 degrees or so for the first week or two, and 75 degrees for a while afterwards. Incidentals include disinfectant, plastic trash bags, and paper towels. Some states also require all breeders to be licensed. A fee may be required. Risks include a glut on the market for a particular breed, so it is wise to check newspaper ads and kennels and stud owners before breeding. Count on at least one buyer trying to return a puppy, Carbonaro advises. The biggest risk, of course, is death by accident or disease.

In all, Carbonaro's per-pup expenses come to an average $50 to $100, leaving a handsome profit, but after a lot of work. "There's a good feeling involved, but you have to really, really love dogs to do this," she says.

More exotic pets—and animals bred for other purposes—can be more clearly lucrative. Fish can be bred as pets, or, with a little space in a rural area, as a food crop. One Ohio man who has made his fortune for years as a home businessman has done very well indeed with bass, blue gill, and a host of related enterprises.

BUSINESS IN THE LAKE

Seldom has a person made more financial use of his property than William M. Gressard of Kent, Ohio. Most recently, he owned and operated Ohio's largest privately-owned fish hatchery on eight lakes surrounding his home. The way Gressard worked his way up to this large-scale home operation is a tale in itself.

Out of the Navy in 1945, Gressard returned to corporate life at Twin Coach Co., a bus manufacturer. But he had a yen for an outdoorsman's career, and set up his first home business in 1946 as a vehicle to reach that goal. Gressard bought 5,000 Navy surplus rubber suits for $1 to $3 each, and with a few alterations he made waterproof suits and full-length gloves for fishermen. He priced them at $10 for the suits and $3 for the gloves and peddled his wares by mail order through ads in outdoorsmen's magazines. He got 15,000 orders from around the world, and sold all he had. Gressard took the money and bought a worn 100-acre farm, where he built a cabin for hunting and fishing. Knowing there were natural springs on the property, Gressard bulldozed a 30-acre lake, stocked it with bass breeders, and within two years had a "glut of fish"—5,000 bass. In the meantime, Gressard also invented his own fishing lure, the Trail Lake Torpedo, and through the years he has sold 200,000 of them at $1 to $1.25 each. He makes the lures in a workshop on his property for 19 cents each.

A college-trained biologist, Gressard knows a little about business productivity, too. He has turned his operation into several profit centers. He sells the lures, and he sells bait. He has stocked his expanded group of lakes with blue gill as well as bass, and he cleans and fillets the blue gill for sale to restaurants at $5 per pound. He sells live fish to other individuals with lakes, turning over about 800 to 1,200 bass per year at minimum two-pound size for $2 per pound. He sells the names of customers of his fishing lures to mail order houses for three cents a name.

He raises hounds and sells them for $300 each. He writes a weekly outdoors column for his local newspaper. And, he has developed in his home operation some gadgets and pesticides for keeping lakes and ponds clean. Gressard sells his cleaning service to neighboring municipalities.

Gressard lives in a home within casting distance of his largest lake, and keeps an office in a bedroom. His wife, Margaret, a business school graduate, does secretarial and other work. It has been, says Gressard, "a lot of fun."

WOLVES IN COLORADO

Even more unusual is the part-time home business of Charles Zanichelli of Harris Park, Colorado, about 50 miles southwest of Denver. A jazz musician and salesman for a New York food importer, Zanichelli once owned a part-wolf malamute that died. In the mid 1970s, he bought a pure wolf to replace it. A year later, he acquired a mate for it. Each wolf cost him $300.

Zanichelli has three acres, and the neighbors in this western town have not really made much fuss—except for the one who used to call anonymously and howl on the phone, Zanichelli says. He built a 50- by 75-foot fenced living area for the wolves, with an eight-foot wooden fence they could not climb, and a concrete fence foundation that prevents them from digging out. He maintains that the wolves must be fenced not because they are dangerous, but because ranchers in the area might shoot them if they caught the wolves running free.

The animals make excellent pets and "good protection," Zanichelli says. "I haven't taught them to protect, but when the male sees anyone around he hasn't seen before, he raises a lot of hell. Anyone who sticks around after that has to be crazy. He protects everyone in the family. He considers us part of the pack." A wolf can have as many as 15 litters in its life, and Zanichelli says he expects about eight cubs per litter. He sells the cubs at $350 each, mainly by word of mouth. Feeding the wolves a diet of half dog food and half meat costs $1 per day per wolf, he says. One drawback to the business is that wolves in the wild mate for life, so that if one dies the other will not mate again (hence the expression "lone wolf"). A domesticated wolf may or may not mate again, inceasing the potential cost of maintaining stock.

For humanitarian reasons, Zanichelli looks for customers who have land and live in remote areas. He'll sell to no one in the city. He refused to sell to one customer who wanted to turn the wolf into a guard dog. "I wouldn't do that to the animal," he says. One of the big surprises in the business is the discovery of how affectionate wolves can be. "They're good to come home to," Zanichelli says.

MDM STABLES

Marilyn Morton lived with her husband, Richard, on a one-acre plot in Texas that gave her just enough room to run a tiny, part-time, animal boarding business. Her love of animals, especially horses, convinced her to try to convert her enterprise into a much larger home occupation. Richard, an electrical engineer, resisted the idea at first. "He didn't want me taking on all that burden, working outside a lot, doing some fairly heavy work. But I'm very ambitious, and knew I could make the thing work. So I said to him, 'Look, I'm the type who is either going to spend money or earn money. Which do you want it to be?' He changed his mind kind of quickly," says Marilyn with a laugh.

In July 1978, the couple moved to a ten-acre piece of land in Cypress, Texas, fitted it out with a mobile home for living quarters, and built a barn and kennel for the boarding and breeding of horses and dogs. Initial cost was $20,000. Morton started by boarding three horses, but the number grew in a couple years to 27.

Recently, she was taking in $1,700 per month in boarding fees, which put the business "fairly solidly in the black," Morton says. Breeding has been profitable, too. She sold one filly in 1980 for $3,000, after paying $250 for stud service and about $50 in veterinarians' fees. Veterinary costs range from $50 to $500 per month for the whole operation, depending on the health of the animals—a range of expense that shows some degree of risk. "The breeding business," Morton agrees, "is a crap shoot. Any number of things can happen to make that a risky investment, disease or injury to the animals, principally."

In the boarding business, the risk "lies in the sometimes shaky financial positions of the owners." They must sometimes sell their animals or switch to stables closer to their homes, she says.

Nevertheless, Morton is expanding MDM Stables. "There is a demand out there," she observes. Morton spent two years as a veterinarian's assistant, and says she finds the psychic rewards in her business as gratifying as the cash. "It's something I really love doing, and would certainly do over again had I the chance. The financial rewards are nice, but I really enjoy taking care of animals, seeing them grow, seeing them flourish."

OREGON BOUQUETS

Irma E. Spreeman has developed a home business in what might be called flower processing, rather than growing. She was running a small janitorial service in Gresham, Oregon, when she saw an advertisement for a floral supply business. She decided to buy it. Earlier, while living in Arizona, Spreeman had run a regular floral shop, but this was different: She bought a business with contracts to supply tiny floral bouquets for the tables of five Oregon restaurants. She acquired Restaurant Floral Supply in May 1980, and soon added two more restaurants to the list.

The restaurants pay 75 cents to $1 per table per week for her arrangements. They also buy vases from Spreeman for 85 cents to $1 each. For each table, she provides three or four flowers tied together with leather or mixed with baby's breath, and she changes designs every week. At Christmas or Thanksgiving, she provides special, festive arrangements. Spreeman has found a business with solid demand; the restaurants find that her arrangements truly attract customers. At least one reports that its business swells on the day Spreeman makes her deliveries, because some customers come in just to take home last week's flowers.

Spreeman makes certain her flowers are fresh enough to last the week, and longer, by spending the time to personally select long-stemmed specimens. She hand-picks her stock at wholesale markets on Monday mornings, and carts them home in an air-conditioned station wagon—a considerable business expense, but one that is tax deductible. She makes the arrangements at home and delivers on Tuesdays. On Wednesdays and Thursdays, she repeats the schedule. Having had experience in flower retailing, Spreeman finds there are some distinct advantages in bulk supply. Mainly, she can control inventory levels and cut waste. "This is pre-sold," she notes. "When I had a flower shop, I had to have flowers on hand, hoping a customer would come in and buy them."

WOOD AND BEAN SPROUTS

At the other end of the spectrum in the plant business is Jack Smith of Akron, Ohio. Canadian-born and built like a lumberjack, Smith's biggest investment is in his firewood business, a home-headquartered enterprise that nonetheless keeps him outside much of the time. On the inside, he utilizes his basement to grow mung and alfalfa sprouts for sale to restaurants and supermarkets.

Smith has $15,000 tied up in equipment for the wood business: two trucks, a tractor, one splitter, and four saws. His profitability does not really depend on pricing of his end product—firewood—because the prices must be kept competitive with those of others in his market area. Without much price flexibility, Smith's business depends on his inventiveness in locating inexpensive supplies. He takes waste wood from lumbering operations, and visits sawmills to buy the tops of trees. Smith also "cleans up" the wooded lots of private landowners, often commercial businesses where appearances are important. The property owners he serves want somebody to remove dead wood from their grounds for aesthetic reasons, so they charge relatively little for what Smith takes. For $800, he takes out 100 cords of wood from a nearby golf course. The pickings are better behind a hotel that is another of Smith's clients. There, he pays $500 for 200 to 250 cords. He sells the wood primarily to residential customers stocking up their fireplace bins for the winter. A recent selling price: $90 a cord, for a gross profit that would make most giant corporations envious.

Smith cannot spend all his time outside, though. His wife, Marilyn, is a teacher, and he has opted for the role of house-husband, taking care of their young son. It was while the boy was napping that Smith got the idea to put the basement to profitable use. He takes mung bean seeds, soaks them for several hours, puts them in crocks and raises them in the dark. It takes about five days to produce edible sprouts. Alfalfa beans must be soaked for four hours, he says, and then grown for seven days, constantly in the light. The mungs sell for between 30 cents and 40 cents a pound, and alfalfa for $1.10 to $1.60 a pound. In essence, Smith, who is interested in the future of world food supplies, has become an indoor city farmer. When firewood is out of season, Smith also works on the 480-acre outdoor farm of a friend, and utilizes one of his trucks to sell produce. Smith has set goals that include an animal business as well: fish farming.

A TWO-HOME PLANT BUSINESS

Southern Florida is a major producer of house plants sold all over the East. The climate, in fact, is hospitable enough that Mickey Carmichael watched as her backyard plant nursery spilled right over to the yard next door. In 1979, she bought the home next door, and now rents that house while using its back yard to add to her growing space. Carmichael is a full-time plant nursery operator whose business recently was producing $10,000 a year of income. "It was something I started as a hobby, and just built up from there," she says. She now spends about 50 hours a week tending to hundreds of ornamentals—orchids, ferns, bonsai and many more. Her original back lot is 70 feet deep; the neighboring lot adds 56 feet more.

Carmichael prefers to stick to the retailing side of plant-raising, and she sells mainly by word of mouth. However, she also uses occasional newspaper advertising, and sometimes rents plants for special shows or conferences. She hires out her plants at $7.50 each, and may allow some to be sold from shows as well.

Christmas is the hot selling season. In the meantime, Carmichael's biggest expenses are water and pots. In 1981, her water bills, which come once every two months, hit $120. She uses $1,000 worth of pots annually. Fertilizer costs come to $150 to $250 per year. Jack Frost is her biggest enemy. A hard freeze can be immensely destructive, and a light freeze can cause nights of lost sleep, when Carmichael stays up with neighbors to keep fires lit to prevent a loss of plants.

PROFIT POTENTIAL

Without a truly innovative idea in animal and plant businesses, big money may be beyond reach for people with ordinary-sized homes and lots. However, extra incomes ranging from a few thousand dollars up to $5,000 or $6,000 per year are readily attainable for a busy part-timer. Full-time work usually requires plenty of outdoor space, and, with animals, proper permits, zoning, and agreeable neighbors. Competition in most animal and plant businesses is right up against professional shops and kennels.

RISK

There is substantial risk of loss of animals and plants from disease and accident. Weather can be a killer in plant businesses. Pet litters are unpredictable in size. Careful and loving attention cannot always prevent loss, making these businesses typically volatile. Plant and animal services, however, are low in risk.

ENJOYMENT

Much greater potential exists for having fun with plants and animals than with many other home businesses. Work is hard. Animal businesses can be tedious and constant in demands on the operator. Plant businesses can simply involve heavy labor. But for those who love their families of green or fur-bearing creatures, there is no comparable way of making extra income.

CHAPTER 15

Garments

Creativity is one of those human qualities—like talent and logic—that occurs through a mental process that no one fully understands. But the consequences of creativity in business are easy to measure in paychecks: Creativity means more zeros in the salary. The same, of course, is true for home-based entrepreneurs, notably in the garment business.

Home garment businesses range from design and manufacturing (the creative end) to repair work. Garment repair businesses are not to be belittled; they have the advantages of quick turnover of items, relatively easy work, low starting costs, and almost nonexistent business risk. There is always a market for garment repair, and inflation is making that market bigger all the time. More and more people, as they try to cut living costs, are buying fairly good-looking but inexpensive clothes. A few months later, zippers break and hems sag and holes appear in the knees of inexpensive children's pants. Millions lack the knowledge or time to fix clothes, producing the demand for garment repair services that are surprisingly hard to find.

Even so, there is much more money in home garment design and manufacturing. But there is more risk: Even the best of the big clothing manufacturers come up with some designs that bomb in the marketplace, and others that boom but later die suddenly in the fickle world of consumer fashion. For those who are looking to make big incomes in garment work at home, however, creating the pieces yields the best odds for success. While garment repair is usually limited to a local market, design and manufacturing can tap a much broader area. There are a number of ways to sell: custom work for individuals, wholesale to retail stores or to chains of stores, retailing from home, or through the assignment of goods to a manufacturer's representative.

Producing garments in volume will require the employment of others. This draws home garment businesses into a web of government regulation that became extraordinarily controversial in 1981. The debate began after the U.S. Department of Labor took a stab at enforcing old legal restrictions on the employment of garment workers at home. The Department sued CB Sports Inc., a Vermont manufacturer of knitted ski apparel which purchased some of its goods from home workers in Vermont and Massachusetts. CB Sports fought back, and some of its suppliers added their voices to that of the company.

At issue was a federal law passed in 1938, and amended in 1942, which prohibited home-based work in seven industries: women's apparel, jewelry manufacturing, knitted outerwear, gloves and mittens, button- and buckle-making, handkerchief manufacturing, and embroideries. To the modern eye, the law was strange to say the least. Making men's shirts at home was legal but women's blouses were illegal. Ear muffs were okay, but gloves and mittens were criminal activities. The law was not written very specifically, but, according to a Labor Department spokesperson, it does not cover the home-based business owner, though it might cover the employees of such a person.

Written at a time when employers forced the poor and underprivileged in garment centers to work at home at subnormal wages, the law was designed to eliminate home sweatshops and discourage illegal child labor. The target industries seemed to be the offenders of that day. The law didn't work. Unscrupulous employers in such garment production spots as New York City continue to exploit their employees. One standard technique is to insist that workers in a small sweatshop-type factory take extra work home with them. Using sewing machines at home, these workers are paid by the piece, often at rates that fall below the minimum wage. Illegal aliens, who comprise part of this work force, obviously cannot complain.

Unfortunately, the law also prohibited home garment work where the worker was not only well paid but labored in pleasant surroundings. Thousands do so. In testimony at a Labor Department hearing on the subject in February 1981, home-based garment workers who sold products to CB Sports testified against the regulations, citing the standard reasons anyone begins a home business: extra income in an inflationary era, a chance to combine working and staying at home to raise a family, eliminating the commute, and so on. Struck with the arguments, and clearly aware of the scope of the home business movement, Secretary of Labor Raymond J. Donovan proposed on May 1 to lift the ban on all kinds of industrial work at home. "We do not believe that working at home should be an underground or illegal activity," Donovan was quoted as saying. Along with the garment industry, one might hope that some city zoning officials were listening!

The dispute appeared to be on its way to a resolution that would eliminate a set of federal rules that were seldom enforced anyway, and really were aimed at exploited home workers. Across the country, other home-based garment businesses have long been run by entrepreneurs who themselves are seeking to exploit something—the opportunity to make a living, or some extra spending money, by mending or making clothes.

A ONE-WOMAN CONGLOMERATE

When she lived in St. Louis prior to World War II, Marge M. McKenzie worked in a garment factory. McKenzie not only learned how to make a dress, but she picked up a few business pointers too. Since moving to Houston, she has established a home business with so many different features that there is always a good level of customer demand. McKenzie does custom dressmaking, custom knitting, sells knitting machines, and gives knitting lessons, working six days a week. She does all this, often working 12 to 16 hours a day, "because it's fun." It also pays. McKenzie says she uses two guidelines in setting prices for garments. She totals her cost of materials and labor, and then doubles that figure. Or, if what she makes copies a style available at a retail store, she sets her price at half that of the store, and still finds she makes a profit. In selling knitting machines and supplies, McKenzie says she takes a standard retailer's markup.

McKenzie is the one who had the clever newspaper ad idea mentioned in Chapter 6. Having moved from St. Louis to Houston, her first ad for custom dressmaking in the Houston *Chronicle* noted that she was "from the East." Within a week, she says, she had 125 dressmaking customers. But in 1970, when she launched the knitting and knitting machine business, McKenzie found she had struck on an even more lucrative market. Recently, only one quarter of her revenues came from dressmaking. Another quarter came from custom knitting, and sales of machines and related supplies accounted for one-half of sales.

With $500 in dressmaking profits, she had purchased three knitting machines—two to use and demonstrate, and one to sell. She spent three years using the machine to become expert in manufacturing knitted garments.

Today, the up-front investment such a business would require is much higher because knitting machines can cost about $500 each. In addition, most of them are Japanese-made, and this can make price-setting more complicated because the cost to buy them wholesale fluctuates with exchange rates on the Japanese yen. But McKenzie has developed ways to cope with that problem. She gets her machines from a wholesale distributor in town who can deliver within a few hours when she orders. Thus, McKenzie can keep her inventory of machines down to just a few, so that she doesn't need to finance them. She keeps about $1,000 worth of yarn and related supplies on hand and estimates that others could launch a home knitting business today for about $2,000. For modest fees, McKenzie has her business registered with the state controller's office, which assigns her a tax number for payment of state sales taxes.

Selling machinery from home may seem an unlikely trade, but McKenzie notes that knitting machines fit well. Because the average customer needs instruction to operate them, many retail stores (where turnover of trained clerks can be rapid) don't seem adept in marketing these items. McKenzie has about 215 regular knitting customers, and says she is happy to give lessons. "When you're in business for yourself, you don't mind teaching beginners every day, because they are future customers for supplies," she says.

McKenzie also enjoys her scheduling freedom at home. She likes to keep the business open from about noon to 10 P.M., but sometimes works straight through until 3 or 4 A.M., and then sleeps in the next morning. "I'm a night person," she declares. "I love to watch TV or listen to the radio while I do designs or pattern-making. The wonderful thing about running your own business at home is that you can work your own hours." The only thing that suffers from McKenzie's long hours is housework. "Before long, your whole home becomes a business," she says. "You start sticking stuff under the beds and in all the closets. We used to really keep house. But as the business grew, something had to go."

SILKS AND WOOLENS

When Jeanne Iguchi got out of design school, her goal was to become a garment designer and manufacturer in her own studio. But, as a low-cost way of getting started and to build up a solid list of customers, she chose to set up shop in her two-bedroom house in Los Angeles. Over the course of four years, Iguchi succeeded in building the business at home. And, by using manufacturer's representatives to sell her silk and wool separates, Iguchi's products have ended up in some of the most prestigious U.S. department stores, including Neiman Marcus.

In the beginning, Iguchi had saved a few thousand dollars from her job working for another designer. She felt it was enough to launch her own enterprise. "I started out very small," she says. "I already had a sewing machine and a few sketches to show some stores. The bulk of the money was spent on fabric, which I bought at retail stores."

Much has changed since then. Iguchi now buys European fabrics from suppliers with whom she became familiar through friends in the business. She stopped trying to peddle her finished goods to retail stores herself. This had taken valuable time away from her designing and manufacturing, and Iguchi found that selling could also become a discouragement. "Because the items you are selling become personal, you feel you have failed if the store doesn't want them," she says. She let her sales representatives in Los Angeles handle marketing. Since her "better wear" for women is uniquely designed, carefully crafted, and made of the finest materials, Iguchi can afford the services of the marketing middlemen. She recently was receiving $70 to $150 per garment, paid to her by her representatives, whose duties included collecting bills from the stores.

Still at home, Iguchi found herself working seven days a week. But the business grew handsomely. She was making enough to neatly exceed raw material and overhead costs that averaged $1,500 to $2,000 a month. "It is my own business, so I really don't mind working as hard as I am," she says.

Iguchi's one regret is that, while she prepared herself for a career in clothing, she did not take business courses in school. She recommends that others do so. "This is a highly competitive business, and many people don't want to tell you anything about it. I was very unsuspecting when I got out of design school.

I trusted everybody and thought everybody was honest. I wish I had had more business experience and taken some business courses," she says.

Some of the problems Iguchi has encountered involve purchasing and getting timely payments. Her materials can cost as much as $30 a yard, and she has had to learn to buy only enough to fill orders. "When you are in a small business and have too much of anything left over, it is a traumatic loss that cannot be recovered financially," she warns. Iguchi also has run across retailers who order goods and accept delivery, but declare bankruptcy before they pay her. In such cases, there is little chance of recouping the debt.

In addition, Iguchi has suffered from one of the banes of home businesses—selling products that are not paid for on delivery. Most retailers have a 30-day payment policy, but Iguchi has discovered that many of them stretch out their payments for as many months as they can get away with. This is typical in an inflationary economy, in which savvy businesspeople recognize that money paid later is cheaper. Iguchi uses borrowed money to pay some of her own bills when her incoming payments are late.

All this means, "I had to learn the business the hard way," Iguchi says. But she has learned. Thanks to the national scope of her sales representatives, Iguchi's blouses, slacks, dresses, and jackets are selling in stores across the United States.

FOR EXTRA INCOME

Like Iguchi, a number of design-oriented home entrepreneurs make their garment businesses full-time ventures. But commercial sewing is very frequently a part-time occupation at home, used to supplement the income of a spouse, or to add to social security payments. Gertrude Konen, a seamstress in Cuyahoga Falls, Ohio, charges by the hour to make dresses or fix garments to earn extra money to add to her husband's pension payments. She keeps the business small and modestly priced— from the minimum wage on up, depending on the difficulty of the job.

With very small home garment operations, it becomes most

important to weigh costs versus income. Konen was able to buy a good used heavy-duty sewing machine in Florida for $200 in the 1970s. Sometimes, the older machines are worthy investments. A number of home-based seamstresses report that the used machines outperform new ones for certain purposes, although they may lack the ability to do some fancy work. Louise Brogdon of Takoma Park, Maryland, still uses a 35-year-old Singer machine that originally cost $125—an exhorbitant sum in those days. She has a newer one that cost $400, and is better at zigzag sewing, but can't match the old one on certain products, such as knits. Like Konen, Brogdon charges hourly rates.

Bigger home sewing operations can afford more machinery, of course, but it is unwise to spend a penny before checking out government regulations that could eventually quash the business and leave the owner stuck with monthly equipment payments. In July 1976, W. Jean Yoder in Seattle put $500 down to acquire $5,000 worth of commercial sewing machines to launch South End Custom Draperies in the basement of her mother's home. Monthly payments on the machinery came to $140. But in Seattle, zoning restrictions prohibited Yoder from having employees in a business run out of a residence. The restrictions threatened to limit the scope of production and income. Yoder's operation was able to continue by becoming a partnership of three—Yoder, her mother, and a neighbor—all owners and none employees. South End sells its draperies wholesale to department stores.

Konen likes to use one cost-reducing technique: She asks her dress-making customers to bring their own supplies and materials, including thread, pattern, material, and interfacing. Konen is one of the home garment entrepreneurs who also takes advantage of booming demand for mending. A lot of store-bought clothing is so poorly sewn now that she says her business in repairs and alterations is very busy, even though she does not advertise. Dry cleaning and apparel shops have contacted her about both repairs and dressmaking.

Because sewing is very close work, and the hours can be long, it is sometimes more enjoyable to keep the business part time. Working full time plus, Iguchi in Los Angeles reports that she feels isolated at times, although she does get out to chat and do business with others in the fabric trade. An active senior citizen, Konen maintains that her job beats "hanging around shopping malls." By keeping her hours short, she is able to take long breaks to play bridge, a favorite pastime. Though sewing can be tedious, there are also some memorable moments in the business, says Brogdon. For example, she has had several calls from men who want her to make them women's dresses. "They say they just like to wear women's housedresses around the house," Brogdon smiles. She demurely declines.

It's smart in a small custom dressmaking or mending businesses to know your customers, or to take deposits from them before starting to work. Every so often, Brogdon reports, she gets stuck with a finished garment for a customer who seems to have disappeared. "I really wish they'd call back and argue about the price. That way at least I'd get something," she says. Konen's requirement that customers furnish the materials helps to ensure that they will come back. One Florida woman who custom-makes slipcovers for furniture at home has a similar method. She has the customer supply the material; she provides zippers. Without much investment in inventory or equipment, the slipcover business provides an extra $1,000 to $2,000 per year as a part-time venture. She finds that is enough on top of social security and her husband's income. "We get along just fine," she says.

CLOTHES FOR KIDS

"I flunked out of three art schools," says Kay Schachtel of Highland Park, Illinois, "but I do have an eye for what goes together." Schachtel makes children's clothes at home, and she has gained a good deal of notoriety. A number of department stores, for example, have called on her without prior solicitation, asking for pieces to display. The reason is that Schachtel's products are original. She redesigns commercial patterns, but usually finishes the garment by appliquéing it with a child's name and a decorative object, such as a puppy or an ice cream cone. She has a mix of business. She makes most of her clothes for individual customers by order, but the department stores place orders with her for their customers who have seen the display pieces. This creates a combination retailing and wholesaling operation.

Schachtel is part of a home-based business family. Her

husband, Joel, operates a photography business out of the house (see The Professionals, page 228). There are children to raise at the Schachtel home as well. In fact, it was just after Schachtel delivered her third child that her mother-in-law gave her a sewing machine to keep the creative juices flowing. Schachtel had never used a sewing machine before, but she was a quick study.

At first, she tried designing clothes for her own children. "Other people saw them and wanted them," Schachtel recalls. "I never really wanted to get into business. It was always an issue of supply and demand. But I knew I was really in business when I started buying supplies wholesale. I'm in business despite myself." Indeed, seven years after she first sat down in front of the machine, Schachtel's business, named KSL, was turning out garments at the rate of 500 pieces a year. Her outfits for kids were selling from about $40 to $70, and she was taking in about 25 percent of the sales price in profits.

With that kind of business volume, the real surprise is that Schachtel has maintained part-time status. She has accomplished that through agreements with five to nine other women, who do sewing in their homes to help produce many of the garments Schachtel designs. Unlike many home businesspeople, who want growth and may even be seeking an eventual location outside the house, Schachtel feels adamantly that she is busy enough already. "Over my dead body would this become full time," she says.

If she felt differently, Schachtel has no doubt that KSL could grow much larger. She is typically inundated with orders, and chooses not to take them all. Oddly, men in particular are always advising her how to make the business larger, and cannot seem to understand that she doesn't want that to happen, Schachtel says. "If I had a nickel for every man who has sat down with me and explained how I could develop my business into a $100,000-a-year company, I could buy a new car. People judge women doing volunteer work as good. But if you start a business and your goal is not to make a lot of money, no one understands."

There is another pressure point: working with the parents of the children. Sometimes, Schachtel says, the parents, who are enamoured with the idea that she can appliqué almost anything on the clothing, ask for all sorts of unrealistic add-ons. "Because my business is special order, they think they can put their kid's whole life story on the front of a dress," she says.

"And," Schachtel adds, "they have no qualms about criticism. Because you are accessible, they can put more pressure on you than the salespeople at Saks."

Schachtel finds she does not need to do much in the way of promotion. She hosts clothing shows at her home twice a year, and that helps boost sales enough in a business she already is forced to hold down so that she can enjoy spending time with her family. "The only risk to my business is everyone's enthusiasm," Schachtel declares. "You get snowed by it and take more orders than you can handle. You get overextended. It's really a problem of not being realistic." Schachtel's happiest moments are when she watches children come by with their parents to pick up clothes. "They are so easy to please," she says. "I love to watch them."

PROFIT POTENTIAL

Sewing at home, by itself, sometimes is not lucrative enough to support a family. It can provide extra income to the tune of $2,000 or more per year part time, depending on the number of hours put into it. The real money is in design and manufacturing. Busy full-timers can make $20,000 per year or more, and there is always the chance of being "discovered" by a design and manufacturing company that may buy homemade designs and patterns for a pretty penny. Start-up and maintenance costs are relatively low, and the cost of materials can be built into one's prices. Customers for custom-made garments also can be asked to supply materials.

RISK

The prime financial risk is being stuck with unwanted inventory, usually of raw materials but sometimes even finished garments. Since at-home garment-makers must buy in bulk to get wholesale prices, there is a need to aggressively push the material in stock when selling to individual or company customers. With careful buying and good marketing, home garment businesses can be relatively risk-free.

ENJOYMENT

A real craftsman behind a sewing machine can rightfully feel pride in her or his work. However, the business can be somewhat repetitive, and it can confine a person to a single sitting position for long periods. At home, where one can arrange comfortable chairs and furnishings to compensate, the business is not so tedious as at most factories. Creative garment businesses, in which the operator is designing and making one-of-a-kind products, can be every bit as satisfying as other creative arts.

CHAPTER 16

Repairing and Restoring

When times are tough, you fix the old and postpone buying the new. That's a time-worn axiom of consumer economics, and the use of it during inflation-wracked years has caused demand to boom for all types of repair services. "Repair people say they are treading water to keep their heads above the deluge of demand," reported the *Wall Street Journal* in January 1981. To the chagrin of original equipment manufacturers in the auto and appliance industries, the *Journal* article was all too true. While production of new "big ticket" consumer goods hovered at consistently low levels, older cars, washers, and refrigerators were heading for repair shops instead of the junkyards.

The bad news for the manufacturers, of course, was good news for those who repair consumer goods. They have benefitted not only from a low level of purchases of new products, but from the fact that machinery seems to be breaking down more frequently than ever. The cause is not so much a lack of quality control on the assembly line as it is the fact that such products as autos and appliances today are so much more complex. With dozens of extra controls and moving parts, the odds that any one will malfunction increase dramatically.

It is difficult to launch home-based repair services for some products. Auto repair, for example, now requires expensive diagnostic tools and other big, heavy equipment not exactly suited to the residential neighborhood or the pocketbook of the home entrepreneur. Yet there are plenty of other opportunities. Appliance repair services can be operated from home. There is a real growth market, too, for furniture and antique repairing and restoring. Home workers in that business can glean plenty of orders from the recent boom in antiques as investments and hobbies. Upholstery work can be tailored to the home shop as well. And, as consumers put money into the restoration of their increasingly valuable homes, there are new opportunities for custom millworkers and carpenters with shops at home. Some wily home businesspeople have even devised ways to tap into the auto repair market with mail order operations.

Repair and restoration businesses can be a little more expensive to start up than some home occupations: Tools are needed, and a stock of parts and materials. The cost will naturally depend on the intended products to be repaired, and on the scope of service that is to be offered. Starting the business on a small scale at home is one way to gradually build enough profit for expansion, and a move to an outside shop if desired.

In any repair business, it is wise to make sure that you have adequate medical insurance—hospitalization and major medical coverage for doctor visits and medicines. Repair services can be hazardous occupations. Machinery repair poses dangers of electrocution and shock, not to mention cuts and bruises from moving parts. In furniture repair and antique restoration, there are less obvious but, perhaps, more insidious dangers. Prolonged inhalation of stripping fluids, for example, can cause lung problems. Even in small-scale home upholstery work, practitioners have to use caution in working with fine fibers that can enter the atmosphere of a room. These, too, can hurt the lungs.

For tips on how to prevent accidents and occupational illnesses, it is a good idea to contact the nearest office of the U.S. Occupational Safety and Health Administration. This agency can send literature and offer verbal advice on safety practices in all the repair and restoration fields. Usually, good ventilation of the home workshop, and the use of safety equipment from gloves to masks, will suffice. Informed and protected, you can join the growing number of home workers who have discovered healthy markets for repair services, good for part-time income, and sometimes lucrative full-time work.

ZEN APPLIANCE

Gail Henning and Steve Ropczynski are two young adults just getting started in the home-based repair field. But they have certainly come up with a unique business name: Zen and the Art of Appliance Repair, also known as Zen Appliance. Henning was the office manager, and Ropczynski the service manager, at an out-of-home appliance shop in southern Florida in

1979. The owners of the shop went on vacation and left the business in the hands of their young subordinates. Henning recalls: "They went away for a week or two and we did it ourselves. We were running the business better than they were."

Having come to that conclusion, the two threw together their savings, became partners, and inaugurated Zen from headquarters in Henning's home. The company does air conditioning and refrigeration repair. The home location was picked for its low overhead rather than as a final resting place. The two needed to buy their own tools, plus a car for Ropczynski to get back and forth to work sites and appliance pickup spots. There wasn't enough cash left to support an outside shop, which is the ultimate goal.

In the early life of the business, Henning was doing the office work for four or five hours a day. Ropczynski handled the repairs for five to six hours a day. The two were getting most of their work from realtors and property managers. They have high hopes to stimulate much more business by the end of 1981. Although Henning felt she could handle a business as well or better than her former employers did, she had to learn advertising and promotion the hard way. The two tried direct mail solicitation, newspaper classified ads, and flyers, but these techniques didn't work very well. Henning concluded that people simply don't pay attention to repair services until they need them. That meant "the *Yellow Pages* were really the only place to be," she says. Zen scheduled a big ad in the 1981 phone book, and that has encouraged the couple. "What's really worked for us so far is word of mouth," Henning says. "If we're in the *Yellow Pages* and also get referrals, we can build the business."

If that happens, Henning and Ropczynski have clear plans for their next move. Zen will graduate from home to shop "as soon as it is necessary," Henning says. Once in a more spacious location, she would like to add another feature to the business— the sale of used refrigerators from the floor of the shop. "It's really easy in this business to pick up refrigerators that people don't want anymore, fix them and sell them," she notes. "You need a shop to do that."

Henning is convinced that by starting at home, the two will be able to build the capital to finance the shop. "What we're doing now is extremely lucrative, partly because our overhead is almost nil. Our service charges give us a good profit," she says. "I'm sure we will move out of the home."

UPHOLSTERY IN THE BASEMENT

Mary McCarthy of Akron, Ohio, has spent more than 35 years reupholstering furniture at home. For the first 15 years, she had to work from the top of her kitchen table. Afterwards, she and her husband Ray moved to a larger home where he helped to build a fully-equipped basement workshop for her. In fact, after his retirement from B. F. Goodrich Co., Ray helped work at the business until he recently passed away. McCarthy has continued on her own and utilizes the business to pull in supplemental income.

Her business includes some sewing, and she did some subcontracting for a time, making draperies and slip covers for a local fabric shop. McCarthy's main work, however, is on furniture. She typically charges $75 to reupholster a basic chair, and $125 for a sofa. Pillows and tufting are extra—$25 to $50. Customers sometimes buy their own materials for the job. Her expenses have been low. Aside from hand tools, McCarthy bought a secondhand Singer industrial-grade machine for $350. She periodically replaces the head, and has a portable machine as well. Her husband built the shelves and tables McCarthy uses, and he installed fluorescent lighting in the workshop. McCarthy has been able to make $5,000 to $6,000 a year in extra cash.

One of the advantages to starting a reupholstery business, McCarthy contends, is that it doesn't require extensive training. She has attended adult education classes on the subject, but says she found she already knew much of what was taught. "I was amazed at how much I had learned on my own," McCarthy declares.

McCarthy is acquainted with the occupational hazards of the business. She suspects that the arthritic pain in her hands comes from years of pressing and pulling heavy fabric, for example. But she is pleased with the rewards of the work, too. Customers come to her by word of mouth, and often "become friends," McCarthy says. "People marvel at my work. I feel challenged and then satisfied."

TOOLS FOR "BUGS"

In the daytime, Nelson Antosh is an editor at the Houston *Chronicle*. In his spare time, Antosh is owner and operator of Volks Tool Supply, an innovative mail order business that puts Antosh in the auto repair industry without ever getting his hands dirty.

Antosh sells specialized tools for working on Volkswagens, in particular, the old "beetle" models that are no longer manufactured or sold in the United States. The old VW's are now the targets of collectors and hobbyists. But these owners, who often like to make their own repairs, have a hard time finding the proper tools to fit the oddly shaped bodies and parts of their cars. Antosh made this discovery himself in 1971.

He had purchased a new VW in 1968 and learned to make repairs at home. Antosh was fascinated with the precision of the engine, and he liked to build and rebuild it. Antosh has squeezed 280,000 miles out of his car, but he began to find in 1971 that even the specialty magazines for VW buffs didn't tell where to buy the special tools he needed. Antosh wrote to the German-American Chamber of Commerce to get the names of importers or distributors of the tools. He had already conceived the idea to tap these sources of supply to start his own sideline business.

Antosh found three importers, plus half a dozen U.S. manufacturers that made at least some of the tools for VW work. He began buying in wholesale quantities, and built an inventory of $5,000 worth of tools. At the same time, he put together a catalogue of his offerings, and began advertising in such magazines as *Popular Science, Popular Mechanics,* and the specialty magazines for VW owners. His ads peddled the catalogues, which Antosh sold for 60 cents each. After that, he says, the business "expanded by itself." He became a recognized source of supply. By the mid-1970s, Volks Tool Supply had sales of about $25,000 a year.

Since that time, Antosh has let the business slack off somewhat. Some of the reasons involved the complexities surrounding his sources of supply. The catalogues list firm prices, but many of Antosh's tools are made in Germany. When the U.S. dollar fell in value in relationship to the German Deutschmark, Antosh sometimes found himself selling products at fixed prices lower than his cost. Recently, there has been a second foreign complication. A number of the tools are no longer made even in Germany. They come from Brazil, a nation with high inflation and a volatile economy that further confounds the currency problem.

Antosh has been weighing whether hassles such as these make it worth the trouble to produce a new catalogue, although he has no doubt about the salability of the tools. With more attention to the business, he says, revenues could reach $40,000 annually without too much trouble. In the meantime, odd as it sounds, Antosh manages to inventory his products at home, but he rents warehouse space for $24 a month to store his packaging materials. The boxes, he says, tend to give the house a musty odor. If he makes a new catalogue, Antosh says he is considering adding VW parts to the tools. Parts carry a higher markup than tools, and VW beetles are off the market now in the United States. "It's really gotten hard," he says, "to find good-quality parts."

FURNITURE AND ANTIQUES

Probably the hottest results from the new interest market for home-based repairing and restoring in correcting the bad taste of some of our predecessors. Cultural historians have not focused much attention on it, but society in the United States obviously experienced a generation-long paint fetish not so many years ago. Off-whites were in. So was a sickly shade of light green. Fine, old hardwood furnishings were coated and recoated. It may have been a post-Depression reaction: Now that the average guy could afford it, he was going to paint that old furniture and make it look modern!

The fashion today is quite to the contrary, and feelings are just as strong. Increasingly scarce hardwood is very expensive, and, therefore, stylish. For some people, a natural finish has been a thing of beauty all along. Antique pieces, in particular, have become investment items as well as objects of general admiration. For all these reasons, there is money to be made in stripping off the paint, removing the scratches, rebuilding, restoring, and refinishing.

Furniture repair and restoration is typically a part-time

home business. Each piece needs the attention and labor of an individual craftsman. There are some, however, who make a full-time occupation of furniture restoration despite the long hours and hard, physical work. One of them is Morris Pearson of Wheaton, Maryland, who says his work week averages 80 hours. "Saturdays and Sundays don't mean anything to me if I enjoy what I'm doing," Pearson says.

Many of Pearson's customers are antique dealers. The dealers can turn a decent profit by picking up old and craftsmanlike pieces for a song because they are marred and painted over. By hiring an outside restorer, the dealers can resell the same items at high prices. A great many sizable, finely built and finely finished pieces go for more than $1,000 retail. Like many restorers, Pearson has a combination business. He works for dealers and private owners, but also tries to find, restore, and sell antiques of his own. He buys his own retail selling license annually for "ten or fifteen dollars," and displays up to $3,000 worth of merchandise at antique shows.

Pearson hopes to start his own shop outside of his home. Many part-time restorers, however, find a home location most convenient and financially practical. Waldemar Reichert, a Chicago-area commercial photographer, spends about 15 hours a week on his furniture stripping and refinishing business. He charges about $10 to $15 an hour for the wardrobes, chairs, desks, and tables that he manually refinishes. Although chemical stripping compounds are expensive, Reichert finds that at his rates the raw materials costs come to only about 5 percent of his gross income. Similarly, Lair D. Tienter of Colorado charges $12.50 an hour for antique restoration, an avocation that is a natural part-time extension of his full-time job as a restorer of historic homes.

Big, out-of-home refinishing establishments often handle pieces in a more mechanized way than home entrepreneurs can. They often use automatic dipping tanks filled with chemical strippers, but these can be expensive for home workers. Reichert in Chicago has seen the tanks selling for $500, and they may take 50 gallons of stripper at $6 a gallon. To support that investment, the home businessperson needs an assured volume of pieces, plenty of extremely well-ventilated space, and adequate safety equipment. Even working on a smaller scale, Reichert uses thick rubber gloves and protective goggles, and he has decided not to expand his practice partly out of fear of the chemicals. Solvents are widely suspected as a long-term health hazard, and manufacturers now print safety warnings all over the containers.

A number of home furniture restorers avoid chemical strippers altogether. Danny DiMauro in Kent, Ohio, says he believes that some of these products remove too much natural oil from the wood. There are a number of alternatives: heat and mechanical stripping machines, for example. Almost anyone can learn to use one method or another to strip and refinish furnishings. The keys to success are the degree of craftsmanship one can develop, aggressiveness in seeking out commercial business or antiques to buy and resell, and plain luck. Thousands of dollars await the fortunate few who can find and recognize a valuable piece at a bargain price at a flea market or similar spot. Unfortunately, a lot of people realize this, and there simply aren't many gullible original owners left.

Even so, there is more than profit that has attracted people to furniture and antique restoration. Pearson views the practice as an art and himself as "an artist." Those who feel that way sometimes find their customers are the ones who prevent full expression. Working on pieces owned by others at an hourly rate, Reichert warns: "You can't treat every piece you do like a Stradivarius. You can put two hours into a piece and turn out a decent product, or four hours and turn out a great product. Most people don't know the difference, and, therefore, aren't willing to pay for the perfect job." That needn't eliminate all the pleasure, however. "There's a tremendous feeling of satisfaction," Reichert declares, "in taking something that looks terribly dilapidated and worthless and turning it into something beautiful."

CUSTOM MILLWORK

"There is no sense in working for someone else," declares Daniel J. Pytell of Denver. That statement may not be surprising (particularly in this book), but Pytell is. Born in 1959, Pytell, at age 22, already had his own business doing custom millwork for home restorations. He was taking in about $18,000 a year.

Pytell spends three or four hours a day in a shop in his garage, making stair railings, windows, columns, posts, and related items. The rest of his day is spent on the job site, installing the pieces, measuring, and repairing. Eventually, Pytell says he would like to have his own shop and do nothing but the millwork. But that's not imminent. He estimates it would cost $15,000 in tools; he has $4,000 to $5,000 worth.

Pytell is surprisingly experienced, though. He started out as a laborer for a remodeling crew when he was 16. Age has created something of an image problem, he concedes. "I'm so young, a lot of people don't think I know what I'm doing. They are not too sure about me." Gradually, however, Pytell is building a reputation in town. He already finds he does not need to advertise to find customers. He also holds his prices down to develop the business. "My prices are reasonable because I'm trying to get known," Pytell says.

Like many cities, Denver is the site of a good deal of restoration work, and that makes a ready market. Some jobs are quick fix-ups for people who want to sell their homes; some are more detailed restorations for people who want to stay put. Pytell gives the customer a choice on price. He will bid on a job, or bill for his time and materials plus 10 percent. Most people are aware of good quality in their homes and want to retain good woodwork and stained glass, yet Pytell still finds that one fringe benefit is the materials he can keep. "I salvage a lot," he remarks. He replaced one fine old oak stairway, for instance, and kept the oak for himself with the owner's permission.

Pytell has one regret. "If I were to do it again," he says, "I'd take a partner who knows business." Mananging the operation "takes a lot of time," Pytell says. But by keeping his office and part of his work at home, he has reduced some of the complexities and a lot of expense. That frees Pytell to do more of what he really enjoys—the work. "I love doing it," he says. "I wouldn't do anything else."

PROFIT POTENTIAL

Because repairing and restoring tends to be a labor-intensive, one-piece-at-a-time kind of business, it lacks the potential in most cases to grow very large while still at home. A home location can, however, be a launching pad to a larger retail service shop or place of production. For part-timers, home-based repair and restoration work can yield extra income at rates of $10 an hour and higher.

RISK

There is more physical risk to the practitioner in many kinds of repairing and restoring than in most other home businesses. Working with solvent chemicals, machinery, and electricity poses clear hazards that call for training and caution. Financially, there is a risk that customers' products might be damaged during repair, or that customers might allege damage even if it doesn't happen. This becomes serious only when the pieces are very expensive. Antique restorers should be certain to have insurance coverage.

ENJOYMENT

Most home repair and restoration workers are in the business for reasons similar to those who make creative products. They enjoy working with their hands, and they are skilled in their crafts. For people who fit that description, repair and restoration can be compelling work. Many who cannot make a real business out of furniture and antique restoration do it as a hobby anyway.

CHAPTER 17

The Professionals

A young attorney in northeastern New Jersey, couldn't help but notice the look of surprise on a new client's face when the discussion got down to money. It was 1980, and the attorney, who had modest offices and did a mix of criminal and civil work, had just announced that his standard fee was $65 an hour. Without waiting for the client to ask, the lawyer gestured toward his surroundings and said: "It's the overhead. The office, the secretary, the taxes. I've got to hussle to make this work even at $65 an hour." It was true. As his client later learned, the lawyer was stretched thin over so many cases that he worked most nights and Saturdays.

The upward-spiraling prices for real estate have been almost universal. Professional offices—for sale or rent—have jumped in cost right along with residential homes. Labor costs for professionals' full-time employees have risen, too, and not the least of the increases have been for legally-required benefits (such as social security) and typical fringes (such as medical insurance). Many municipalities, caught in an unstable economy and facing a citizenry opposed to voting in new state or local income taxes, have raised property taxes to all-time highs.

A glance at a recent classified ad section of *The New York Times* drives the point home. One ad offers to rent 916 square feet of space on 42nd Street—five or six blocks away from the seamy Manhattan pornography district—for $2,200 a month. Another offers to sell three rooms set up for a dentist in a slightly nicer part of town for $180,000, plus a $290 per month charge for maintenance. Across the Hudson River in a distinctly middle-class part of crowded New Jersey, mediocre little offices were renting for nearly $500 per month.

Figures like these go a long way toward explaining a shift among thousands of professional workers to offices at their homes. Professional people, unlike businessmen who manufacture products, do not usually face much of a problem in purchasing raw materials. Office overhead is the great expense, and it has pushed professionls' fees so high that many clients have become price-oriented shoppers in the marketplace for these sophisticated services. It is no coincidence that as this is happening, more lawyers and doctors, for example, are now advertising for customers than ever before.

When office overhead becomes a major determinant of the price of one's services, the notion of eliminating that overhead almost entirely becomes extremely attractive. By switching the office to the home, the professionals simply remove office rental or mortgage costs from their structural expenses. Moreover, they begin to deduct from taxable income a portion of the cost of home mortgage interest or rent, and utility and property tax bills. Many learn to use outside contractors for secretarial and related services (see Information Processing, page 156). Some worry that a home location diminishes the reputation, or limits contact with other professionals. But economics have become a greater concern, and the home practice will cease to appear odd to clients or colleagues as it becomes more common.

Professional is a word of many meanings. Here, let's use it to refer to those occupations that require long periods of higher education for entry. That definition covers a lot of ground, and it should. There is a host of highly educated or highly trained types of service workers who have the option to switch their offices to their homes—or to start them at home. Unlike home-based manufacturers, whose space may limit the potential for profit compared with outside factories, professional workers can earn more money at home. They can price their services competitively with others in the market, but enjoy a higher margin of net income because of lower expenses. By eliminating the commute, they also can squeeze more paid working hours into the day without cutting into time spent with family or in leisure pursuits.

Professional offices at home have become more practical and affordable because of electronics. More sophisticated telephones, and machines that connect to them, can remember and automatically dial certain numbers, record messages, and be utilized to pay bills. Calculators and minicomputers offer a full range of at-home mathematical and word processing capabilities for professionals. Not surprisingly, many professionals who are moving home are those that rely on crunching numbers and words—including accountants and public relations people.

Teaching and tutoring, an old home-based profession for

music instructors and for those who help children who have learning difficulties, is increasing at home as well. The boom in interest in adult education, and in what might be called "recreational instruction," have created new opportunities. In one Houston neighborhood that is peppered with home businesses, one couple teaches square dancing at home, and runs a related operation—selling square-dance clothing to the students. As the baby boom generation ages, the possibilities for teaching at home should steadily increase.

There has been solid growth in the number of professional and technical workers in the United States. As measured by the Department of Labor, employed professionals totaled 11.5 million in 1972, or 14 percent of the entire work force. In 1980, the number reached 15.9 million, or 16 percent of the work force. Some of the faster-growth occupations have been the same ones in which home working has become most attractive: accounting, public relations, computer work, psychology, and higher-education teaching. But these are far from the only work-at-home professions, as New Yorker Peggy W. Gowan demonstrates.

SEVEN LANGUAGES AND A CONVERTED DEN

Once you learn foreign languages, says Peggy W. Gowan, "you can use them forever." You also can use them from an office based almost anywhere in a cosmopolitan city where such language skills are in high demand. Gowan runs her own translating and interpreting service from her large apartment in Manhattan. She regards her home location as something that is already becoming standard in New York, and is certain to grow. "Because of inflation, I know a lot of women who do something at home to make extra money," Gowan says. "One sews. Another designs jewelry. Another has become a premier costume designer for ballet. Working at home is a matter of thinking of the future."

Since 1972, Gowan has operated her language service from a converted den at home. She can interpret and translate French, Italian, German, Spanish, Portuguese, and Arabic into English, and vice versa. Her experience and educational background are vast. A graduate of Vassar who received additional training at several institutions in the United States and abroad, Gowan has worked for corporations, the U.S. State Department, the United Nations as a "whispering" translator, and for a number of other public and private clients.

Her office was often based outside her home in her early years, but she took a chunk of time off work to raise her children. "When the kids were ready to go to college, I asked myself what I should do. The answer was, why not the same thing I've done all my life?" Gowan remembers.

Her choice, then, was to get an outside job or begin her own business, with low overhead, at home. She was confident enough of her skills to decide in favor of self-employment, and the pick of an office location was easy. "I need complete peace and quiet for this work," Gowan says. "I am also one of those people who works better under pressure when I am at home. There is no one around me there. I'll never work in an office again. I can't take the phone noise or the coffee breaks or the socializing. And," she adds, "I make more money now than I could as a company employee."

Gowan prices her services by the job. Recently, she says she has been doing more translating than interpreting, and she can quickly scan a piece of printed information and offer a price to translate. Her income and hours vary, but Gowan clearly works a professional's long hours fairly often, and commands good pay. "I might get a thousand-dollar job one week, or an eighty-dollar job for a day," she says. "I am my own boss, and I pick my turnaround time on every project. There are times when I work from six A.M. to midnight." Gowan is well known among agencies and companies that frequently need translation, including advertising firms, so she does no promotion for her business.

Indeed, she says that good translation is important enough that reputations are passed by word of mouth. "If you get a bad translator to save some money, it could cost you thousands of dollars extra in a ruined legal contract or other document," she notes. Gowan translates speeches, corporate annual reports, medical and legal documents, letters, educational documents, newspaper and magazine articles, industrial and cultural brochures, and advertising copy. She does interpreting for business conferences, court proceedings, and for business and government visitors and travelers.

There are some problems in the business, but they are more

related to the profession than to Gowan's location. For example, some clients ask for interpreting services on technical subjects without giving much prior notice. A government agency once called Gowan in at the last minute to do interpreting for an international conference on patent law and legal rights for choreographers.

As owner of the business, however, Gowan also sees much more significant opportunities ahead. She makes some extra income already by taking a percentage from work she farms out to other translators who may be better in a particular language or special subject. Next, she says, she might establish a consulting business to advise clients, such as advertisers, about such things as the nuances of word meanings in other languages.

Although she waited until the children were ready to leave the nest to set up shop, Gowan found that there was still a connection between them and her work. The home language service, she notes, helped "enable us to put two kids through Vassar and Princeton at the same time."

ACCOUNTING AND TAXES FROM 9 TO 5

The drastic reduction in overhead costs at home offers a major nonfinancial benefit to professionals. It mitigates the need to work extra long hours to pay for office rent, mortgage, or utilities. The professions are marred with workaholism, either to pay the bills or because of the inner drives of the practitioners. Hugh Hoffman, a Fort Lauderdale bookkeeper and income tax preparer, has structured his business to avoid that syndrome.

After leaving the service in 1949, Hoffman moved to Fort Lauderdale and went to work for an established accounting firm. He did tax returns for $1 each. By 1956, Hoffman could see a better life was open if he could start his own business. He did that, at home, after winning a fight with Cty Hall over zoning.

But Hoffman has set up his business carefully. In the 1960s, the untimely deaths of several colleagues convinced him that workaholism was too great a risk. Back then, he recalls, there were some 70 accountants in town, and "not counting overdrinking, five dropped dead in March" of one year, apparent victims of overwork. At the time, Hoffman gave his secretary a key to the office, which occupies about one quarter of his home. He told her to make sure he walked away at 5 P.M. every day and to lock up behind him. "If I don't walk out at five o'clock," he told her, "I'll give you five dollars." He hasn't spent much.

More recently, Hoffman has found he does not even need the secretary. His costs are pared to the bone. He uses an outside answering service, and maintains two desks and two chairs. Without employees or long hours, Hoffman may sacrifice some revenue, but his low expenses increase the profitability of each revenue dollar. He has about 300 regular clients for income-tax preparation, and charges them between $40 and $75 per return. For a monthly fee, Hoffman also does bookkeeping for local companies, and makes out income statements and W-2 forms for some of them.

The business has been lucrative enough within a normal set of work hours that Hoffman was able to take trips around the world in 1959 and 1973. Although he declines to tell his personal income, he notes that his own tax payments and charitable contributions totaled about $16,000 in 1980.

Some other home-based accountants have much larger operations. In Littleton, Colorado, Gay G. Luke employs six in the basement of her townhouse, headquarters of G. G. Luke and Associates. Luke's main reason for wanting to locate at home was to be near her children. Like Hoffman, she does not seek out long hours, but Luke is sometimes forced to work them to support the bigger organization. Still, she says she finds this easier to do than if she had an outside office. "I'm not a workacholic," she declares, "but if the work has to be done, I'm there. If I wake up at five A.M. I may do it then. If I had an office outside, I would not get dressed and leave. But there are times when I'm under pressure and delighted to be able to throw on a robe and get to work."

MORE PHOTOS, LESS BUSINESS MANAGEMENT

A highly successful photographer in Highland Park, Illinois, Joel Schachtel finds he is typically booked up between two and three years in advance for portraits, special occasions, and commercial work. His headquarters are at home. Given the volume of his business, Schachtel says he could easily justify opening an out-of home studio. It is an idea he has considered and rejected. "Opening a retail studio would mean I would have to become more of a businessman and less of a photographer," Schachtel says.

Working at home is standard in the Schachtel family. Joel's wife, Kay, is a home-based designer and producer of children's clothing (see Garments, page 207). However, Schachtel's photo business didn't start in an orthodox way. He went from college into the teaching profession, and it was while he was employed as a teacher that Schachtel bought a $90 camera to try out photography as a hobby. He liked it enough to begin serious study, and Schachtel worked as apprentice to a professional for a year. One day, Schachtel's sister showed some friends black-and-white portraits that Schachtel had made of her children. The friends asked him to photograph their children, and Schachtel's business was born.

That was in the early 1970s. Nine years after launching the business at home, Schachtel was as busy as he wanted to be. About 40 percent of his work is at weddings, Bar Mitzvahs, and similar occasions. Another 40 percent is portrait work, and 20 percent is commercial. His fees recently ranged from $600 to $1,000 for occasions and portraits, and $1,000 per day for commercial work. At first, Schachtel maintained and used his own darkroom in the basement, but he later found it preferable to send his film to labs for developing and printing. He makes a percentage on the lab work in addition to his fees. Schachtel's promotion is strictly word of mouth; he says he has never advertised, other than with a listing in the *Yellow Pages*.

The Schachtels feel their children have adjusted well to a duo of home businesses. Joel recalls that when the children were young, it was hard for them to distinguish between his roles as father and in-house business operator. "They used to go down to the basement and mess around with the negatives," Schachtel says. "But the kids appreciate the business more and more as they grow older."

Schachtel estimates that he works about 40 hours a week. With the office downstairs where "you can always get to it," the exact length of the workweek becomes difficult to pin down, he says. Schachtel's backlog of orders and his instant access to work give him the flexibility to adjust his income. "I'm my own boss. The harder I work, the more I'm rewarded," he says.

Schachtel does find that because he works at home, some of his customers assume they can call him anytime to see if their prints are ready—and to nudge him along. Undoubtedly, there would be at least a little less of this if he owned an outside studio. But Schachtel doesn't find the problem serious enough to alter his thinking about where he would like to work. "I prefer the less commercial aspect of a home office," he says. "The work is more personal and more creative."

PIANO WITH THE WINDOWS CLOSED

Gladys M. Kendall learned how to play the piano as a child in the San Luis valley, a rural spot in southern Colorado. By the age of 14, she was good enough to begin teaching others at her home. Kendall is now over 65, living in Denver, and still teaching piano at home. Hundreds of students have come and gone; there has rarely been a shortage. Kendall has never found it necessary to advertise, and she often has a waiting list. She handles between 25 and 30 students regularly, though at times the number can swell to 50.

Teaching piano is one of the oldest at-home professional businesses, and it remains a very widespread practice. Like many jobs in teaching, it is a hard way to get rich, although prices for the service have increased. Kendall can still remember charging 50 cents a lesson in her early years. More recently, her prices were $10 an hour for adults and $6 for 45 minutes for children. And in some parts of the United States, those prices would be considered bargain rates. In the New York area, 45-minute lessons for children can be double Kendall's price.

Even so, home music instruction is most often done to supplement a family income rather than to supply it all. The same is usually true for tutoring schoolchildren, another long-established business that can be performed at the home of the student or the home of the instructor. Yet, teaching is a growth area for home entrepreneurs, particularly where the students are adults. Across the country, people with a thirst for new knowledge and skills are spilling over from adult education institutions into the homes of those skilled in fashionable arts and pastimes: gourmet cooking, dance, computer operation, painting, and many more.

To be a credible instructor whose business will last, one needs real expertise. Kendall attended a music school in Denver for four years after high school, and she did some teaching in New York, where she lived for six years before returning to the West. Kendall also taught for a brief time in a Denver piano store that contained studios. But she found teaching at home to be "more convenient and safer."

Kendall lives in an older home whose architecture is known locally as a "Denver Square"—a cubic sort of two story structure with four rooms on each floor. She has two pianos and an organ spread between two of the first-story rooms, and holds both lessons and recitals there. Unlike some home teaching businesses, music instruction has the potential to bother some neighbors, so Kendall keeps her windows and doors shut during lessons. But several of her neighbors ask Kendall now and then to open them up for a little free entertainment, especially during recitals. What they hear must be good, because a number of people in the neighborhood have sent their children to Kendall for lessons. Recently, one of her former students was the pianist at the well-known Teller House hotel, 35 miles west of Denver in Central City, a former gold mining camp.

Watching her former students put their talent to use has been gratifying. And Kendall has found additional rewards to her practice. Widowed in 1967, she has seldom been without company and meaningful work. Since her husband's death, Kendall says music has "filled the time and the emptiness and the loneliness."

IMAGE AND PUBLICITY

U.S. society is known for its idiosyncrasies. Americans have been called a nation of counters and record-keepers, of the rootless looking for roots, and, perhaps above all, a nation of communicators. The evidence is everywhere. Billions of words are laid down daily in what is probably the most diverse print media establishment in the world, and billions more hum along the ubiquitous phone lines and through the air waves.

Business is a big part of this act. The private sector has to get its messages across about its products, and also about itself—its image, its accomplishments, and its needs. The public relations industry performs that second function, and it has been growing in size and sophistication. Even during the 1970s, when inflation and periodic recessions tempted businesses to cut back on all nonessential employment, the number of public relations practitioners in the United States increased impressively. The Labor Department counted 87,000 of them in 1972 and by 1977, the number had jumped 38 percent to 120,000.

With a substantial market that is growing, especially in the booming cities of the South and Southwest, the opportunities in public relations are plentiful. Most PR people work for corporations or agencies, but a number of independents have launched businesses of their own at home, usually serving smaller business clients who cannot afford a full-time public relations employee. For these independents, the range of pay is quite broad. That is because clients will generally pay for the value of the service they receive, and a public relations agent may be employed merely to polish up an annual report, or to do something with a much greater financial impact.

What the PR person accomplishes depends as much on his drive and imagination as it does on his assignment. There have been some ideas in the profession as important to the financial health of an employer or client as any discovery in the research lab. One is reminded, for example, of Robert Lane, a public relations executive at Goodyear Tire & Rubber Co., who backed the idea that the company fly blimps to keep the Goodyear name in the minds of consumers.

In Los Angeles, Karen Dardick, a public relations consultant who works out of her one-bedroom apartment, was recently charging a monthly retainer of $1,000 to $1,500 to her clients. In Denver, Irving M. Seidner billed at higher rates—$1,200 to $2,500 per month. Seidner had spent 20 years in public relations in Chicago before switching to a home-based business out West.

Though the rates vary with experience, location, and the capabilities offered, there is a commonality to the business in expenses. For those based at home, the cost of doing business can be extremely low. Marjorie Maxfield, who runs the Max Agency from her Houston home, spent about $1,000 to get started. That covered a phone, office furnishing and supplies, and an answering service. She says her office operation expenses come to about $200 per month. She does contract out for expensive printing services for company annual reports, brochures, advertisements, and the like, but these costs are passed along to the client in Maxfield's billings. Public relations agents typically have high entertainment and travel expenses as well, but these are all tax deductible. Dardick spends about $3,000 annually on business travel in her car, plus about $4,000 a year on entertainment and all other overhead.

Dardick figures that by keeping her office at home, she can retain as much income as she would with a larger operation outside. "If I grew to the point where I needed an [outside] office and an assistant, I would be working twice as hard and don't think I would be earning that much more money," she says. "The business would also become more complicated, and I want to leave it as simple as possible."

Isolation is seldom a problem for an at-home public relations person. The profession is one of contact with people, and Maxfield, for example, reports that she spends a good deal of her time at the offices of her clients. Now and then, a client visits her office, and Maxfield recalls one time when that was helpful. A real estate developer in Houston was about to begin a major construction project, yet he seemed disinterested in the kind of publicity that Maxfield felt certain she could deliver. She needed him to authorize her to proceed with media contacts.

"I called him on the phone and I saw him at his office, and he was just obstinate," she says. "Finally, I decided to invite him over to see me after work. I sat down with him in the living room in a very relaxed atmosphere, and we chatted about everything but the project. Finally, I brought it up, and he agreed to use me on it. I really think the home setting in that instance had a lot to do with it."

FREEDOM VERSUS PRIVACY

Jeff Sulkin spent some time working for an architectural firm. He says it was "invaluable experience," but boring. Still in his twenties, he launched his own architectural company from the first floor of his two-story loft in Venice, California. The new business, still young, is coming along. Sulkin's low overhead has enabled him to build the practice gradually by charging lower fees than are standard in the industry. Many architects, for example, charge clients a percentage of construction costs. Sulkin charges by the hour at rates that range from $15 to $35, and he adds fees for printing and structural consulting to his bills. Sulkin's pricing methods have helped to keep him working steadily in a profession where demand can be extremely volatile.

He likes the flexibility and the environment of work at home. But, like photographer Schachtel in Chicago, he sacrifices some privacy. Sulkin does a good deal of residential architecture for families, and his clients do not hesitate to call at all hours. Many of them are building new homes that represent the family's biggest investment ever, so the emotions can run high as well. "I can get caught in the middle of marriages," Sulkin says. "The wife will call up and want to know what her husband said about a project, and then she'll tell me to forget what he said. The husband calls later and tells me to forget whatever his wife told me. It's crazy."

Yet Sulkin is an ardent commute-hater, and he loves the loft. "This place is like a romper room, and the work becomes entertainment," he says. Like many in Southern California, Sulkin finds himself facing steep home rental costs—recently $850 per month. But unlike the commuters, he can both generate income from his property and write off a portion of each month's rent from his taxable income. When the general economy sours, individual and business clients have a tendency to postpone new building projects, so low overhead can be especially attractive in architecture.

In Chicago, Edward S. Hall, formerly a partner in an 18-member architectural firm, finds that his earnings potential is nearly one-third greater in a home-based business he recently began. "There is a lot lower ratio of operating costs to income here," Hall says. "And you can put in more work. The ratio of financial rewards to effort expended is much higher in this job."

Hall has specialized in architectural marketing consultation at home. Using his contacts in the industry, he takes construction projects still in the idea stage and brings together a proper team of architects, contractors, engineers, and interior designers to do the work. Hall offers other services as well, and for 55 to 60 hours of work per week he can earn a distinctly upper-middle-class annual income.

But Hall does not share the view of many home workers about commuting and the bustle of work outside. He misses some of that. "The lack of change of scenery can get me down," he says. "If you work in an office building, the very process of getting out, going to work, and moving around in the building can be exhilarating." However, Hall does not miss some of the internal goings-on between employees at a big company. "I am totally in control of my own success here," he says. "Success is not dependent on personalities or the politics of an office, but on my own initiative and sales ability."

PROFIT POTENTIAL

Professional work is one activity that in all likelihood becomes more profitable at home than outside. This is not true if the professional is a business owner who reaps profits from the work of many others, in addition to his own work. But most professionals tend to be paid largely for their own efforts, and office overhead is the prime factor that determines how much income can be saved. A home location can easily cut overhead costs by half or more.

RISK

There is almost no difference between professionals' risks at home versus outside. The only serious consideration is a positive one for home workers. By spending less to launch the business at home, there is less likelihood that the professional will need borrowed funds. That reduces financial liability in case of failure.

ENJOYMENT

The financial gains from working at home may be a greater lure than the pleasure of doing so. Many professionals enjoy and profit from contact with their peers, and some of this contact may be lost in a home location. On the other hand, professional practices that require quiet, undisturbed surroundings are ideal for at-home location, as long as families are small or understanding and cooperative.

Index